胡野秋 | 主编

（汉英版）**微观深圳**

Chinese-English Version

SHENZHEN: Dynamic and Diverse

CHIEF COMPILER | Hu Yeqiu

丛书策划：	聂晓阳　周洪波
主　　编：	胡野秋
副 主 编：	伍呆呆　韩湛宁
编　　委：	（按姓氏笔画排列）
	王绍培　邓康延　伍呆呆　张晓燕　胡野秋　姜维勇　聂蔚琳　韩　洁　韩湛宁
撰　　写：	（按姓氏笔画排列）
	伍呆呆　吴俊忠　张晓燕　陈燕燕　胡野秋　姜维勇　黎　明
摄　　影：	（按姓氏笔画排列）
	王德强　韦洪兴　文锡泉　宁少贤　吕　翔　任小涛　苏贝妮　李伟文　肖玲玲　吴忠平　何思慰　何耀华　宋　城　张小惠　张元辉
	陈大元　林浩生　南兆旭　禹　安　姜维勇　顾一兵　郭　颂　黄伟钊　黄雪红　梁向荣　梁崇汉　喻楚迪　曾刘秋　曾　衍　谢权荣
	詹裕升　阙永福　褚文铭　蔡一宁　魏珏珺
英文翻译：	梅　皓（美）
英文审订：	赵春燕
中文审读：	肖淼晨
责任编辑：	刘婷婷
书籍设计：	亚洲铜设计顾问

Chief Producers:	Nie Xiaoyang, Zhou Hongbo
Chief Compiler:	Hu Yeqiu
Deputy Compilers:	Wu Daidai, Han Zhanning
Editorial Board:	(Surname Stroke Order)
	Wang Shaopei, Deng Kangyan, Wu Daidai, Zhang Xiaoyan, Hu Yeqiu, Jiang Weiyong, Nie Weilin, Han Jie, Han Zhanning
Writers:	(Surname Stroke Order)
	Wu Daidai, Wu Junzhong, Zhang Xiaoyan, Chen Yanyan, Hu Yeqiu, Jiang Weiyong, Li Ming
Photographers:	(Surname Stroke Order)
	Wang Deqiang, Wei Hongxing, Wen Xiquan, Ning Shaoxian, Lv Xiang, Ren Xiaotao, Su Beini, Li Weiwen, Xiao Lingling, Wu Zhongping, He Siwei, He Yaohua, Song Cheng, Zhang Xiaohui, Zhang Yuanhui, Chen Dayuan, Lin Haosheng, Nan Zhaoxu, Yu An, Jiang Weiyong, Gu Yibing, Guo Song, Huang Weizhao, Huang Xuehong, Liang Xiangrong, Liang Chonghan, Yu Chudi, Zeng Liuqiu, Zeng Yan, Xie Quanrong, Zhan Yusheng, Que Yongfu, Chu Wenming, Cai Yining, Wei Juejun
English Translator:	Mei Hao（USA）
English Reviewer:	Zhao Chunyan
Chinese Reviewer:	Xiao Miaochen
Executive Editor:	Liu Tingting
Art Design:	asiatondesign

序 言
PREFACE

我与一夜之城的一世情缘

胡野秋

试图迅速而准确地描述深圳，是一件困难的事情。虽然她只有短短的四十岁，但她的丰富性和复杂性超过中国其他任何城市，甚至在世界上也是独一无二的。

在人类的建城史上，城市都是一步一步叠加式地累积而成，在漫长的累积过程中，建构了城市的自然风貌和人文传统，形成了此城与彼城的分别。

深圳则不然。

准确地说，深圳不是建成的，而是"造"成的，她的出现让人猝不及防，于是人们只能用"一夜之城"来形容她。

"1979年，那是一个春天，有一位老人在中国的南海边画了一个圈"，这首耳熟能详的歌曲，起首便道出这座城市的特别。多年前我写过一本书《触摸：设计一座城市》，当时我在拍一部电影纪录片，采访了和深圳相关的设计师们，片子拍完了，我也得出了结论：

这是一座设计出来的城市。你可以想象一下，在一片荒凉的海滩上，搭积木一样地搭出了一座城，而且这座少年之城居然一跃而起，与历史悠久的北上广大佬们平起平坐，被划进一线城市。这样的速度被命名为"深圳速度"，在世界建城史上成为叹为观止的孤例。

正是在这个高速旋转的陀螺的带动下，中国的城市化脚步也因此大大加快，我们仿佛用了一个弯道超车，就集体地从乡村模式插队进入城市模式。小说家余华在他的长篇小说《兄弟》后记里，写下过这样一段话："一个西方人活四百年才能经历这样两个天壤之别的时代，一个中国人只需四十年就经历了。"

快则快矣，唯解读便成为万难。

因此，当商务印书馆总编辑周洪波先生约我编一本《微观深圳》时，我一则以喜，一则以惧。深恐因为我的不胜其力，既误了一座新晋的城市，又误了一家老牌出版社。但洪波兄是我数十年的老友，他对我的信任，让我决定放手一试。

我知道，在此之前作为洪波兄的得意策划，"微观中国"系列已经"微观"过西藏、新疆、内蒙古、西安、杭州，这些地方都有相对成熟的风格乃至性格，我们甚至可以用一个关键词去给这些地方一个不太离谱的界定，比如神秘的西藏、大美的新疆、缤纷的内蒙古、厚重的西安、窈窕的杭州……

但是深圳呢？

至今有太多的人到过深圳，写过深圳，但是却无人能够为深圳找到一个众望所归的关键词。在很多年里，人们认为这里到处是黄金，所谓人傻钱多是也，当年"东西南北中，发财到广东"的人中，有一多半是冲着深圳而来；还有一些人认为深圳是一个暴发户，缺乏底蕴，略显肤浅，这里可以是事业的疆场，但不是宜居的温床；还有人以为这里充满着冒险家的争夺，商人们在尔虞我诈中获得快感，到处是灯红酒绿与刀光剑影，胆小者勿进；当然也有人把这里视为天堂。

而只有在这里生活了一年以上的人，才能明白这座城市的形式与内容有多么与众不同，随便你怎么想象她，她都在你的想象以外，无论是好，还是坏。

认识一座城，总是由表及里的，正如认识人。

我的朋友南兆旭长期致力于研究深圳的生态文化，他在《深圳自然笔记》中对一线城市的自然环境曾有过透彻的比较，他写道："在北上广深四个一线城市里，深圳是唯一同时拥有城区、山岭、溪流、湖泊、森林、田野、古村、海洋、岛屿和中国最美海岸的城市；多样的生境为多样的生命提供了栖息地。"根据南兆旭和他的团队长达十多年的考察，深圳陆地面积只占全中国陆地面积的 1/5000，却飞翔着全中国 1/5 的鸟类，奔走着 10% 的哺乳动物和 20% 的爬行动物物种；深圳的海域只占南中国海的 1/10000，生命物种却超过 20%。在这块不大的温暖湿润的土地上，50% 的土地草木覆盖，已记载的植物有 2979 种，超过整个欧洲大陆。

外表之外，内里又如何呢？

在我眼里，深圳是一个对追梦者来说充满魅惑的村姑。她出生在一个小渔村，却多年与一母所生的亲姐妹隔河相望，历史老人最终还是让这对并蒂花一同绽放，她们对走进新时代的人们有着神秘的吸引力，一批又一批年轻人和不太年轻的人都前赴后继地南下寻梦。有的梦做成了，有的梦还在路上。

在我眼里，深圳是一个有点儿鲁莽的小伙子。这里曾经尘土滚滚、脚架林立，到处是"坑"，到处是"围"，到处是"岭"。然而，对于到深圳寻梦的人来说，小伙子还是挺帅的。他没有什么不敢试，没有什么不敢闯，创下过辉煌，也犯下过错误，但他始终坦然地朝前走，像背着双肩包的旅行者。

在我眼里，深圳亦是一位性格温和的儒生。这里以读书为荣、以读书为乐，因为读书而受人尊重。从曾经的一书难求，到买书习惯用小推车，每个区都拥有一座巨大的书城，每个社区都有自己的图书馆。图书在这里随处可借，也随处可还。联合国把"全球全民阅读典范城市"的美誉给了他。

在我眼里，深圳还是一位包容谦让的绅士。他的口头禅是"来了就是深圳人"，这里一直用"英雄不问出处"作为对陌生人的标准。在斑马线上，踽踽独行的老人不必担心汽车会与之抢道；在纵横交错的街道，迷路者可以放心地向路人问道，他会详细告诉你怎样到达，如果有空的话，他会陪你走上一段。

当然，更多的眼里会有更多的深圳，无论哪一种，都可能颠覆你曾经的想象。

所以您即将打开的这本书，不是一本教科书，而是通过众多的微博体词条，为您提供打开深圳的若干把钥匙，也许是一处风景、一座老宅、一道美味、一位故人。这里有的是细节，有的是过程，但我们不采用宏大叙事，不提供简单结论。

用微博体来表达深圳，其实是一种天作之合。

如果说北京、上海、广州各是一本长篇小说，那么深圳就是一台无场次的先锋话剧，当北上广在讲述一个完整故事的时候，深圳每天都在演绎着各自独立、互不干涉的传奇，中国的城市中本土居民比例最少的唯有此城，这种与生俱来的碎片化、多元化、杂处化，使得一条又一条 140 个汉字的组合，与这座城市构成了极具象征性的互文关系。

无论从哪个角度我们都可以进入深圳，都可以获得关于这座城市的印象，但没有一个印象具有唯一性和覆盖性，你只有把它们全部连缀起来，才可以得到这座城市的三维图像。多年前，在全国的话剧会演中，北京有《茶馆》，上海有《七十二家房客》，广州有《三家巷》，它们的共同点是具象的、可描述的。而深圳带去的则与之迥异，这台话剧叫《城市魔方》，只有用"魔方"才可以表述这座城市，"魔方"呈现的不可描述性，正是这座城市的恰切象征。

《微观深圳》面世的时候，正逢中国改革开放四十周年，人们都在重新审视这个改革开放的新生儿，这本书希望能为大家提供解读这个新生儿的一些全新的视角，只要您能捕捉到您认为有价值的一鳞片爪，吾心足矣。

是以为序。

2018 年 8 月 3 日
于深圳鸠兹斋

序 言
PREFACE

My Lifelong Love for an Overnight City

Hu Yeqiu

Writing a book that accurately describes Shenzhen is a difficult task. Even though the city is only 40 years old, its richness and complexity exceed that of any other Chinese city; it may even be described unique in the world.

Humans build cities step by step, superimposing elements they create upon the ground where these cities arise. As this long process continues, these urban amalgamations accrue their own flavours and cultures, making them distinct.

This is not the case with Shenzhen.

Accurately speaking, Shenzhen wasn't built, but rather "created"; its rise has been astonishing to observers. It is almost as if the city sprung from the ground overnight.

The song *Story of Spring* is familiar with listeners in China; it describes the city's unique character. A number of years ago, I wrote a book titled *Contact: Designing a City*. At that time I shot a documentary film where I interviewed a number of designers involved with Shenzhen, and after I finished, I arrived at a conclusion: this is a city that was designed. You can imagine what it's like, for a huge youthful metropolis to just pop up along what was originally a remote and desolate beach, becoming a first-tier city on the same level as Beijing, Shanghai and Guangzhou. This pace has become known as "Shenzhen Speed"; the tempo of the construction of the city has become a singular case which has marvelled at by observers worldwide.

Like a rapidly spinning top, the urbanisation of China has been a whirlwind in recent history, events proceeding at a breakneck pace with the feeling of overtaking a car on a curved lane as we transform from villages to cities. Novelist Yu Hua thus described it in his novel *Brothers*: "A westerner would have to live four centuries to see this heaven-and-earth difference in eras, but a Chinese would only need forty years."

Great care has been taken in the assembly of this volume to accurately reflect the nature of the city it describes.

When editor-in-chief of the Commercial Press Zhou Hongbo contacted me to organise this publication, I was both delighted and afraid. I worried that I wouldn't be up to the task, up to doing right by this new city and China's oldest publishing house. However, Mr. Zhou is my friend of decades, and trusts me, thus I'm determined to try my hand at the task.

I was familiar with the "One-Minute China" series: previous volumes have told the stories of Tibet, Xinjiang, Inner Mongolia, Xi'an, and Hangzhou, showcasing the unique characteristics of these cities and regions, all with long histories. For those books, it was easy to find adjectives or phrases to sum up their subjects: Tibet, so mystical; Xinjiang, vast and beautiful; Inner Mongolia, colourful and magnificent; Xi'an, steeped in history; Hangzhou, gentle and graceful.

But what about Shenzhen?

Many people these days have been to and written about Shenzhen, but nobody's come up with a simple summation of the city's characters. Over the course of many years, people think it's a city full of money, and people without enough sense to spend it. The city has, in the context of people viewing Guangdong Province as a central location for making profit, been flocked to by many. Some view it as a city of nouveau riche, lacking depth—an occupational battlefield without culture, not a nice place to live in. Still some others see it as a free-for-all kind of atmosphere full of explorers and raiders, everyone for themselves, with debauchery, feasting, revelry and gaiety all about, merchants at each other's throats—no place for the weak-hearted, yet a paradise for players of a certain breed.

Only after living here for at least a year can one understand how special this city is compared to others; no matter what you imagine, the city can exceed—whether in dimensions good or bad, however, is not something guaranteed.

Getting to know a city is a process which progresses from outside to inside, just like getting to know a person.

My friend Nan Zhaoxu has worked for a long time researching the ecological culture of Shenzhen. In his book *Notes of Landscape in Shenzhen*, he provides a clear comparison of first-tier cities' natural environments. He wrote within: "Shenzhen, one of the four first-tier cities along with Beijing, Shanghai and Guangzhou, is the only city to have an urban area, mountains, streams, lakes, forests, fields, ancient villages, ocean, islands, and China's most beautiful coast. Varied environments provide various resting places for life." According to the research results of Nan's crew over the course of many years, whilst Shenzhen only occupies 1/5000th of China's land area, it's home to 1/5th of China's bird species, and has more than 10% of the mammalian and 20% of the reptilian species. Its maritime territory is only one hundredth of a million of South China Sea's total, yet has 20% of the total species. It's a city that's hot and moist, and has more than 50% green coverage, with 2979 plant species documented, which is more than continental Europe.

Aside from the outward appearance, how is the inside of Shenzhen?

In my eyes, Shenzhen is a city full of charm for those looking to pursue their dreams. It's a place that was born as a fishing village and later went to exceed all the neighbouring cities, blooming like a magnificent flower, walking into the modern age on a par with Hong Kong, it's neighbour separated from it by just a small stream. It's a city occupied by the young and not so young, somewhere where dreams come true.

In my eyes, Shenzhen is like a reckless youth. It may have come from relatively rough roots, but it's grown into something diverse, strong, and mighty. For those that have come here to pursue their dreams, this brash child is actually quite handsome; there's nothing he doesn't dare try, nowhere he doesn't dare go. Accomplishments and mistakes are both present in number, but he always pushes forward, like an intrepid backpacker.

In my eyes, Shenzhen is also like a warm-hearted Confucian scholar. Reading is celebrated, enjoyed, and respected here. The city has progressed from a time when books were smart to a time when people need carts to carry all their purchases. Every district has a huge book-selling shop, and every compound has its own library. Books can be borrowed and returned everywhere. The United Nations even designated the city as a "Worldwide All-Citizen Reading Model City".

In my eyes, Shenzhen is a tolerant and humble gentleman, who says that all who come are locals. One here asks not from where heroes come. Elderly making their way across the streets need not fear traffic, and those in need of directions find themselves provided with detailed advice—if the one you ask has time, you will even find yourself accompanied part of the way.

Of course, the more people you ask, the more opinions you'll hear about the city. No matter what you hear, it will exceed what you have imagined.

Thus, when you open this book, I hope you see it as not just a textbook, but rather a vehicle through which you can come to understand the city in small pieces, with each entry describing a scene, a residence, a flavour, a person… Everything within is details and processes, rather than grand narrative; there is no simple conclusion to be drawn.

I believe that the format of this book is precisely suited for describing a city of this character.

If one views Beijing, Shanghai and Guangzhou as long-format novels, then Shenzhen can be seen as an avant-courier production with no posted end date. If the productions of the aforementioned three cities contain complete stories, then Shenzhen's performance is an impromptu one with its own legends. This is China's city with the shortest history, one that's fragmented and diverse; in these stories that are less than 140 Chinese characters in length in their original text, we see the immense intertextuality between them and the city they represent.

No matter from which angle we enter Shenzhen, we can gain an impression of the metropolis, whilst at the same time not having a fixed or comprehensive view. Only by gathering all these small distinct views can we have a full picture of the place we are observing. A number of years ago, there was a national joint performance of popular stage plays by troupes from different cities: Beijing had *Teahouse*, Shanghai *House of 72 Tenants*, and Guangzhou *Three Family Alley*. They all had their characteristic points and were describable and attributable. Shenzhen is quite different, however. This play is called *Magic Cube of the City*, because only a magic cube can be used as a metaphor to describe such a place.

Shenzhen:Dynamic and Diverse comes out just as the fortieth anniversary of China's opening up and reform is upon us. As we examine all of that which Shenzhen has brought us, this book comes out with the hope of showing this newly born city from a new angle.

It's my earnest hope that you enjoy the stories within.

August 3, 2018
Jiuzi Zhai, Shenzhen

目 录
CONTENTS

自然 · 天成 — 1
Nature and City

讲古 · 述今 — 29
Now and Then

此岸 · 彼岸 — 49
Here and There

特区 · 特色 — 69
SEZ and Features

移民 · 风情 — 97
Migration and Feelings

科技 · 金融 — 123
Tech and Finance

创意 · 设计 — 139
Creation and Design

读书 · 读城 — 161
Books and Reading

深商 · 化蝶 — 179
Commerce and Change

艺文 · 活色 — 207
Culture and Life

索引 — 237
Index

Nature and City

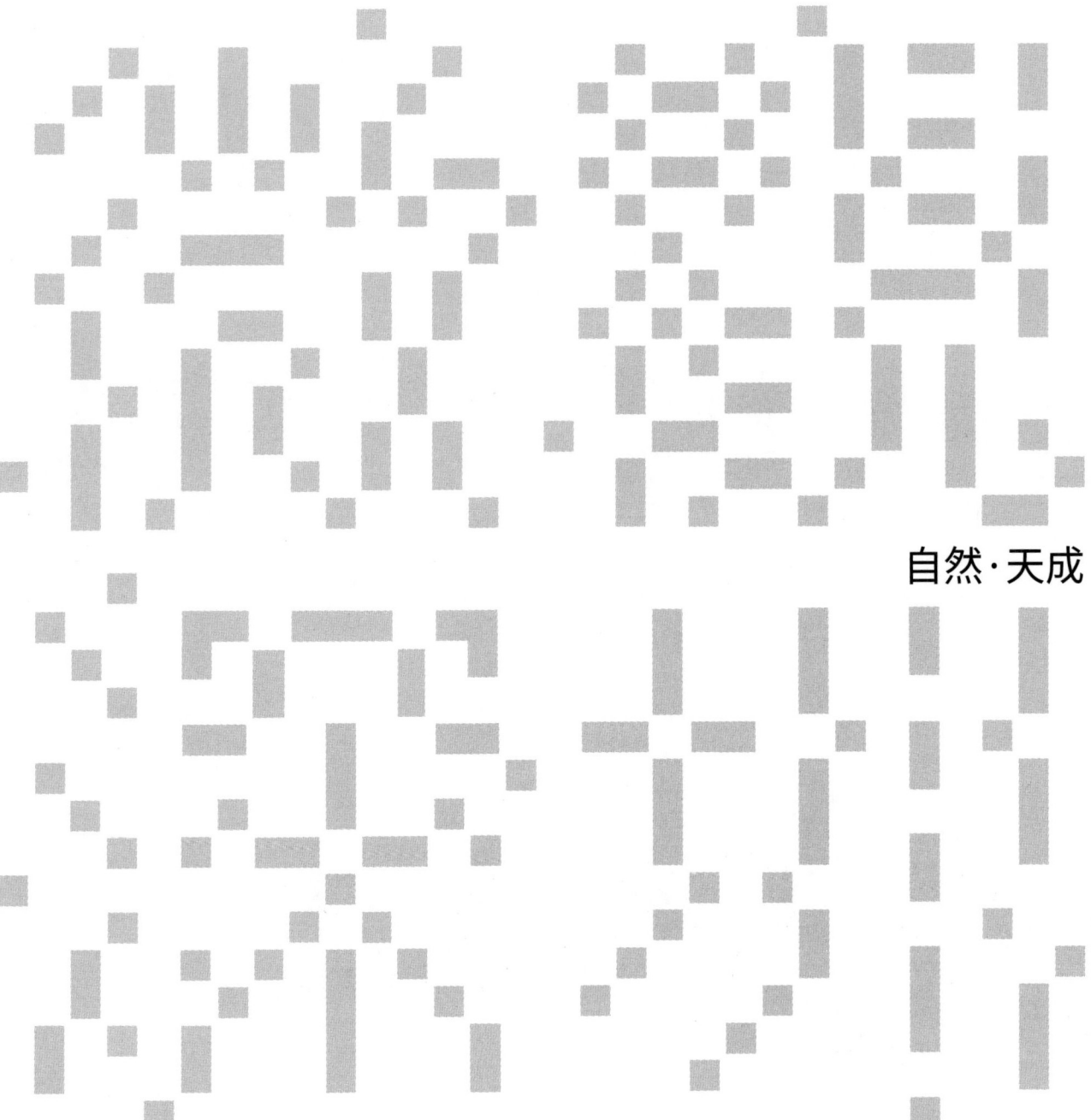

自然・天成

在深圳玩雪 001

深圳无雪更无冰，四季皆然。但市民多为北方移民，心中怀念有雪的故乡。愿望催生了国内最大的室内滑雪场：世界之窗"阿尔卑斯冰雪世界"。嬉雪场里大人可以从五层楼高的雪道冲下；小朋友玩20米的迷你滑道，更可以打雪仗。游人躲过南国似火骄阳，一脚踏进冰雪世界，乡恋瞬间沁入心扉。

Alps Snow World

Shenzhen has no snow, much less ice—this is how it is year round. However, with many of the residents of the people hailing from the northern portions of the country, there is a market for those who miss the weather of their hometowns. This led to the construction of the country's largest indoor snow park: Window of the World's "Alps Snow World". Adults can slide down a five-storey slope, and children can enjoy a 20-metre mini-slope, as well as snowball fights. Visitors to the city can avoid the scorching heat here; just take a step inside and let your spirit fly.

树林里的潜伏者 002

噪鹃，听名字就不招人待见，昼夜不停的响亮叫声吸引着观鸟者，但几乎无人见过此鸟。深圳的噪鹃多为华南亚种，每日清晨凄厉开叫，扰人清梦。夏季在公园及树木浓密处，均可闻其嘹亮的鸣叫。禽鸟专家说，噪鹃能在城市出现，说明这里生态环境极好，此鸟数量日稀，已入世界濒危物种红色名录。

赤湾天后宫的香火袅袅 003

天后又称妈祖，为沿海地区渔民共同信仰的海神。赤湾天后宫始建于宋代，明朝郑和下西洋，曾以此为一站，遂成海上丝绸之路的重要节点。鲁言于《香港掌故》记载："由于赤湾天后古庙宏伟，每年农历三月廿三天后诞，香港、九龙水陆居民都前往赤湾天后庙去贺诞。"至今香火仍袅袅不绝。

Lurkers in the Bush

The Chinese Koel is a bird that lurks in the foliage, calling out day at night, but is rarely seen. The variety common in Shenzhen is that of the Southern Chinese subspecies. Every day as the sun rises it lets out shrill and forlorn cry, waking those sleeping nearby. In the summer it's often about in the dense trees of parks and forests, and its call can be heard everywhere. Ornithologists say that for the koel to appear in a city, the environment must be exceptionally good. The bird is rare, and has been placed on the red list for endangered species.

Smoke from the Temple

Mazu, the goddess of the ocean, is widely worshiped by the local coastal fishers. The temple in Chiwan dedicated to her was built in the Song Dynasty, and was a stop on Zheng He's route when he sailed the ocean in the Ming Dynasty. It also became an important site on the Maritime Silk Road. Lu Yan, in *Hong Kong Memories* notes: "As the temple to Mazu at Chiwan is large in size, on the twenty-third day of the third lunar month, people from Hong Kong and Kowloon as well as those living upon the water come to the temple to celebrate her birthday." Even today large curls of smoke rise there from the incense being burnt in offering.

从湿地看风水 004

明永乐八年（1410年），历史上首次出现"深圳"一词，本地人称小河沟为"圳"，深圳因而得名。广东人普遍迷信，深圳背山靠水，风水极好。已被发现的几块湿地被保护起来，芦苇茂盛，草长莺飞。对此现代科学另有诠释，湿地乃城市之肾，调节气候，改善水质。特区成立至今，得风藏水，全赖斯也。

Feng shui from the Wetlands 004

The name "Shenzhen" was first used in the 8th year of the Yongle Emperor's reign in the Ming Dynasty (1410). "Shen" means deep and "zhen" is a ditch between fields. Cantonese people are widely superstitious, and believe that the city, both situated on the sea and abutted by mountains, has excellent Feng shui. A number of wetlands that have been discovered are protected, with reeds and grasses growing thickly and birds flying about. Modern scientists explain that they function like the kidneys of the city, regulating the environment and improving water quality, an important function for the urban environment after the establishment of the Special Economic Zone (SEZ).

大华兴寺隐于观音山 005

大华兴寺矗于三洲田，其之"大"不在庙大，而在佛像大，镇寺之宝为观音坐莲宝像。大华兴寺的观音坐莲宝像是目前世界上最大的，也是唯一集四尊不同观音像为一体的佛像。常见都市中各路忙人，抽暇登山入寺。听钟鼓之音阵阵，闻弥漫檀香缈缈，立时心静如水。站在山顶俯瞰山海，万般烦恼皆抛于九霄。

Dahuaxing Temple 005

Dahuaxing Temple towers over Sanzhoutian. The "da", meaning big, refers not to the size of the temple, but rather to its statute of Avalokitesvara. The statute of her seated upon a lotus is the world's largest, and the only one depicting her four incarnations. People in the city climb the mountain to visit when they have time. Listening to the beat of the drums and smelling the thick smell of incense, you feel as if your heart has been purified. Standing upon the mountain looking out over the sea, you feel all your worries and troubles float away in the wind.

"花园"深圳

Shenzhen Garden

深圳被国际植物学界誉为"全覆盖的花园"。一个不大的城市居然有1000多个公园，绿化覆盖率几近50%，绿色是这座城市最得意的"颜值"。2017年，第19届国际植物学大会在深圳举办。国际植物学大会是该领域规模最大、水平最高的学术会议，被誉为植物科学界的"奥林匹克"。大会历经百年，首次花落中国。

Shenzhen is noted for its very high degree of green coverage. The city has over 1,000 parks, and more than fifty-percent vegetative coverage, making it full of natural beauty. In 2017, the 19th International Botanical Congress was conducted in Shenzhen. It is the largest conference in the world of botany, with the highest level of academic discussion—the "Olympics" of the botanical world. The congress has been conducted for a century, and this was the first time it took place in China.

海滨栈道任徜徉

深圳有两条海滨栈道。一条是世界最长的海滨栈道——东部大鹏湾栈道，东起沙头角，终点背仔角，全长20千米，有木头道、水泥道，可骑行、可步行。另一条是西部深圳湾栈道，栈道的对岸是香港米埔，沿着海岸长廊行走，海面碧波荡漾，海岸红树林逶迤，海天之间，数万只候鸟翔集，深圳湾不再寂寞。

A Walk Along the Beach

Shenzhen has two plank pathways along the ocean, one of which is the world's longest. In the east of the city is the Dapeng Bay Plank Pathway, which originates in the east at Shatoujiao and terminates at Beizaijiao, for a total length of 20 kilometres. It has a plank pathway, and a cement pathway, and can be walked or biked upon. The other plank pathway is in the west, at Shenzhen Bay, opposite the Mipu preserve in Hong Kong. It runs along coast, undulating like the waves of the sea, winding alongside the mangroves. In the vast blue sea and sky migratory birds fly, providing accompaniment to the landscape.

梵音悠扬弘法寺 008

弘法寺1983年始建，是中华人民共和国成立后首座新建寺院。由于地处改革开放前沿，毗邻港澳，面向东南亚，中国佛教协会对其寄予厚望：要办成中国一流的佛教文化寺院，成为同海外佛教界联谊的纽带。1992年正式对民众开放，南禅临济宗第44代传人本焕长老升座方丈。2012年本焕以106岁高龄圆寂，坐化得舍利子。

Hongfa Temple

Hongfa Temple was built in 1983, making it the first new temple built after the founding of the People's Republic of China. In the context of opening up and reform, as it is near Hong Kong and Macao and faces towards southeast Asia, the China Buddhist Association had great hopes for it, to make it a first-rate Chinese Buddhist cultural site, and establish links with Buddhist associations abroad. Formally opened to the people in 1992, the 44th generation Linji practitioner Ben Huan served as abbot. He passed in the seated position in 2012 at 106 years of age, and some sarira remained from cremation of his body.

Mangrove Forest

绿色的红树林 009

The expansive forests of this subtropical evergreen tree, interspersed with shrubs, function as embankments that shield against waves. Located on the north bank of Shenzhen Bay, they look out across the sea at Hong Kong. In 1984, a protective zone for them was formally established. Prince Philip of the United Kingdom and Prince Henrik of Denmark have both visited for birdwatching, remarking that the site is a "green pearl".

红树并非某种植物的专称，红树林亦非红树之林，乃是10多种热带、亚热带的常绿灌木和小乔木群落，常起护堤防浪作用。深圳红树林位于深圳湾东北岸，与香港隔海相望。1984年正式设立红树林保护区。英女王丈夫菲利普亲王、丹麦女王丈夫亨里克亲王，都曾专程到此观鸟，并惊叹于这串"绿色明珠"。

生态广场拥抱幽静

人类若要与自然和平相处，首先便要顺其自然。华侨城生态广场循此原则，广场上的人文和自然景观均依照原始地形随势而建，虽有楼宇在侧，但犹如在山野之间。眼前便是山丘、溪流、瀑布、芦苇、绿荫和鲜花，人虽置身都市之中，却又拒喧嚣于外，是一个可以拥抱诗意和远方、发呆的好去处。

Ecological Park

For people to coexist with nature peacefully, we must follow its course. The ecological park in Overseas Chinese Town (OCT) follows this principle, with human and natural vistas following the native shape of the land. Although there are buildings to the sides, it still feels as if one is deep in the mountains, with hills, streams, waterfalls, reeds, the shade of trees and flowers all about. You may be in the city, but you're isolated from the clamour and noise. This is a place full of feelings of poetry and distance, a nice place to let yourself go.

Dutch Village

The Holland Flower Village in Shenzhen is a place that combines the culture, creativity, relaxation and art of Shenzhen. It was formerly the Nanshan Floral World, and was opened in its current form in 2011. It has the three Dutch essentials: clogs, windmills and tulips. There are many flower shops here, and the sculptures of tulips are all about. There is also a small lake full of reeds in the village, with calm water only slightly rippling. With water, lotus flowers, and green leaves, this is a great spot to take pictures.

花卉小镇的荷兰风情

荷兰花卉小镇是深圳文化、创意、休闲、艺术的集群地。前身是南山花卉世界，于2011年开园。荷兰三宝——木鞋、风车、郁金香皆汇于此。小镇里花卉园艺店面众多，随处都有郁金香的雕塑。镇里有一小湖名为"芦趣"，水面平静，微有波澜，靠岸多处芦苇摇摆，红莲碧叶杂陈其间，倒是小资拍照的好地方。

Lizhi Park

Autumn in Shenzhen can't really be called autumn, as it still has the feeling of summer. Blue skies, green grasses, bright flowers, clear lakes—beauty is all around. All kinds of flowers bloom in the park, and fruit hang from the branches of trees. Green grass flourishes. Lizhi Park is an excellent place to go to appreciate the osmanthus blooms, which open in early autumn, brilliant yellow with a wonderful fragrance. One feels refreshed in the heart and gladdened in the mind as the soft breeze blows.

荔枝公园的秋意

深圳的秋天绝不能简称"深秋"，因为仍然是夏意。蓝天、绿草、鲜花、湖泊，处处温馨美丽。公园里各色鲜花绽放，路边果树硕果累累，草坪绿意盎然。荔枝公园是赏桂花的好去处。秋天桂花开了，黄灿灿的小花挂了一树，空气中散发出阵阵清香，沁人心脾。你还可以在湖边感受一下微风拂面。

荔枝花开 013

初夏，开园不久的香蜜公园10万平方米荔枝花海，让游人流连忘返。荔枝是深圳的特产，三四月开荔枝花，五六月结荔枝果。花香果甜齐名，眼福口福皆饱。荔枝花总是密密麻麻地排列在一起，站在香蜜公园的中部栈道，大片大片金黄的荔枝花扑面而来，花香四溢，蜂蝶飞舞，福田香蜜，此言不虚。

蝴蝶谷在梦幻中闪亮 014

一群斑蝶在长途迁徙途中，来到一处僻静、隐秘的栖息地。它们聚在一起，层层叠叠地挤在树干上休息，有时候翩翩起舞，翅膀在寂静处会发出美妙的声音，犹如花开一般。这就是马峦山的蝴蝶谷。《深圳自然笔记》作者南兆旭说："11月，我可以和同伴们去看看那几万只斑蝶回来了没有。"

蓝色的抛物线伸向远方 015

深圳是个令无数人羡慕的滨海城市。碧波荡漾，惊涛拍岸，潮起潮落间，沧海桑田变迁。大鹏半岛海岸被《中国国家地理》评为中国最美的八大海岸之一，其中东涌、西涌更是深圳的"黄金海岸"。但如今，许多海岸线被填埋、修建、占用。我们应该真正学会珍惜。

Lychees Blooming

At the start of summer, the recently-opened Xiangmi Park, with an area of 100,000 square metres, becomes a sea of lychee flowers. Lychees are a local product in Shenzhen; they bloom in March and April, and bear fruit in May and June. The flowers are fragrant, and the fruit sweet—a true treat. The inflorescences of the lychee trees are dense clusters. Standing on the plank pathway in Xiangmi Park, surrounded by lychee flowers, you're drenched in their fragrance, as bees and butterflies fly about.

A Dreamy Atmosphere

A group of Ursula butterflies come here to take a rest on the route of their long migration. They gather together on the tree branches, occasionally fluttering their wings, making a beautiful sound as they fly about, their movements resembling blooming flowers. This is the Butterfly Valley of Mount Maluan. The author of *Notes of Landscape in Shenzhen* Nan Zhaoxu says: "In November, I can come with my comrades here to see if the tens of thousands of butterflies have returned."

A Long Blue Curve

Shenzhen is an enviable coastal city. The surface of the water ripples as mighty waves crash against the coast, rising and falling with the tides. The coast of the Dapeng Peninsula has been listed as one of the eight great coasts in China by the magazine *Chinese National Geography*. Dongchong and Xichong are both "golden beaches". However in modern times, a lot of the coast has been filled in, built upon, or occupied. We need to learn how to treasure these landscapes.

以深圳人命名的昆虫

毕业于深圳大学的黄宝平是一个"追虫子的人"。他先后在坪山和大鹏半岛发现了两种蚁甲科的新种。一种以其母之名命名为"亚连中华锤角蚁甲",另一种以其外婆之名命名为"珠带寡节蚁甲"。这是世界首次以深圳人的名字命名昆虫。在"追虫人"心中,一个水洼就是一片海洋。

Insects Named by a Local

Graduate of Shenzhen University Huang Baoping is an insect chaser. On Pingshan District and the Dapeng Peninsula, he found two new species of pselaphids, one named for his mother, and one for his grandmother. This was the first time that a Shenzhen local had named a new insect species. Working at the scale he does, a puddle of water is practically an ocean.

如火的簕杜鹃

烈日暴晒,台风肆虐,全然改变不了簕杜鹃在南国热土上娇艳多姿和绚烂夺目的盛放。这种学名为"三角梅"和"九重葛"的花儿是深圳市的市花,花型硕大,花色鲜艳如火。它来自遥远的南美,折枝便可扦插成活,如同来自全国各地的深圳人一样,一旦在这片新土扎根,便不畏风吹雨打,怒放生命。

Bougainvillea

Under the hot sun and the intense rain of typhoons, the bougainvillea still grows beautiful and strong in Shenzhen. Bougainvillea glabra is the city flower of Shenzhen, with large, fiery-red blooms. Originally from South America, one can simply snap off a branch and plant it to propagate the plant. Just like the people who come to Shenzhen from all over the country, once it takes root, it can withstand rain and strong wind, and thrives with a will to survive.

"山城"深圳

"青山行不尽,绿水去何长",崔颢的诗句仿佛字字都道出深圳的形貌。除去绵长的海岸线的拥抱,这座城市似乎静卧在起伏的山脉之间:梧桐山、笔架山、观音山、羊台山、马峦山……山山不同,各有姿彩。想知道它们的不同,用你的脚去丈量吧!深圳也成为全国最早开展民间登山、探险运动的城市之一。

Mountain City

There are countless mountains to climb and rivers to follow—the words of Tang Dynasty poet Cui Hao seem almost as if they were meant to describe Shenzhen. Aside from the long coastline, Shenzhen also has a large number of peaks and valleys: Mounts Wutong, Bijia, Guanyin, Yangtai, Maluan… There are so many different mountains with different characters here. If you want to know the character of each one, you must walk it with your own footsteps. Shenzhen is one of the earliest Chinese cities in which hiking and exploration became popular in modern times.

自然的爱与愁

深圳自然学者南兆旭说到深圳的自然生态总是滔滔不绝：600 年仍然郁郁葱葱的古榕树，在鹏城上空自由飞翔的鸟类，四季常青的山野里恣意生长的珍稀植物，海底世界种类繁多的珊瑚……他用了十几年在深圳的山海间行走，写下《深圳自然笔记》，用文图留住地上的一片绿，并记下他对自然的爱与愁。

Natural Feelings

Shenzhen-based naturist Nan Zhaoxu has so much to say about Shenzhen: a 600-year-old banyan tree, the various birds that fly freely in the sky, the blankets of vegetation upon the mountains, green year round, all the kinds of coral that grow in the sea. He has spent more than a decade exploring the mountains and waters of Shenzhen, writing a book *Notes of Landscape in Shenzhen*, using pictures and text to describe in detail all the green spots of Shenzhen and his feelings of love and worry for them.

深圳下雪

雪，对深圳人来说无异于一个美丽的童话。这个童话故事在 2016 年初春让深圳人大喜过望。一则深圳"下雪"的消息引来梧桐山下车水马龙，市民纷纷前往山顶"赏雪"。然而，市气象局表示，大家看到的只是低温后的雾凇，以及类似白雪的冰粒。下山者将车头用雪粒堆成的雪人上传网络，果然美得像童话。

Snow in Shenzhen

Snow is like something out of a fairy tale for the people of Shenzhen. This tale came to Shenzhen in 2016, when the weather forecasters predicted snow. The roads below Mount Wutong were jammed with traffic, everyone summiting to enjoy the "snow". The meteorological agency noted that in fact it was technically rime that had formed after a low temperature period, small white snow-like balls of ice clinging to the vegetation. People posted pictures of little snowmen they made out of them online, making the fairy tale a reality for others to witness.

梧桐烟云 021

住在梧桐山下的文人禹安曾写诗描述梧桐烟云："梧桐翠壁山径微，仙湖深秋仍芳菲。敢问弘法觉海在？拈花一笑看落晖。"其实雨后的梧桐山最美，山色翠绿，却被浓雾萦绕，花草树木的叶子上都凝聚着一层露珠。此时行山，总会恍惚，以为自己是误入凡尘的仙家。如此，梧桐山遂成"深圳八景"之首。

泛红的毛棉杜鹃节 022

三月末，绿了一冬的凤凰台开始星星点点地泛红，从山腰到山顶，近20亩的毛棉杜鹃陆陆续续地盛开，深深浅浅的红色铺成了一片壮观的花海。历时半个月的毛棉杜鹃节，吸引了众多的市民上山观赏。当人们一步一步地走向远离市区的海拔高处，愈走近花的海洋，便愈走近心灵放飞的地方。

Clouds on Mount Wutong 021

Man of letters Yu An wrote about the smoky clouds on Mount Wutong, their beautiful appearance evoking thoughts in the autumn as they drifted about. The mountain is in fact most beautiful after a rain, with green everywhere that's shrouded in mists, small drops of dew cleaning to the leaves everywhere. Walking the mountain at this time, one feels as if in a trance, as if one has entered a fairy's home in our mortal realm. It's for this reason that Mount Wutong is the foremost of the "eight sights of Shenzhen".

Rhododendron Moulmainense 022

At the end of March, Fenghuang Terrace, which has been green all winter, becomes flecked with points of red everywhere. From the middle of the mountain to its peak, more than 3 acres of land are covered with the blooming rhododendrons, forming a striking sea of red flowers. This half-month-long sight draws many people from the city to admire it. As you walk in this high-up place far from the city, you look out over the sea of flowers as your spirit flies.

自然·天成　18

窗外有片相思林

"楠榴之木,相思之树。"相思可以成林,亦可以成园。深圳银湖度假村内,便有一座小小的相思林公园。山顶的烽火台虽是人造,却刻着岁月的痕迹,可以鸟瞰整个银湖美景,清幽的山泉自山顶倾泻,优雅地从公园中缓缓淌过。时光飞逝,当年热闹的度假村游人渐少,而流水依旧,林中的相思依旧。

Acacia Forest

Acacias can form both forests and gardens. At the Yinhu Resort Village in Shenzhen, there is a small park forested with acacias. Although the beacon tower at the peak is man-made, it still shows the traces of years of wear. From here one can look out over the entire lake into which spring water slowly flows from the mountain, passing quietly through the park. Time passes, and even visitors to the resort village become few, the water continues to flow and the forest continues to stand.

人与兽的角色互换

深圳野生动物园是国内首个放养式动物园。人在笼中坐,猛兽自由行,让游人大感新奇刺激,并发展成为国内最早集动物园、植物园、科普园为一体的新型园林生态环境风景区。北有连绵青山为屏,南有巨型动物石雕,东有葱郁的荔枝林,西有澄碧的西丽湖。园内处处皆佳景,景景皆迷人。

Switching Places

Safari Park Shenzhen is the first free-range zoo in the country, where people are in cages and beasts roam freely. It's an exciting experience for the visitors. It's also the first site in China to combine a zoo, a botanical garden, and a science park. In the north there are continuous green mountains, in the south giant rock sculptures of the animals, in the east a lychee tree forest, and in the west the Xili Lake. There are all kinds of wonderful things to see here.

茵特拉根小镇的穿越

如果没有钱也没有闲去欧洲,那么你可以去深圳的茵特拉根小镇。那里山青水碧、鸟鸣谷幽、云遮雾绕,又有古老的森林小火车、典雅的度假酒店,小镇的每一个角落都突显着浓浓的瑞士风情,无处不散发着浪漫优雅。在亚欧这两个同名小镇之间穿梭,仿佛是一场时空的穿越。

Interlaken Is Here

If you don't have the time or money to visit Europe, you can visit the Interlaken Village in Shenzhen, where there are mountains, water, birds, and clouds. You can ride the small forest train, stay at the luxurious resort hotel, and feel Swiss culture in every corner of the complex. It really is like travelling through time and space being here.

榕树寿星见证生命

在深圳这片古老而年轻的土地上生长了数百年的生命令人敬仰。南园村615年的老榕树是深圳植物中最年长的生命。半天云村的风水林中，最老的枫树已经超过了400岁。纪伯伦说："假如一棵树来写历史，那也会像一个民族的历史。"深圳人书写深圳的历史，而深圳的树木沉默地见证着深圳的历史。

Old Trees

There are some quite impressive trees in the both old and new city of Shenzhen. The oldest of them is a 615-year-old banyan in Nanyuan Village; the oldest maples are more than four centuries old in Bantianyun Village. Writer Kahlil Gibran remarked that trees could write history just in the way that people could. The people of the city write their histories in words, and the trees stand there as quiet testaments to the passage of time.

翠竹之园

竹乃岁寒三友之一，其傲骨临风的品格深得千百年来文人心。深圳市区内有一处清幽之地——翠竹公园。园内绿烟蔽日，翠玉凝露，竹林景致，沁人心脾，将游人与闹市的喧嚣隔离开来。漫步其间，清风徐来，竹自林立，自有一番风格。难怪清人郑燮赋诗云："一节复一节，千枝攒万叶。我自不开花，免撩蜂与蝶。"

Cuizhu Park

Bamboo, along with the pine and plum, is one of the "three friends of winter". It stands tall and strong against the winds and ravages of time. There is a nice, quiet place in the urban centre—Cuizhu ("green bamboo") Park. Within there are many bamboo trees growing with dense foliage, the sight of which refreshes the onlooker. Deep green leaves filter the sunlight, making for a wonderful scene, and shielding visitors from the noise of the city. Taking a slow walk through the park amidst the tall stalks, one experiences a different feeling. Qing Dynasty poet Zheng Xie wrote a poem about such scenes: "Trunks support branches from which leaves rise. I keep to myself as to not disturb the bees and butterflies."

一脚回到远古 028

比人类诞生更遥远的时间被定格在生物化石之中。深圳古生物博物馆坐落于仙湖植物园古化石森林旁，展馆外形酷似一块巨大的岩石城堡，收藏的上千件古生物化石，是远古时期的历史见证。整个博物馆内部都是仿原始地形地貌，蜻蜓、蜥蜴等化石散落在四周，一脚踏进，恍如瞬间穿越，回到了远古时代。

Back to the Past

Freeze-frames of time before humanity are recorded in the fossil record. The Shenzhen Museum of Palaeontology is situated next to the Fairy Lake Botanical Garden's petrified forest. It's constructed in the form of a giant stone castle, and displays more than a thousand petrified objects, testaments to the past. The entire museum looks like a primeval landscape, with dragonflies and lizards fossils all about. Walking in, you feel as if you've entered a previous age.

新安古城 029

新安古城又称南头古城，现存古朴雄伟的南门。城内原有县前街等九条街道，故又俗称"九街"。南头建城史最早可溯源至汉元封元年（前110年），古时为珠江口东岸海防要塞、交通贸易重镇，是深圳之根，也是粤港澳地区历史源头，附近为伶仃洋。古城静处都市中，现代繁华和历史厚重在此融合。

Xin'an Ancient City

The Xin'an Ancient City is also known as the Nantou Ancient City, and still has its old, ancient south gate. Xianqian Street is one of the nine thoroughfares within; the city used to be known as "Nine Streets" in common parlance. The origins of the site can be traced back to the first year of the Yuanfeng Emperor's reign in the Han Dynasty (110 BC). In ancient times it was an important defensive location, as well as a site for commerce. It can be seen as the root of Shenzhen, as well as the origin of the history of Guangdong, Hong Kong and Macao. It's situated near the Lingdingyang Estuary. It now rests calmly within the city, a site that combines the modern and ancient, the wild and calm.

三洲田问茶 030

风云变迁，沧海桑田。三洲田村因1900年爆发"庚子起义"闻名，1958年修建水库时沉入湖底，现开发为东部华侨城茶溪谷景区。该地群山环绕，气候独特，山间茶树层层叠叠，优质乌龙茶引爱茶人士趋之若鹜。在三洲田，品香茗一盏，迎山林晚风，望碧波万顷，观古典茶艺，赏悠扬茶曲，犹如身处世外桃源。

青青世界 031

青青世界居于大南山西麓，养在深闺，是一个容易被人忽略和遗忘的生态观光农场。歌手那英为这里演唱的主题歌让这里名声大噪。热带雨林植物生机茂盛，侏罗纪公园遇见恐龙在飞奔，蝴蝶谷里万蝶起舞弄清影，瓜果园让五谷不分的孩子大长见识。有人在此起航，开启青春；有人在此回归，重拾青春。

Evergreen Resort 031

Tea in Sanzhoutian 030

Time brings great changes to the world. Sanzhoutian became famous in 1900 during the Boxer War, and in 1958 was submerged after the construction of a reservoir. It's now the OCT Tea Valley Scenic Area. Encircled by mountains, it has unique climate. Tea trees grow densely upon the surrounding slopes, and tea enthusiasts scramble for the Oolong tea that grows upon them. This is a wonderful place to have a cup of tea, enjoy the calm night breeze, look out over the lush landscape, and appreciate a tea ceremony, taking in the music, as if you are in paradise.

The Guangming Farm 032

In 1958, the government arranged a location for overseas returnees—the Guangming Farm. People have intense memories of returning to China and arriving here. Now it's been called the "back garden of Shenzhen". Forestry, animal husbandry, farming and fishing both flourish here, and the "Guangming Milk" and "Guangming Pigeons" are both quite famous. There are many entertainment activities here now, as well: one can enjoy both grass skiing and bungee jumping.

归国华侨的光明之地 032

There is a wonderful site at the lower reaches of Mount Danan that is easily ignored or forgotten; famous singer Na Ying even described it in one of her songs. Rainforest plants grow thickly here, beasts fly, butterflies flutter, fruit gardens give education to children... If you get a chance, you should take a visit to the Evergreen Resort and enjoy a world of green.

1958年，为安置东南亚纷纷归来的华侨，深圳建立了光明农场。有人回忆，当年拖家带口的华侨们一踏上这片祖先之地，立刻长跪不起，热泪涟涟。如今这里被誉为深圳"都市后花园"。农林牧渔诸业兴旺，"光明牛奶"和"光明乳鸽"最为闻名；观光娱乐项目丰富多彩，滑草、蹦极让青少年大感刺激。

坝光遗世独立 033

坝光的名字自带美感,"深圳的九寨沟"等美称也不及。居于深圳最东端边界,偏僻让坝光得以保留纯净;古树众多,有处罕见的银叶树群,被称为"中国最古老的银叶树群"。甘蔗林、沙滩、海浪、贝壳、简陋码头,客家老屋,坝光遗世而独立地美。随着开发建设,坝光的容颜却也在一点儿一点儿地褪去。

海山公园 034

依山而建,布局巧妙,结合中式园林和西式建筑风格,街心花园的容量,营造天人合一的气场。"天石"拔地而起,挺拔昂扬。建有中国最大的景观象棋盘,面积达680多平方米,棋子重130斤,如此巨型棋盘棋子,考验棋手智慧,更考验体力,只有与天对弈的高人可下此棋。"山呼""海应",公园点眼之笔。

Haishan Park

Built next to the mountains, this is a site with a wonderful layout that combines Chinese gardening and Western architecture. It's an excellent getaway within the city centre. Amazing stone structures rise from the ground here. This is also the site of the largest chess set in China, more than 680 square metres in area, with each piece weighing more than 65 kilogrammes—playing this game is not just a test of wits, but also strength. Here mountains call, and the sea answers.

Remains of Baguang

Baguang is renowned as a beautiful site in Shenzhen, comparable with Jiuzhaigou in Sichuan. Situated in the far east of Shenzhen, its remote nature has allowed it to remain pure, with a large number of old trees, and a rare Heritiera littoralis forest which is renowned for being the oldest in China. There are also groves of sugarcane, beaches, waves, shells, a simple quay, and an old Hakka residence. As development progresses, however, this simple countenance is slowly fading.

溪谷生态园 035

溪流穿凿山石，无尽光阴，在深圳东侧园山中切割出嵯峨山峰，打磨出光滑岩石。溯溪而上，两岸连山，植被茂盛，鸟语花香，泉水欢唱，负氧离子醉人，被称为"深圳又一处后花园"。徒步健身外，可赏花、摘草莓、玩刺激的CS游戏、吃纯正农家菜。假期周末，约三五友人，生态园内自助野炊，更是乐事。

玫瑰海岸 036

玫瑰遇上大海，浪漫从此无以言表，这里是新婚夫妇的必到之地。廊桥、相思林、同心锁、情之涯，是为美好爱情、婚礼设计的背景。作为深圳及周边地区年轻人喜欢去的婚纱摄影地，华南地区最大的婚庆产业基地之一，玫瑰海岸传递的是浪漫温馨。停留在玫瑰花海中的时光虽短，记忆里却是永恒。

西涌情人岛 037

离西涌海滩约1海里，深圳最东的一块陆地，孤悬于海上。海水蔚蓝清澈，沙滩细腻爽白，红树林茂密葱茏，海鸟蹁跹飞舞，恋人谈情说爱的圣地，被奉为"人间天堂""深圳最后的一块净土"。在十里银滩，年轻人牵手漫步海边，在海风中山盟海誓，它原本的名字"赖氏洲"已被遗忘，为"情人岛"取代。

Creek Valley Park

This is a site of craggy peaks on the Mount Yuan on the eastern side of Shenzhen; the rock formations here are a sight to behold. A river flows within, and thick plant coverage is all about. Birds sing and the fragrances of flowers flow throughout the air. The water is clear and the oxygen in the air intoxicates visitors; this is a natural site better than humans could design. Taking a healthy walk through the area, appreciating flowers, picking strawberries, playing airsoft, or eating delicious country food are all activities available here. It's a great place to gather up some friends on a weekend and have a barbecue.

Rose Coast

It's a very romantic scene where rose bushes abut on the ocean, and makes for a wonderful place for couples to visit. A gallery bridge, an acacia forest, a love lock spot, "The End of the World"—this is a site that's designed for weddings, and one of the top spots for young couples to take wedding photos on the outskirts of Shenzhen, as well as one of the major sites for the wedding industry in southern China. The Rose Coast is truly a place of romance. Although one may only spend a short while here, the memories will last for a long time.

Lovers' Island

Only one mile away from Xichong Beach lies Shenzhen's most easterly point, standing alone in the sea. Sitting in the clear azure sea with beaches of fine sand, this is a place where mangroves grow and birds soar overhead. It's a popular spot for lovers, and has been called a "paradise", as well as "Shenzhen's best preserved natural site". The long beach is an excellent place for a lovers' stroll, where one can look out at the beautiful ocean. The original name "Laishizhou" is hardly ever used, with everyone now calling the place "Lovers' Island".

马峦山访梅

马峦山不以高峻取胜,而以水秀闻名。龙潭瀑布群为深圳最大,"白练当空挂,银河落九天"。在马峦山不仅可观海,如果运气好,更可欣赏到海市蜃楼的人间仙境。尤其在那青色依依的树丛中,盛开着万株幽幽的梅花,用手轻抚着一束束幽花,感受她"零落成泥碾作尘,只有香如故"的"高风亮节"。

Plums in Maluanshan

Maluanshan, or "Mount Maluan", isn't famous for having high peaks, but rather for having beautiful waters. It has the largest spring waterfall in Shenzhen, which shines majestically with white spray. Here, one not only can view the sea, but, if luck is good, can also see a wonderful mirage. There's a wonderful forest in which plum trees grow, making for an excellent sight when they bloom. It's a wonderful place to get away and enjoy nature.

Facing the Sea

There are two places named "17 Mile" in the world: one is on the Monterey Peninsula in California, and the other is on the Dapeng Peninsula upon which Shenzhen lies. They're both mountainous, and have gentle beaches and soft waves. Vanke has the slogan "We can maintain distance with the world", which it uses to attract city dwellers. "Facing the sea, the flowers of spring bloom" is the feel that it sells, playing to the desire of people to return to nature, and have a separation from that hustle and bustle of everyday city life.

Mystic Tree

Generations come and go over the course of centuries among humans, but trees remain. The plumeria tree beside the Wu's Ancestral Hall in the Fenghuang Compound on Pinghu Sub-district is over 500 years old. It is tall, strong, and has thick foliage. In 2006 it was entered into the list of ancient trees of the Longgang District. It offsets the ancestral hall, and is a guardian of the spirits of the Wu clan. It blooms year round with great fragrance; its flowers can be sunned to make material for a tisane, which can treat headache and fever. It's known as the "Mystic Tree" by local residents.

面朝大海，春暖花开

世界上有两个"17英里"，一个在美国加州蒙特利半岛，一个在深圳大鹏半岛。都是山海相拥，都是滩缓浪柔。万科希望以"我能与这个世界保持的距离"理念吸引渴望山海的都市人，"面朝大海，春暖花开"的居住环境，正满足了他们回归自然的幻想和期望，凭栏望海，潮起潮落间大有回看尘世之感。

神仙树

春秋更迭数百载，清风徐来花自开。位于平湖街道凤凰社区伍氏宗祠旁的鸡蛋花古树，树干高大，枝叶繁茂，树龄已500余年，2006年被列入龙岗区古树保护名录。古树与古祠相伴，是伍氏族人的心灵寄托。古树四季有花，花开时带有鸡蛋香，花瓣晒干冲茶，可医治头痛发热，功效神奇，被居民称为"神仙树"。

Now and Then

讲古·述今

Chiwan Bay Left Fort

Chiwan Bay is located at Mount Yingzui in Shekou District, and in ancient times boats travelling between Guangzhou and the Southeast Asian countries would all pass by here. In the Ming Dynasty, a pier was erected to combat pirates, and in the 56th year of the Kangxi Emperor's reign in the Qing Dynasty (1717), forts were built—they have already been 300 years. During the time of the Opium Wars, Lin Zexu, when garrisoned with troops at the Pearl River, had the forts repaired. In modern times only the left fort stands silently, a complaint of ages past. A bronze statue of Lin Zexu stands, a monocular held in hand looking out over the Lingdingyang Estuary, face full of determination.

赤湾炮台的诉说

赤湾雄踞蛇口鹰嘴山，古代船舶往来广州与南洋诸国，皆经此地。明代已设墩台以防海盗，清康熙五十六年（1717年）始建炮台，迄今已300年。鸦片战争期间，林则徐布防珠江口时重修炮台，现仅剩左炮台默立山头，诉说着一个时代的悲剧。林则徐铜像，手握单筒望远镜虎视伶仃洋面，满脸的不屈与坚忍。

大鹏所城

深圳别称"鹏城"，源头在此。明洪武二十七年（1394年），为抗击倭寇而在大鹏半岛鹏城村设立"大鹏守御千户所城"，简称"大鹏所城"。所城赖氏将军家族曾孕育"三代五将"，其数量之多、品位之高，实为中国军史所罕见，素有"宋朝杨家将，清代赖家帮"美誉。岁月淘淘不再，古城雄姿依旧。

Dapeng Fortress

Shenzhen is known as Pengcheng (the Roc City). In the 27th year of the Hongwu Emperor's reign in the Ming Dynasty (1394), in order to combat Japanese pirates, upon the Pengcheng Village in Dapeng (Big Roc) Peninsula, a "Dapeng Fortress to Protect the 1,000 Households" was erected, also known as Dapeng Fortress. Generations of people lived here and served in the military with distinction. Even in modern times, Shenzhen is referred to as "Pengcheng". The families of ancient times may have drifted away, but the name remains.

The Intersection

Looking down from above, in the Dongmen Laojie Street area, Jiefang Road and Renmin Road meet at a cross-shaped intersection; this is called "The Intersection" by the people of old Shenzhen. In times past, farmers from outside the city would come into town barefoot carrying fowl and vegetables to sell them here. As time has passed, The Intersection has been built up with tall buildings, and is packed with all manner of new and fashionable stores. It's still "The Intersection", however, a centre of trade, albeit with a new face.

东门十字街

从空中俯瞰，东门老街的解放路和人民路交界的地方是一个大"十"字，老深圳们称之为"十字街"。当深圳还是新安城的时候，郊外的农民打赤脚挑着肉禽蔬菜，从十里八里外聚集到此叫卖。时光飞逝，十字街高楼迭起，取而代之的是各种新潮时尚店铺和大超市。而十字还是那个十字，生活只是翻了一页在继续。

得宝者安

深圳原属宝安县，宝安境内有一山，名曰宝山，山中有宝，得宝者安，故而得名。宝安县东晋咸和六年（331年）始设，广府文化、南粤文化、客家文化于此并存；改革开放后，又加入移民文化、工业文化、海洋文化等，表里均显多元。区内文物古迹众多，以曾氏大宗祠和铁仔山古墓群遗址为代表。

Bao'an District

Shenzhen was originally within the jurisdiction of Bao'an County. Within the county there is a mountain, called Mount Bao ("Treasure Mountain"), and within there was treasure, thus the name. Bao'an County was established in the 6th year of the Xianhe Emperor's reign in the Eastern Jin Dynasty (331), and has traces of the Cantonese and Hakka cultures. After opening up and reform, elements of migratory, industrial and maritime culture were added in, making for an even more diverse landscape. Within the district there are many traces of cultures past, with the Zeng's Grand Ancestral Hall and the ruins of the ancient tombs of Mount Tiezai being representative.

风雨伶仃洋

伶仃洋又称"零丁洋",曾是中国南大门上的一道防线。鸦片战争前,伶仃洋和伶仃岛被英美鸦片贩子用快艇强占,沦为侵略者对我国走私鸦片的跳板。民族英雄文天祥曾写下千古正气诗篇《过零丁洋》,其中"惶恐滩头说惶恐,零丁洋里叹零丁。人生自古谁无死,留取丹心照汗青!"更成传世绝唱。

Lingdingyang Estuary

Lingdingyang Estuary used to be a major southern line of defence for China. Before the Opium Wars, Lingdingyang Estuary and Lingding Island were occupied by the English and Americans, perverted by invaders as a gangplank for the dealing of opium. National hero Wen Tianxiang once wrote in his classical-style poem "Passing Lingdingyang Estuary" of tragic usage of this location. The words he penned later became well-known lyrics to Chinese people which denounced the wrongs wrought upon these lands.

过街 006

"过街"在客家人口中并非指人人喊打的"老鼠过街",而是到亲戚邻居家串门。从前大家都住平房,房子与房子之间无围墙隔离,无防盗网遮拦。夏日的傍晚吃罢饭,你到我家,我到你家,孩子嬉闹,大人八卦,客家乡音里,一句东家长,一句西家短,欢声笑语不断。后来,楼渐高,街渐宽,便不"过街"了。

Crossing the Street

In Hakka culture, "crossing the street" refers to busting into a relative's house for a visit. In previous times, everyone lived in large structures without partitions between them, and no grates on the windows. In the summer after eating dinner people would just walk into each other's houses, children playing and adults gossiping, everyone living communally. Later, as buildings grew taller and streets grew wider, these customs gradually died out.

不讲粤语的广东人 007

外省人和广东人对话,总有"鸡同鸭讲"之感。因为广东人讲的"白话"粤语太难懂了。其实,广东人不一定都会讲"白话",广东方言不仅仅是粤语,还包括客家方言、闽方言,大不相同。深圳很多人讲客家话,而粤东沿海的潮汕地区讲的则是闽方言中的潮州话。众多方言杂陈,各自相安无事。

No Cantonese

It can be difficult for people from other provinces to communicate with Cantonese people, as the local language can be hard for outsiders to understand. In fact, people from Guangdong don't necessarily speak Cantonese, as dialects such as Hakka and Hokkien are also endemic to the province. Many people speak Hakka in Shenzhen, and in the Chaoshan area many people speak Teochew dialect, which is a Hokkien language. The linguistic scene is varied, but everyone gets on well enough.

甘坑小镇的客家凉帽 008

甘坑客家小镇是深圳原住民的聚居地,是一个拥有300多年历史的村庄。客家话中,"坑"是指小溪流,甘坑泉眼遍布,溪水甘甜,因而得名。甘坑从古至今以凉帽闻名中外。史载:"甘坑山,瑶人居之,多产赤竹。"用赤竹做成的凉帽实用而精美,"甘坑凉帽"已被列入广东省非物质文化遗产。

Hakka Hats

The Gankeng Hakka Town is a place where the original residents live, with more than 300 years of history. In the Hakka language, "keng" means a small stream. There are many springs with sweet water in the village, and this is where it gets its name from ("gan" means "sweet"). The summer hats of Gankeng Town have long been famous, and are even remarked upon in historical texts. Made of bamboo, they are practical and pretty, and have been listed as an intangible cultural heritage of Guangdong Province.

观澜炮楼群

在深圳,现存炮楼 500 余座。观澜镇在民国时期被称为"小香港",拥有规模最大、格局最完整的炮楼群。为了抵御外敌,保卫家园,自清以降,深圳几乎村村有炮楼。这些炮楼建筑风格各异,多数能守能攻,且与邻近民房相通。如今这些炮楼带着旧日的传奇,成为历史遗迹,在现代建筑的夹缝中独善其身。

Guanlan Blockhouses

In Shenzhen, there are more than 500 blockhouses still standing. In the Republic of China era (1912-1949), Guanlan Town was known as "Little Hong Kong"; it had the largest-scale and most complete blockhouses. In order to combat outside invasion and protect homes, from the time of the Qing Dynasty, almost all of the villages in Shenzhen had blockhouses. These structures are built in all manner of styles, most serving offensive and defensive functions, and are linked with surrounding residences. These blockhouses carry the legends of the past, and serve as relics of an age bygone, squeezed in between modern structures.

骨子里的文明城市

"礼让斑马线"已成为深圳的交通习惯,在没有信号灯的路口,车辆主动停下,行人优先通过。行人也会向司机竖起大拇指,彼此报以微笑。大多数深圳人都是彬彬有礼的,若有人问路,多半能得到热情相助。随处可见 U 站和义工,路边无人采摘的杧果、人群中坦然觅食的小鸟……这就是文明深圳。

Cultured City

Yielding to those in the striped crosswalk is already a part of Shenzhen culture. At intersections without a traffic signal, cars will stop and let pedestrians cross. Pedestrians will give the thumbs up to drivers, and they will smile at each other. Most people in Shenzhen are very polite. If you ask for directions, people will happily help you. You can see volunteers everywhere, fruit ripe for the picking on trees, birds foraging for food amongst people. This is cultured Shenzhen.

解放路的"金三角"

解放路在深圳人嘴里不叫解放路,叫东门。特区成立前的解放路是贯穿城市东西的交通要道,如今的解放路成了供游览和购物的步行街。过去这条路上有个老深圳们都知道的"金三角":深圳戏院、工人文化宫和新安酒家。如今无数新"金三角"代替了老"金三角",步行街上拥挤着饮食男女。

Golden Triangle

Jiefang Road isn't thus called by the locals—it's the "East Gate" (Dongmen). Before the SEZ was established, it was the major east-west corridor for the city. Now Jiefang Road is a major shopping pedestrian street for tourists. Walking this road, there is a "golden triangle" that all locals know: Shenzhen Theatre, Worker's Cultural Palace and Xin'an Restaurant. Now many new golden triangles have replaced the old one, and the pedestrian street is full of people wining and dining.

最早的军事驻防

唐开元二十四年(736年),新安县南头城设立了一个独立于地方政府之外的军事机构——屯门镇,驻军2000余人,防线从南头一直布到香港青山下的海岸边,这是深圳最早的军事驻防。沧海桑田,当时严密的防线早已没有踪影,妈湾港的小山坡上,一座老炮台安静伫立。

美哉七娘山

有峰七座,连绵蜿蜒,面朝大海。相传有七位仙女云游于此,被大鹏湾迷醉,遂不愿返回天庭。玉帝闻之大怒,派雷神追缉,仙女们宁死不从,于是玉帝将她们幻化成七座山峰。七娘山为深圳第二高峰,山高谷深、溪涧纵横、瀑布高垂。最壮观的莫过于海面水汽化为云雾,山峰时隐时现,宛如仙女重现。

The Earliest Military Garrison

In the 24th year of the Kaiyuan Emperor's reign in the Tang Dynasty (736), an independent military organ named as Tunmen Town was established in Nantou Town, Xin'an County. It had more than 2,000 soldiers, its line of defence extending from Nantou all the way to the coast below what is now Castle Peak in Hong Kong. This is the earliest military garrison in Shenzhen. Time brings about great changes. The defensive line is long gone, and only an old fort stands upon a hill above Mawan Port in Shenzhen.

Qiniangshan the Beautiful

This is a beautiful winding mountain that has seven peaks, and faces the sea. Legend says that seven fairies roamed here, and were intoxicated by the Dapeng Bay, and thus became unwilling to return to heaven. The Jade Emperor of Heaven was infuriated to hear of this, and dispatched the God of Thunder to pursue and capture them, but they would not comply; thus the Jade Emperor turned them into the seven-peaked mountain. Qiniangshan is the second-highest mountain in Shenzhen, with great height, deep gullies and vast valleys. It faces the great mists of the vast sea, and when enshrouded in them, is quite a sight.

职业参会者

都说深圳人"敢为天下先"。20世纪90年代，深圳招商会主打亲情牌，少不了送家乡土特产做礼品，这就诞生了一批专门去拿免费土特产的职业参会者。他们派头十足，名片上的头衔大得吓人，在会场侃侃而谈，酒足饭饱，提着礼品满意而归，再无下文。当然，他们拿走的礼品也部分起到了广告效应。

My Goodies

People in Shenzhen dare to be the first—in the 1990s, meetings for investors were everywhere, and an essential component was local specialities as gifts. This gave birth to a class of people who attended these conferences almost professionally in order to take the goodies. They show up with name cards bearing fancy titles, and talk the talk, enjoying nice food and drink, and leave with freebies, never following through. Of course, this still serves as advertising for the organisers.

晒布路无布晒

晒布路原来是个岭，传说当年深圳墟有不少染坊，染好的布匹都拿到岭岗上晒，因此得名晒布岭。晒布岭旁有条上大街，整条街都晾晒五颜六色的布匹绸缎。20世纪50年代，解放路扩建，晒布岭上的店铺都改成了住家。特区成立，晒布岭渐渐又恢复商业街本色。晒布岭无布晒，只剩下随风飘荡的传说。

深圳墟

"墟"同"圩"，客家人说"墟"，就是"集市"的意思。清嘉庆、道光年间，新安县共建有36个墟市，深圳墟为其中最繁华的。深圳墟在十字街人民路南边，当年趁墟的多是大脚客家婆和操围头话的本地佬，如今步行街上多了许多满口普通话的外来者。旧日的墟市只剩下墙壁上那一杆铜秤，隐喻着曾经的繁荣。

Shenzhen Market

During the Jiaqing and Daoguang Emperors' reigns in the Qing Dynasty, Xin'an County had 36 markets, with Shenzhen Market being the most active. Shenzhen Market was at the site of the current Renmin Road; back then, Hakka ladies and locals speaking Weitou dialect would come here, whereas now the location is full of outsiders speaking Mandarin. Only a copper scale on the wall remains in modern times, a sigil of past glory.

Shaibu Road

Shaibu ("sunning cloth") Road was originally a small ridge. It's said that Shenzhen Market originally has a number of dyehouses, and that dyed cloth would be taken up to the ridge to be sunned. The Shaibu ridge had an avenue next to it, and one could see all colours of cloth here. In the 1950s, Jiefang Road was expanded, and all the structures on Shaibu Road were transformed into residences. After the SEZ was established, Shaibu Road gradually returned to its commercial nature. Now no cloth is dyed there and only the name remains.

大隐于市的戏院

深圳戏院隐藏在繁华的东门步行街的大厦里，20 世纪 50 年代末，是广深一带最豪华的戏院，时常有东方歌舞团、广东粤剧团等名团演出。香港人爱听戏，便坐着火车过来，步行几分钟便到戏院。往事如烟，60 年过去，戏院重建了，门口的人流也变了，当年一票难求的戏院如今也靠放映电影营利。

Theatre and the City

The Shenzhen Theatre is hidden in a building upon the busy Dongmen pedestrian street. In the late 1950s, it was a top-tier theatre in the region. Famous troupes such as Oriental Song and Dance Company and Guangdong Cantonese Operas Troupe all performed here. Fans from Hong Kong would take a train here, walking a few minutes to the theatre. As 60 years passed, the theatre was rebuilt, and the clientele changed. Back then, it was hard to buy a ticket; now the theatre has to screen films to stay open.

抵达梦开始的地方

在作家纯野笔下，"抵达深圳火车站，便是抵达梦开始的地方"。深圳站始建于 1950 年，与香港仅一桥之隔，和罗湖口岸紧密相连，南下香港、北上广州，必经此站。1991 年，新深圳站改建后，邓小平为其题下"深圳"二字。从当年的绿皮火车到如今的动车，站台里进进出出的，多是南下寻梦人。

Field of Dreams

According to author Chun Ye, "when you arrive at Shenzhen Station, you're arriving at the place where dreams start". The station was built in 1950, right next to the border with Hong Kong, abutting Luohu Checkpoint. To the south was Hong Kong, to the north Guangzhou—it was a point all had to pass. In 1991, the station was rebuilt, and Deng Xiaoping calligraphed the name of the city for the grand sign. The old green trains have been swapped out for the new high-speed carriages, yet the character remains.

宋少帝陵

南宋最后一个皇帝赵昺出生的那年，忽必烈建立元朝，因此他的出生注定是场悲剧。元兵饮马长江，南宋国势危急，赵昺八岁即位。崖山决战，宋军大败。左丞相陆秀夫背负少帝跳海，南宋灭亡。黄袍尸身漂至蛇口赤湾村，被礼葬于此。史界素有"崖山之后无华夏"之慨。在今日看来，乃是王朝更迭而已。

Song Imperial Tomb

The year that Emperor Zhao Bing of the Southern Song Dynasty was born, Kublai Khan established the Yuan Dynasty; for this reason, the site of his life was destined to be a tragedy. Yuan troops advanced and the Southern Song faced a crisis; Zhao Bing ascended to the throne at eight years of age. Battles transpired and the Song Dynasty was decisively defeated. The Left Prime Minister Lu Xiufu jumped into the sea with the young emperor, and the Southern Song Dynasty was extinguished. The body of the young emperor floated to Chiwan Village in Shekou, where it was buried. It was a tragedy, but it is only natural that dynasties change over time.

Floating Firewood

More than one century ago, Shekou Port was untouched land. Fishing was a seasonal activity with great yields. When there was a great famine in Haifeng, eastern Guangdong, people fled to Shekou, leading to a dramatic increase in fishers there. They collected floating wood from the harbour and dried it to use as firewood. After 1949, these people came ashore, and established Yu'er Village in Shekou, becoming residents of the modern city.

咸头岭文明

都以为深圳年轻,殊不知咸头岭的考古发现,把这座城市的年龄前推了7000岁。在大鹏半岛西岸的迭福湾内那片沉睡的沙丘上,发掘出大量新石器时代的陶器,远古的器物慈祥地打量着今世,岁月没有暗淡它们的光泽。咸头岭遗址被评为中国十大考古发现,这些7000年前的文明碎片让深圳不再是文化浮萍。

"水流柴"上岸

100多年前,蛇口港还是野草横生的荒地,从海丰来此捕鱼的渔民先是季节性捕捞,清明过后到蛇口,临近春节回海丰。粤东曾爆发大饥荒,从海丰逃至蛇口的渔民剧增,他们捞水面漂流的柴晒干用于生火,所以被称为"水流柴"。1949年以后,"水流柴"上岸,在蛇口成立渔二村,现已全部转为城市居民。

Cultured Xiantouling

People who think that Shenzhen is young don't know about Xiantouling, which when discovered pushed the age of the city to 7,000 years. On the west coast of the Dapeng Peninsula at Diefu Bay on a sleepy sandhill, Neolithic pottery was discovered, lustre undimmed by the ages. The Xiantouling discovery has been classed as one of the ten major archaeological discoveries in China, these 7,000-year-old pottery fragments attesting to the long history of Shenzhen.

Guardians of Lianhuashan

In the mountaintop square behind the Civic Centre, at Lianhuashan Park, stands the statue of Deng Xiaoping, dressed in a dust coat, imposing and grand in appearance, taking a big step forward. This is the first statue in China erected to comrade Deng Xiaoping; he originally encouraged the growth of this city, and there he still stands as the protector of the metropolis. Standing on the peak of the mountain, looking down below, it's as if the statue can see all the development that is happening.

Nostalgic Restaurant

The Xin'an Restaurant is a landmark with more than 50 years of history. The former Vice-Premier Tao Zhu attended the foundation laying ceremony, and great marshal Ye Jianying cut the ribbon at the opening ceremony. The actors from Guangxi Opera Group working on the play of *Liu Sanjie* were the first VIP clients. In early years when Hong Kong residents visited their relatives in the mainland, they loved to meet up at the Xin'an Restaurant to eat and drink tea. Today's Xin'an Restaurant is always packed. Here you can see history, and have a nice nostalgic meal.

莲花山的守护者

在市民中心后面的莲花山公园山顶广场上，邓小平同志身披风衣、气宇轩昂、大步前行的姿态栩栩如生。这是全国第一座以城市雕塑形式竖立的小平同志塑像，曾经他催生了这座城市，现在他依然在此伫立，他是这座城市的守护者。站在山顶，放眼远眺，仿佛能看到已经展开的百年新画卷。

吃回忆的酒家

新安酒家是50多年前的城市地标。陶铸同志参加了它的奠基仪式，叶剑英元帅为它开业剪彩，广西剧团《刘三姐》剧组的演员成为它的第一批贵宾。早年香港人回乡，最喜与亲朋好友相约新安酒家接头，在此吃饭喝茶。至今酒家生意仍然常常"爆棚"。在这里，人们满眼看的是历史，吃的是回忆。

特区中的"特区"

一条长不足 500 米、宽不足 7 米的街道，在中国却无人不知。中英街街心以"界碑石"为界，深港商铺相向而立，深港警察各管半边。中英街又被称作特区中的"特区"，你要进入中英街，首先要去公安局办理一张"边防通行证"，方可进入港方店铺购物。自 2018 年起，办证工本费正式取消。

A "Special Zone" in the SEZ

A road less than 500 metres long and 7 metres wide is known to all the Chinese. Zhongying Street is marked by a stone stele; it straddles the border, with one side belonging to Shenzhen and one to Hong Kong. A special permit is required to visit the street, with applicants having to visit the Public Security Bureau, but the fee has been formally cancelled in 2018.

CTSOC

There is no Heping Restaurant on Heping Road, but rather an Overseas Chinese Hotel, which is full of tropical plants, flowers and birdsong. The hotel also has a marquee of China Travel Service for Overseas Chinese (CTSOC), by which many locals recognise it. Previously, when overseas returnees came back to China they would frequently stay here when in Shenzhen. It's said that both Wang Guangmei and Tao Zhu stayed here.

侨社

和平路上没有和平饭店，倒是有一座华侨大厦，里面种满热带植物，一片鸟语花香。因为华侨大厦也挂着"中国华侨旅行社"的牌子，老深圳们习惯称它为"侨社"。当年海外华侨从外面回来，到了深圳，都很习惯住在侨社，据说王光美、陶铸等都在这里住过。

Xichong

When tourists go to the beach in Shenzhen, Kuichong and Xichong are the most famous locations. The character for "chong" is often misread by Chinese, however, as it's normally pronounced "yong". While "yong" is used for easy reading, sometimes, this character is pronounced "chong" as in "flush" rather than "yong" in "stream". Situated in the eastmost area of Shenzhen—Nan'ao on the Dapeng Peninsula, Xichong is one of Shenzhen's longest and most beautiful beaches, known as "Hawaii of the Orient".

"西涌" = "西冲"

来深圳的游客，大部分会去海边游览，其中"葵涌""西涌"知名度最高。但是，这个"涌"字，读对的人不多。其引申义是像水涌出，在这里读作"冲"。西涌也名西冲，位于深圳最东端——大鹏半岛南澳，西涌海滩是深圳最长也是最优美的海滩之一，有"东方夏威夷"之美誉。

Here and There

此岸・彼岸

喜新不厌旧 001

20世纪80年代，香港的一切都受到追捧，包括二手冰箱、沙发和汽车座椅。那时，家具店还未兴起，从海外回来的华侨和原村民在渔民村建起了一栋栋小楼，却发现有了新楼、没有家具，于是村里兴起了深圳第一个旧货市场——卖香港二手家具。深圳人喜新不厌旧，二手货也环保，如今深圳最大的旧货市场有几万平方米。

In with the New

In the 1980s, everyone loved everything about Hong Kong, from secondhand fridges, to sofas and car seats. At that time, furniture stores weren't a big thing. People who returned from overseas and the locals in Yumin Village built many little buildings, but found they had no furniture for these new structures, thus the first secondhand market in Shenzhen appeared—one that sold used furniture from Hong Kong. Shenzhen people appreciate the new stuff, but don't eschew the old. Secondhand goods are environmentally friendly. Shenzhen's largest secondhand market today is tens of thousands of square metres in area.

TVB Shows

In the past Hong Kong TV shows were quite popular, similar to the craze for video games now. Lawyers in office buildings in Central, crazy happenings in Mong Kok—the characters and settings across the border intrigued the locals on the other side. TVB is Hong Kong's first commercial broadcaster. From the incredibly popular *Warrior Huo Yuanjia* to *Legend of the Condor Heroes*, these productions gained huge numbers of fans. Back then, every house in Shenzhen had a high-gain antenna pointed towards Hong Kong.

TVB 电视剧 002

当年追港产剧的热情，不亚于今天打游戏的痴迷。中环写字楼里的律师、旺角街头的古惑仔，TVB的人物和其背后的彼岸生活，吸引着此岸观众。TVB是香港第一家商营无线电视台，从万人空巷的武侠片《霍元甲》，到成为一代人记忆的《射雕英雄传》，都吸粉无数。那些年，深圳家家户户都有鱼骨天线朝向香港。

窄屋外的宽阔人生 003

没有姹紫嫣红，名字却叫"花园"，地界并不开阔，也公然称为"广场"。其实，这就是很多人眼中的"小区"。这种夸张的叫法，源自香港，传至深圳，很快就普及到全国各地。细想起来，香港寸土寸金，屋檐窄小，这一叫法寄托着香港人对屋外宽阔人生的向往。

Narrow Houses, Wide Outdoors

Places without flowers still are called "garden". Places with no wide open space are still called "plaza". These are common naming conventions for complexes here. These grandiose styles come from Hong Kong, and after being imported to Shenzhen, quickly spread across the nation. As land in Hong Kong is very expensive, these names reflect the desires of Hong Kong for a wide open world.

神秘的『二线关』

2018年1月15日,有36年历史的深圳"二线关"撤关,成为市民的休闲步道,特区内外不再有别。当年外地人来深必过此关。这条深圳特区内外的83.5千米管理线,设立于1982年,功不可没,也带来诸多不便。深圳还有一条独特的"一线关",源于英国人强租香港的历史,这条7.5千米的边境线撕碎多少家庭。

On January 15, 2018, the "second border" between the Shenzhen SEZ and the rest of China was dismantled, becoming a walking path for city residents. In the past all people coming from other places to Shenzhen had to pass through this border. The 83.5-kilometre-long border was established in 1982 and served an important purpose, but also brought about a good deal of hassle. Shenzhen still has a unique "first border"—when the English leased Hong Kong, the 7.5-kilometre-long border split a number of families in half.

街头的时尚启蒙

在不知道阿玛尼的昨天,佐丹奴就是时尚的代名词。它和鳄鱼恤、金利来、班尼路等香港本土品牌一起,成为最好的时尚启蒙教材,唤醒着深圳人的爱美之心。其广告语"没有陌生人的世界"十分感性,令人记忆至今。20世纪90年代,深南东路经常可以看到佐丹奴大促销,买一件穿上,秒变潮人。

伸入深圳的手臂

深圳地铁4号线(龙华线),就像香港伸入深圳的一条手臂。其由港铁深圳公司投资,运营有效期从2010年到2040年。浓厚的港铁车站建筑风格、港式瓷砖装修,尤其走进莲花北站的一瞬间,会恍惚觉得到了香港金钟站。龙华线站点也和香港有缘,白石龙站,就曾是香港沦陷时的文化名人营救总部。

Fashion in the Streets

Before people knew about Armani, Giordano was the big thing. Along with other local Hong Kong brands such as Crocodile, Goldlion, and Baleno, these formed the introduction to fashion for the people of Shenzhen. Its slogan "World Without Strangers" is full of feeling. In the 1990s, Shennan East Road, Giordano sold well here; putting on an item of their clothing, you were instantly fashionable.

Extending Reach

Shenzhen's No. 4 underground line (the Longhua Line) is like an arm that Hong Kong extends into Shenzhen. It was invested in by MTR Corporation (Shenzhen) for operation between 2010 to 2040, and is built in the style of the Hong Kong MTR with MTR-style cars and stations decorated in the tiles of the HK MTR. When you are in the Lianhuabei station, you feel like you are in the Admiralty station of Hong Kong. The Longhua Line does have a bit of a fate connection with Hong Kong—Baishilong station is the site of the rescue headquarters from the period of Japanese occupation.

The Most Profitable Expressway

People flow, cars flow, money flows. Then Guangzhou-Shenzhen expressway links Guangzhou to Shenzhen and then Hong Kong. The construction of the expressway started in 1987, and open to traffic in 1997, it is known as the most profitable expressway in China. Shenzhen and Guangzhou both have populations of more than 10 million, and the "factory of the world" Dongguan lies between them. The number of cars on this route is the highest of all the expressways in China. Drivers coming here for the first time will be shocked to see that there is still congestion in the middle of the night.

最赚钱的高速公路

人流，车流，钱流。广深高速公路是联系广州、深圳和香港的重要通道，1987年动工，历时10年通车，有"中国最赚钱的高速公路"之称，广深都是千万人口大城市，"世界工厂"东莞夹于其间，车流量至今仍是中国高速公路之冠。初次到此的司机，会对时间有恍惚感，因为凌晨仍会塞车。

一桥馨香 008

阿芳每天送儿子到对岸的港岛上学。清晨，沐着朝阳，跨过罗湖桥，她目送那抹小身影奔进校园，她便怀抱电脑，坐在街头咖啡厅里开始一天的工作；黄昏，她在校门口迎来他的雀跃入怀，牵起小手，回到桥的这一边。一座桥，连接每日充满期盼的亲情往来。世界琳琅，一桥馨香。

Sweet Bridge 008

A Fang sends her son to Hong Kong each day to attend school. In the morning, bathed in sunlight, they cross the bridge at Luohu Bridge. As the child disappears into the campus, she carries her laptop to a cafe and begins the day's work. At dusk, she meets him at the school gate, and holds his hand as they head back over the bridge. This bridge connects the two halves of this family's world. In a beautiful world, it's a sweet connection.

Che Gong 009

Che Gong, also known as Generalissimo Che, is a famous general from the Southern Song Dynasty who is worshipped by the people of the area. There is a place named as Che Gong Temple in the Xiangmi Lake area of Shenzhen, which mirrors the famous Che Kung Temple in Hong Kong's Sha Tin District.

出门迎车公 009

"不得车公终不乐，已教红袖出门迎。"这是宋人诗句，诗中"车公"又称车大元帅，相传为南宋末年勇将，因其生前忠贞英勇，人们立庙供奉。深港两地都笃信车公，两地皆有"车公庙"。深圳的车公庙位于福田区香蜜湖对面，是地名；香港的车公庙实至名归，是新界沙田区一座纪念车公的庙宇。

李嘉诚的预言 010

成功的花朵，你看到它现时的明艳，看不到它当初的芽儿，浸透了血和泪。超人李嘉诚说过，对深圳改革开放取得的辉煌成就感到振奋，体会到深圳的毅力和决心，相信深圳的投资和国际化营商环境会不断优化，深圳跻身顶尖国际大都会行列指日可待。10年过去了，李嘉诚的预言实现了一大半。

Li Ka-shing's Prediction 010

When you see a beautiful flower, you see its present striking colours, but not what the plant looked like as it sprouted. Li Ka-shing said he was moved by the success that Shenzhen had had in its growth, and felt their will and dedication. He believed that investment and internationalisation would continually improve in Shenzhen, and that Shenzhen would become a first-tier global metropolis. Over a decade, most of what he said has already come true.

信息两栖人 011

做深港生意的老板,就要同时关注深港信息。早年,同时看两种《经济日报》蔚为潮流。内地的《经济日报》,由国务院主办,权威性和公信力极强,报名由邓小平题写。《香港经济日报》,则是和《信报》齐名的严肃报章,影响力极大。老板们参研报纸,研究政策和经济形势,想的多是寻找商机。

城心难寂 012

近朱者赤,近城者喧。香港和深圳似乎没有一刻能静下来。其夜生活之繁华,可媲美任何国际大都会。从邓小平铜像广场远望,深圳中心区流光溢彩,青春旋律让人振奋;对岸香港维多利亚港灯火璀璨,在夜间乘坐天星小轮横渡海港,或是乘山顶缆车登上太平山山顶,都能感受到迷人夜色中香港的律动。

Amphibious Data 011

Those who do business with Hong Kong must keep track of the situation in both cities. It used to be the trend to read two economic dailies. The *Economic Daily* is run by the State Council, and is very authoritative; the masthead is calligraphed by Deng Xiaoping. the *Hong Kong Economic Daily* is as famous as the *Hong Kong Economic Journal*, and has great influence. Bosses read the papers, researching policies and economic trends to identify business opportunities.

In the City 012

The city is a busy place. Hong Kong and Shenzhen almost never quiet down. The nights are fully of activity, on par with any major global metropolis. From the bronze statue of Deng Xiaoping looking out over the square to the lights of downtown, the youthful rhythm excites you. The lights of Victoria Harbour sparkle brilliantly in Hong Kong, where you can ride the Star Ferry to and from the island, or take the tram up Victoria Peak to take in the beautiful view of Hong Kong at night.

女人天生爱逛街

女人天生爱逛街，千金散尽还复来。逛街，就是女人的一种生活方式。深圳女人街，位于繁华的商业区华强北，地标是1995年开业的"女人世界"，闻名全国，也是女游客来深购物首选之地。香港女人街，就是旺角的通菜街，因经营的商品绝大部分是妇女用品和衣物而得名，也是游客必到的购物点。

Women Love Shopping

Shopping is a way of life for women. The Ladies' Street in Shenzhen is situated in the prosperous business district of Huaqiangbei, and the Ladies' World, opened in 1995 is famous throughout the country. It's a first choice for female tourists looking to shop, with most of the stores there being of brands that specialise in products for women; it's a must-hit destination.

深港"飞地"落马洲

落马洲，南宋年幼的宋少帝曾驻扎于此，行人路过必下马以示敬意，因而得名。落马洲一端在香港，一端在深圳，深圳这端今称为皇岗，香港沿用旧名。落马洲河套区原属深圳行政边界，1997年后，香港拥有其土地业权，深圳河的新旧河道将其三面包围，成了一个四面环水的小岛，这是深港间一块天降的"飞地"。

围着垃圾桶"打边炉"

曲不离口，烟要离手，深港两地都推行禁烟。2014年，深圳推出《控制吸烟条例》，违者最高罚款500元。在此七年前，香港就实行了室内全面禁烟，违者最高罚款5000港元。吸烟危害健康，也迫使他人吸进二手烟。事实上，深港两地的街头，常见烟民围着垃圾桶吞云吐雾，自嘲"打边炉"。

Hot Pot

Both Shenzhen and Hong Kong are conducting activities to impose limitations on smoking. In 2014, Shenzhen rolled out anti-smoking rules, with violators being punished with a fine of 500 yuan. Seven years before this, Hong Kong passed a universal indoor smoking ban, with violators facing a maximum fine of 5,000 HKD. Smoking is harmful to health, and also creates secondhand smoke. In fact, in both cities you can see smokers huddling around rubbish bins that have ash trays in the top, forming little "hot pots" that spew out smoke.

Lok Ma Chau

Lok Ma Chau ("horse disembarkation point") is the site of where the last emperor of the Southern Song Dynasty lived; when people passed by, they had to get off their horses to show respect. Part of Lok Ma Chau is in Hong Kong, and part in Shenzhen, where it is now called Huanggang, whilst Hong Kong continues to use the old name. The bend of Shenzhen River near Lok Ma Chau used to be the site of the Shenzhen administration border. After the 1997 handover, Hong Kong holds the land rights; the Shenzhen River's new and old courses surround it on three sides. It has become a little island surrounded by a water on four sides, and enclave between Shenzhen and Hong Kong.

深圳河 016

深圳河，发源于深圳梧桐山牛尾岭，途经深圳湾，流入香港米埔附近的后海湾，在历史上曾经被称为"明溪"，是深圳与香港之间的界河，也是香港地区最长的河流。牛尾岭上溪流小，雨滴顺道入沙湾，因此有"深圳河，沙湾水"之说。这条水量不丰的长河，静静地淌着涓涓细流，见证了历史上《香港英新租界合同》的签订。

Shenzhen River

Shenzhen River, originates on the Niuwei Peak of Mount Wutong, and flows by Shenzhen Bay into Deep Bay in Hong Kong. It was originally called Ming Creek, and served as the border between Shenzhen and Hong Kong; it is also the longest river in Hong Kong. The stream on Niuwei Peak is small, and the overall flow of the river is minimal, although its course is long; this is attested in the lease the English signed for the New Territories.

A Life of Two Cities

It was previously a slow trip that few cars made over poorly maintained roads to get between Shenzhen and Hong Kong, one that took half a day, and required a long wait at the border. Then later a railway was built, then a high-speed railway, and now there will even be a Guangzhou-Shenzhen-Hong Kong express rail link. However, the people who enjoy a life in both cities still miss the slow old days.

双城生活 017

从前慢，深圳往返香港车辆不多，公路破破烂烂，开车要走上半天，过关排队亦是麻烦。后来有了铁路，又有了动车，如今广深港高铁即将开通，香港人到深圳"叹茶"，只需要足球比赛中场休息的时间便已足够。然而，享受着快节奏"双城生活"的人们却难免怀念起从前慢的日子。

Intellectual Online Celebrity

There are all kinds of online celebrities now. At City University of Hong Kong, Shenzhen Research Institute professor Lv Jian's team had the results of their research published in the journal *Nature*, and became internet famous. This kind of celebrity is known as an "intellectual online celebrity", who blow up quickly, but not without much effort.

知识网红 018

如今流行网红，微博网红、微信网红等数不胜数。香港城市大学深圳研究院吕坚教授带领团队取得的科研成果刊登在《自然》杂志封面上，该团队也成了网红。这种网红被称为"知识网红"，红起来很快，红的过程艰苦，和其他网红一样，有一句关于虾蟹的笑话可以形容他们：想红就得忍着。

孟父三迁

老孟卖掉深圳宝安的房子，到高新区另买了一套房子，是为了儿子将来能够在这里上大学。因为随着《"深港创新圈"合作协议》的签署，香港大学等六所知名院校在深圳高新区设立大学研究院。朋友们笑老孟不嫌搬迁麻烦，老孟却得意地戏言说古有孟母三迁，今有"孟父三迁"，为了孩子的教育，值。

Mr. Meng's Three Moves

Mr. Meng sold his house in Bao'an District, and bought a new house in the Shenzhen Hi-Tech Park, so that his son could go to university here. In accordance with the *Shenzhen-Hong Kong Innovation Sphere Cooperation Agreement*, six universities and other educational institutions established research institutes in the Hi-Tech Park. Friends say that Mr. Meng doesn't mind moving. He jokes that Mencius' mother moved three times to better her son's education, thus he will do the same for his son as his surname is also "Meng", like the philosopher.

白龙王喝过的丝袜奶茶 020

有一点儿性感，有一点儿突兀，又有一点儿简单。把煮好的锡兰红茶过滤，加奶加糖，过滤茶叶的纱布用久后变成了深褐色，像女人穿的丝袜，这就是丝袜奶茶。由香港中环兰芳园创办人林木河发明，泰国白龙王也是其长年客。深圳街头的奶茶店，也会冲丝袜奶茶，喝起来却少了香江的味道。

Tea Drank by the White Dragon King

It's a bit sexy, a bit abrupt, and a bit simple. Take Ceylon Black Tea, filter it, add milk and sugar, and the cloth for filtering the tea will turn deep brown over time, like a woman's silk stockings. This is "silk stocking milk tea". Invented by Lin Muhe at Hong Kong's Lan Fong Yuen, it was frequently enjoyed by Zhou Qinnan, a Thailand guru known as the "White Dragon King". Tea stands in Shenzhen also make the drink, but it lacks the Hong Kong flavour.

逃港村的陈迹 021

这里已杳无人烟，大石头上长满了绿油油的青苔，古老的土房子是用糯米砖建成，迄今还屹立不倒，但已被顽固的蔓藤包围。50多年前的黄昏，房前还坐着抽水烟的男人，石板上阿婶还在捡拾豆子中的石头粒。某夜之后，村子里的人都到海对面去了，只留下一片寂静。如今还有谁会逃港？

不夜城 022

深圳是个不夜城。除了马路上通宵不停奔驰的汽车，酒吧里迷醉到天亮的音乐，24小时书吧永不熄灭的灯光，还有东门步行街商业圈一年一度的68小时通宵营业。这是深港购物一族"血拼"的黄金季节，东门步行街人群密密匝匝，都沉浸在购物的狂欢之中，热闹程度不亚于美国的"黑色星期五"购物节。

Things of the Past

This is a remote and desolate place, stones covered in thick green moss; adobe houses built with glutinous rice bricks still stand but are covered in vines. More than 50 years ago at dusk a man sat in front of one of these houses smoking a bong, as an auntie picked stones out of a pile of beans on a stone board. Time passed, and one night the village was finally completely empty, everyone having fled to Hong Kong, leaving a quiet scene. Who would choose to flee to Hong Kong now?

Night Activity

Shenzhen is a city that never sleeps. Aside from the cars that never cease traversing to the roads, the bars playing music until dawn, and the 24-hour bookstore, at the Dongmen Pedestrian Street business area, once a year there is a 68-hour long period of continuous opening. This is a prime opportunity for shopping addicts, when the Dongmen Pedestrian Street is packed with people absorbed in a buying frenzy, similar to the Black Friday phenomenon in the USA.

Wenjindu Checkpoint

The film *Bargain Under the Noose*, made by Shanghai Film Studio in the 1980s, has a number of scenes that were shot at the Wenjindu Checkpoint. The depiction of the border crossing in the film is as busy and complex as the real thing, the Shenzhen area a dirt road where dust flies, and on the Hong Kong side a road that winds like an intestine up a mountainside. Today, below a rotary interchange and new buildings, the road is still packed with cars everywhere, just like the checkpoint of old days.

TV Shows from Hong Kong

In the 1970s, one of the biggest attractants to Hong Kong from the people in Shenzhen separated only by a small river, was TV shows. People who had relatives in Hong Kong giving them a little TV would carefully install a fishbone antenna, and at night the room would be packed with people gathering to watch the programs. At the start of the 1980s, the ban on Hong Kong television was lifted, and all of sudden everyone was busy learning the lyrics to the theme songs of shows.

文锦渡口岸

上海电影制片厂在20世纪80年代拍摄的电影《绞索下的交易》有许多场景取景于文锦渡口岸。影片中的文锦渡与现实中一样繁忙与复杂，深圳地界是黄土飞扬的土路，香港那边，山脚的公路像羊肠一般蜿蜒。如今，在环形立交和高楼大厦之下，通往口岸的马路上车流滚滚，老口岸的风采灿烂依然。

香港电视开禁

20世纪70年代，与深圳仅一河之隔的香港对深圳人最大的吸引之一，大抵就是电视节目了。谁家若是有一台香港亲戚送的小电视，再小心翼翼地装上一条鱼骨天线，家里一到晚上就会被挤得透不过气来。80年代初，香港电视开禁，街头顿时流行起那些日子大家在黑灯瞎火中学会的电视剧主题歌。

香港邮票

看惯了内地的邮票,香港邮票无疑让人眼前一亮。回归之后,香港邮票英国色彩渐渐褪去,却仍然保持着中西文化荟萃的特色,香港动感之都之面貌跃然纸上。现代化、国际化与市民化、生活化和谐共处。方寸之间,有科技,有优雅;有风水,有早茶。粤港澳大湾区其实早已经在邮票上开始了。

Hong Kong Philately

When one used to stamps from the mainland of China looks upon those from Hong Kong, he will be surprised by their vibrance. After the handover, the English style of the stamps gradually faded way, yet they maintained their fusion of Chinese and Western culture, and the energetic appearance of the city. They have a modern, international, urban, lively character. In small area they contain science, elegance, Feng shui, and morning tea. The Guangdong-Hong Kong-Macao Greater Bay Area has long been a thing in the stamps.

夏雨隔牛背

深港多雨,夏日无伞不出门。气象播报最常听到的是"预测本港今日大致多云,有几阵骤雨"。骤雨,本义为暴雨,这里指的是为时不长的降雨,其强度变化很大。常常是"东边日出西边雨,道是无晴却有晴",因而有"夏雨隔牛背"之说法。牛背的这边下雨,那边却滴雨不下。

香港 + 深圳 = 香圳

从卫星上看地球的夜景,在一片连绵耀眼的灯光下出现两座隔海相望的美丽城市。美国学者理查德·弗罗里达看到的是香港和深圳,他将其命名为"香圳"。这个美好而浪漫的词是弗罗里达的愿望:他认为"香港+深圳"很有可能取代东京的地位,成为与纽约、伦敦站在一起的第三大"世界城市"。

HK+SZ="Hong Zhen"

Looking at the earth by night via a satellite, in the sea of lights there are two coastal cities that face each other that you can spot. American scientist Richard Florida saw Hong Kong and Shenzhen, and named them collectively "Hong Zhen". This name for the cities reflects Florida's wish that the two cities together could replace Tokyo, becoming along with New York and London the third largest "world city".

Patchy Rain

It rains a lot in Shenzhen and Hong Kong—one should always take an umbrella when heading out in the summer. The most common weather forecast is "Hong Kong and Shenzhen will be mostly overcast, with patches of heavy rain". The heavy rains come and go quickly, and can be quite intense. It can be raining in one part of the visible sky and sunny and clear in others.

粤语难于上青天

习惯吃粤菜容易,习惯讲粤语很难,对于北方人更是遥不可及。究其原因,北方讲普通话,是四个音调,而粤语有九音六调,所以,很难掌握细微差别。广东人讲粤语掷地有声,香港人讲粤语软糯动听,而北方人在讲自以为流利的粤语时,广东人和香港人是听不懂的,能听懂他们的粤语的大都是北方人。

Bank of China Tower

Hong Kong has a BOC Tower, and Shenzhen has a BOC Tower. A grand work of master I. M. Pei, Hong Kong's BOC Tower holds serious weight in the architecture scene of Hong Kong, rising out of the ground high in the sky, representing the continual rise of the bank. Its unique geometric design has sparked much controversy. Shenzhen's BOC Tower stands across from Lianhuashan Park, and its design with red curtain walls has also courted much controversy.

中银大厦和它的孪生兄弟

香港有一座中银大厦,深圳亦有一座中银大厦。作为贝聿铭大师的杰作,香港中银大厦在香港建筑群中举足轻重,它意喻破土而出、节节升高的外形,代表着银行业务蒸蒸日上,它独特的几何图形曾引起很大争议。深圳中银大厦位于莲花山公园对面,其红色幕墙的设计亦引发诸多争议。

Difficulties with Cantonese

Getting used to eating Cantonese food is easy, but speaking Cantonese is not; it's a very hard goal for people from the north to achieve. Mandarin has four tones, whereas Cantonese has nine tones and six tone pitches; it is very difficult for outsides to differentiate between them. Cantonese spoken in Guangdong is forceful and lofty in tone, whereas in Hong Kong it is soft and energetic. Northerners may think they speak fluent Cantonese, yet people from Guangdong and Hong Kong are unable to understand them, only other northerners being able to make out what they are trying to say.

珠宝城与金饰街

深圳女子爱美,喜珠宝者为美得物超所值,多去水贝国际珠宝交易中心购买珠宝,其始建于2004年,是深圳黄金珠宝产业集聚基地内最重要的交易、文化、信息交流平台。与之相似且邻近的是香港金饰一条街,位于旺角弥敦道,其中有周生生、周大福、六福、谢瑞麟等,都是香港有名气的金铺。

Jewelry City and Gold Street

Shenzhen's women love beauty, and value jewelry highly. Many go to the Shuibei International Jewelry Centre to shop. Built in 2004, it's the most important site for the gold and jewel industry in Shenzhen in terms of transactions, culture and information exchange. Similar to it is Nathan Road in Mong Kok, where there are all kinds of gold sellers, such as Chow Sang Sang, Chow Tai Fook, Lukfook, and TSL.

SEZ and Features

特区・特色

山环水抱的大道 001

滨海大道是一个婉约的女子,北环大道是一个粗犷的汉子。滨海大道临海,蜿蜒地从南山通往罗湖,时有美景;北环大道靠山,几乎和滨海大道平行。仁者乐山,智者乐水。山环水抱,自然有情有义。两条大道东端相接,成了一个环形,罗湖、福田、南山环列其中。东南形胜,"道"此为佳。

春江水暖"银"先知 002

改革开放之初的中国,除了国有的中农工建四大银行,并无其他银行,但深圳例外。有人说深圳银行多过米铺,毫不夸张,这里除了国有四大银行,还有本土的发展、招商、中信等银行;更有种类繁多的外来银行渣打、汇丰、南洋、东亚等。商海逐利,特区遍地开花的银行最早闻到了财富的气息。

The Boulevards 001

Binhai ("abutting the sea") Boulevards is like a girl graceful and unrestrained, and Beihuan ("north ring") Boulevards is like a rough man. Binhai Boulevards runs along the sea, curving from Nanshan to Luohu. There are always beautiful sights to see. Beihuan Boulevards abuts the mountains, and is more or less parallel to Binhai Avenue. Sages reside in the mountains, whereas hedonists prefer the sea. Surrounded by mountains and girdled by a river, these are interesting places. The two roads meet in the east, forming a loop, encompassing Luohu, Futian, and Nanshan. The roads are some of the nicest geographical features here.

The Banks 002

When China began its process of opening up and reform, aside from the four major state-owned banks (BOC, ABC, ICBC, and CCB), there were no other banks, but Shenzhen was an exception. It's no exaggeration to say there were more banks in Shenzhen than rice shops. Aside from the local Shenzhen Development Bank, China Merchants Bank, and China CITIC Bank, there were also foreign banks: Standard Chartered, HSBC, NCB, BEA, and so on. As a SEZ, all kinds of banks got their first whiff of the scent of Chinese money here.

欢声笑语的"大客厅"

有一个地方大多数深圳人都很熟悉，被称作深圳人的"大客厅"，那就是市民中心楼顶通往莲花山的平台。书城看完书的情侣在这里约会，带孩子的父母来这里休憩，也有人什么都不干，就在这里远眺宽阔的红荔路两端。市民相互微笑，似乎确认过眼神，CBD 的壮美令人神往，何人不起家园情？

Big Hall

There's a place that most of the locals in Shenzhen are familiar with and it's been called the "Big Hall" of Shenzhen. On the platform upon the Lianhua Hill on top of the Civic Centre Building, couple meet here after visiting the book city, and parents with children come here to rest. There are also people who come to do nothing at all, simply looking down over Hongli Road. It's a nice vista, taking in the sights of the city, the beautiful and mighty CBD; one really feels at home here.

方形的围屋

004

深圳客家围屋有百余座,年代为元明清各朝,多以圆形呈现。有的简朴原始,有的雄伟壮观,有的则精巧玲珑,各富特色。建于乾隆年间的大万世居,为古堡式围屋形制,则是全国最大的方形客家围屋。围屋曾为中原移民族居之所,封闭建筑为自我保护,其饮食也多偏北方口味,语言亦保留中原古音。

Hakka Enclosed Residences

There are more than a hundred traditional Hakka enclosed residences in Shenzhen, dating from the Yuan, Ming, Qing Dynasties, most of which are round. Some are simple and primitive, some are strong and bold, and some are exquisite in construction, all having their own character. The famous Dawan Shiju, was built in the style of an ancient fort, and is the largest Hakka enclosed residence in the country. These structures were originally residences of those that migrated from the central plains, and were maintained during the feudal period. The culinary customs are those of the north, and the language spoken has the character of the old language of the central plains.

钟声唤醒黎明

华联大厦也叫大钟楼,在当今深南大道鳞次栉比的高楼大厦中显得有些娇小,但作为深圳标志性建筑之一,曾被誉为"亚洲第一钟"。1988年,大钟楼作为国庆献礼工程,钟声正式敲响。建设之初,要求楼应高于100米,于是便借鉴武汉和上海的模式修建为钟楼。每天清晨,鹏城钟声悠扬,行人步履匆匆。

人潮人海似蛇阵

多年前,途经深圳回内地的华侨、港澳同胞甚多。逢年过节的时候,仅有的两个关口人龙盘缠,排队的人们拖儿带女,大包小包,挤在一起,密密麻麻如同一团团盘在一起向前蠕动的蛇,被本地人称为"打蛇阵"。如今口岸虽多,仍赶不上粤港融合的大步流星,节假日,各个关口依然是"打蛇阵"。

安置梦想的家园

打工者暂住的"冬瓜岭",是一个在很长时间内,都在容纳来自天南地北的外乡人的安置区。门口菜档卖的菜很新鲜很便宜,安置区内人们的笑容很简单很温暖,那不是一个单纯安置吃饭和睡觉的地方,而是一个安置梦想的家园。别时容易见时难,旧貌新颜,冬瓜岭早已荡然无存,现名彩田村。

Daylight Bell

The Hualian Building is also called the Big Bell Building; it appears relatively small compared with the rows upon rows of high-rise buildings in the present days, but it still functions as a landmark in Shenzhen. It was once known as "the number one bell in Asia". In 1988, the building was listed as a national-level site, and the bell was formally rung. Before it was built, it was stipulated that it must be more than 100 metres in height, and be built in the style of bell towers in Wuhan and Shanghai. Every day at dawn, the sound of the bell rings out over the streets as people walk them.

Running the Snake Train

A number of years ago, as a number of people from abroad or Hong Kong and Macao passed through Shenzhen on the way to their ancestral hometowns, the two border crossings saw themselves absolutely slammed. People carrying sons and daughters, bags large and small, packed together, forming huge queues like slithering snakes; thus this phenomenon was called "the snake train" by locals. Even today, although there are more ports open, there are still masses of people at these crossings, and especially at holidays, everyone runs "the snake train".

Home of Dreams

Workers from elsewhere reside at Donggua ("winter gourd") Ridge, which has been for a long time a resettlement area for workers from other areas. The vegetables at the entrance to the area are fresh and inexpensive, and the people inside are comfortable and happy. It's not just an area to sleep and eat, but rather a home of dreams. We're talking about the past, however—Donggua Ridge no longer exists. Upon its former site is now the development known as Caitian Village.

"东方神曲"高，深圳和者寡

名噪一时的"东方神曲"，是深圳以神话故事为主题的景点。高大上的景区以中国神话《西游记》为主题，分为天园、地府、人间，其中有唐僧师徒"西天取经"历险故事中的妖洞，还有斗鸡场与斗狗场表演节目。短暂的热闹后，曲尽人散，这个独特题材的主题公园，看来真是水土不服。

Oriental Divine Comedy

Once quite popular was the "Oriental Divine Comedy", a theme park based on fairy tales in Shenzhen. Using the lofty vistas of *Journey to the West* as a theme, the Tang Monk journeys through heaven, the netherworld, and the realm of humans to seek scriptures, seeing all kinds of sights including cockfights and dogfights. After a short period of excitement, the park closed down and the crowd dispersed. Some peculiar parks aren't for everyone.

登顶"地王"为怀乡

20年前，最浪漫的事可能是带着恋人登顶"地王"，鸟瞰罗湖，指点香江，编织梦想。383米、69层的地王大厦，为当时亚洲第一高楼。推出的主题性观光项目"深港之窗"，高悬于巍峨挺拔的大厦顶层，也是亚洲第一个高层主题性观光游览项目。多少独在异乡的深圳异客在上面回望北国，常怀故乡。

On the Peak

Twenty years ago, possibly the most romantic thing was climbing the Diwang ("Land King") Building and looking down over Luohu, pointing at the river, and dreaming. The 383-metre, 69-storey building was at the time the tallest in Asia. The view as promoted as a "window to Shenzhen and Hong Kong", the view from the top floor being the highest in the continent. So many people from elsewhere in the country stood there, and looked out towards their homes.

东湖丽苑的第一缕清风

东阳直挂能添暖，丽苑台高接新春。东湖丽苑是中国第一个商品房小区，1984年顶着骂名和风险竣工，因为采取前所未有的"深圳出地、港方出钱"模式，一时大哗。开盘后直接向公众出售，一房带三个户口，引来一夜售罄。此后深圳土地被盘活，全国纷纷效仿。丽苑居民起居照常，亦习惯被参观。

East Lake Feelings

Donghu Liyuan is China's first commercial housing estate, infamously built in 1984, critics noting "Shenzhen contributes land and Hong Kong contributes money". It was directly opened for sale, and all units were gone in a single day. Afterwards, the sell-off of land in Shenzhen was triggered, and the rest of the country gradually followed suit. The residents of the complex are used to being viewed as an attraction.

让魔咒成为传说

Curses to Legends

劳伦斯魔咒说,"摩天大楼立项之时,是经济过热时期;而摩天大楼建成之日,即是经济衰退之时"。深圳摩天大楼闻名世界,城市天际线越来越高,第一是平安金融中心、"春笋"还是深港国际中心?第一之后又是谁?哪些将成为过去,哪些又将代表未来?勇立潮头,自强不息,魔咒就是个传说。

Andrew Lawrence, a property analyst at Kleinwort Hambros, has noted that skyscrapers are built as an economy is booming, and completed as it busts. Shenzhen's skyscrapers are world-famous, with the city's skyline ever rising. Will the foremost be the Ping An International Finance Centre, Huarun Group Headquarters Building or Shenzhen Hong Kong International Centre? Then who's second? Who's next? All that can be done is to continually raise the bar.

春风又绿试验田

早在1979年1月,蛇口敢为天下先,率先迈出了基建体制改革的第一步——实行工程招投标。随后的1980年3月,率先实行干部、职员公开自由招聘制,实施公开招聘、民主选举;率先改革了劳动分配制度,改变吃"大锅饭"现象。之后的深圳改革更是开风气之先。深圳特区一直被模仿,很难被超越。

书记三问

2010年,时任广东省委书记的汪洋,要求深圳围绕"特区成立30周年"认真回答三个问题:"第一,深圳'三十而立',立起了什么?第二,30周年的今天,深圳能做什么?第三,未来30年深圳再做什么?靠什么去实现?"深圳人记住了书记的问题,用粤港澳大湾区的新蓝图交出了一份满意的答卷。

Forefront of Revolution

Early in January 1979, the first steps of the opening up and reform were taken in Shekou District, with bids made on construction. In March 1980, workers were able to seek their own jobs, and hiring as made open. Elections were held. The system of employment changed, and one-track employment started to erode. Shenzhen became the forefront of this revolution. The trends in Shenzhen were emulated elsewhere, but rarely exceeded.

Three Questions

In 2010, Wang Yang, the Secretary of the Provincial Party Committee of Guangdong Province asked three questions of Shenzhen upon the 30th anniversary of the establishment of the SEZ: "First, what did the 30th anniversary mean? Second, on the 30th anniversary, what can Shenzhen do? Third, what can Shenzhen do in the next 30 years? How can that be accomplished?" The people of Shenzhen responded to those questions, using the new blueprint of Guangdong-Hong Kong-Macao Greater Bay Area to give a satisfying answer.

海上世界耀明华 014

蛇口海岸边停着一艘巨轮，原为法国总统戴高乐的专用邮轮，后被中国购买，改名"明华轮"。曾被派往越南、柬埔寨接回侨民，并载中日友好代表团访日。1983年，明华轮停航，被改造为酒店。1984年1月26日，邓小平登船，并题写"海上世界"。30多年过去，"明华"更加熠熠生辉，喜观深圳巨轮远航。

Houses on Heping Road 015

There used to be a number of small buildings on Heping Road in the traditional style, with red walls and green roof tiles, exquisite in construction, each with its own characteristics. It was like a European fairy tale setting in the middle of an old city. Most of the houses were built by returnees from overseas, and were thus called "overseas Chinese houses". As time has gone by, most have been demolished, replaced by large skyscrapers, with only Luohu Checkpoint remaining.

Rely on Yourself 016

At the start of opening up and reform, the SEZ attracted a number of young dreamers. It's natural to rely on those you know when you arrive somewhere new, but as everyone was grinding, even family members could only lend limited support to those that came to join them. You had to rely on your own abilities and resources when starting out in Shenzhen.

World on the Seas 014

On the coast in Shekou there is a huge passenger liner which used to belong to Charles de Gaulle, which was later purchased by China and renamed "Minghua". It has previously been dispatched to Vietnam and Cambodia to transport Chinese returnees, and has also visited Japan as part of Sino-Japanese friendship exercises. In 1983, it was decommissioned, and transformed into a hotel. On January 26, 1984, Deng Xiaoping boarded the boat, and calligraphed a scroll reading "World on the Seas". After 30 years, "Minghua" still stands there, serving as a landmark on the coast of Shenzhen.

和平路上的侨房 015

和平路边曾经有很多尖顶的红墙绿瓦小楼，伸出小楼外的大阳台，每一栋都很别致，且不重样，当时在古旧破烂的小城里，像从天而降的欧式童话。房子多是归侨所建，所以也叫侨房。时移世易，如今的侨房多已拆迁。变了的是剑指云天的摩天大楼，不变的是川流不息的罗湖口岸。

出门也要靠自己 016

改革开放之初，特区吸引了无数怀揣梦想的年轻人。初来乍到，投亲靠友，理所应当。不过他们的圆梦之旅，客观上给早到的亲朋带来了不便和困扰。特区生活不易，于是"我可以请你吃饭，但不能借钱给你"不知不觉成了深圳人约定俗成的规矩。既然闯特区，不靠自己，何以在特区生存？

巨资买号为哪般?

因为"8"和"发"谐音,开放之初的国人发财梦酣,追捧"888"自是无人免俗。1994年,在深圳首次移动电话号码拍卖会上,靓号9088888引发了39次激烈竞价,最终以65.5万元成交。那个年代智能手机尚未诞生,模拟机大哥大一枝独秀,更是身份的象征。只是不知当年买号的那位,究竟因此大发或是相反?

Big Number, Big Money

Because the number "eight" is auspicious in Chinese culture, "eight" and "make a fortune" being homophonous, after the start of opening up and reform, clamouring for these numbers was unavoidable. In 1994, the "cool number" 9088888 was auctioned off after 39 bids for 655,000 yuan. Smartphones didn't exist back then, but the huge first-generation mobiles gave even more face. As to that person who bought the number, did that make him cool, or the opposite?

Huanggang Doesn't Close

通宵畅行的皇岗

Huanggang Checkpoint is China's largest combine passenger and freight port, and the only one that operates 24 hours a day. To the south of the port is the Huanggang-Lok Ma Chau Bridge which connects Shenzhen and Hong Kong. The port has many cross-border routes, and travellers can take a bus that arrives directly at the Lok Ma Chau Control Point, and then take a bus or train directly into the Hong Kong urban area. Residents of the two cities don't have to worry about partying too late.

皇岗口岸是中国最大的客货综合性陆路口岸,也是唯一24小时通关的口岸。口岸南面的皇岗—落马洲大桥横跨深圳河连接深港两地,口岸有多条跨境交通线路,旅客过关后可乘坐"皇巴"直达落马洲管制区,再乘巴士或铁轨列车到达香港市区各地。深港两地民众再也不用担心购物或游玩入夜无法回家。

离海很远的海滨城市 019

深圳这座海滨城市其实离海很远。市民节假日一般不愿去海边玩，原因很简单：堵车。2018年五一期间，东部景区大鹏半岛试行小客车预约通行。王京生先生一篇《四月，我们看海去》，表达出深圳人心里其实都有那片汪洋："四月，我们看海去。夏天说早了，春天说迟了，然而，我们选择四月。"

A Coastal City Far from the Seas 019

Shenzhen is a coastal city, yet quite far from the ocean. City residents usually don't go to the beach for fun, for a simple reason: traffic jam. For the May 1st holiday in 2018, the eastern scenic area Dapeng Peninsula tried a reservation scheme for small passenger vehicle permits. Mr. Wang Jingsheng wrote an essay "I'm Going to the Ocean in April", in which he expressed the sediments of Shenzhen residents: "In April, let's go to the ocean. Summer is too early, and spring is too late. Thus, we choose April."

全民炒股，于斯为盛 020

作为 A 股的发源地，酒店小弟、卖菜阿婆、公司职员、金领、白领、蓝领，多少人跳入股海翻腾，但有几人笑到最后？股市大涨，个个喜笑颜开，仿佛天上掉馅儿饼；股市大跌，个个愁眉苦脸，捶胸顿足。人生亦如股市，波澜起伏，忽涨忽跌，投机岂能长久。股海莫测，一片汪洋都不见，知向谁边？

全民友好型城市 022

来过深圳的游客大多对深圳印象不错：市容整洁大气，餐饮服务到位，问路彬彬有礼，行人面带微笑，一个词概括为"友好"。按《深圳市城市总体规划（2016—2035）》的设计，未来的深圳将打造成一个儿童友好、人才友好、老年友好、国际友好的全民友好型城市。推己及人、善行善心的友好将继续延伸。

Stock Market 020

As a place that issues A-shares, the bro at the hotel, the old lady selling vegetables, office workers, gold, white and blue collar workers, all play the stock market. Who has the last laugh? When the stock market rises, everyone's happy, as if money is raining from the sky. When the market slumps, everyone's sad. Life is like a stock market, with its ups and downs, rises and falls. Speculation can't continue for a long time.

Shanghai Hotel 021

In the 1980s, the most famous hotel in Shenzhen was named "Shanghai"; situated in a prosperous area it functioned as the origin coordinate of Shenzhen city, and a common meeting spot for friends. All kinds of office workers headed out for various locations in the city from here. When a plan came about to demolish and reconstruct it, it was met with waves of opposition from the residents of the city. The property owner respected people's wishes, and for this reason the original structure with only 163 guest rooms was retained.

A Friendly Place 022

Almost everyone has a good impression when they come to Shenzhen: the city is broad and clean, the food is good, it's easy to ask for directions, pedestrians smile as they walk around; it's friendly. According to the *Urban Overall Planning of Shenzhen City (2016-2035)*, the city is going to form an environment in which everyone is friendly to children, talents, seniors and international guests. Through being considerate, friendliness and kind behaviour can propagate throughout the city.

上海宾馆 021

20 世纪 80 年代，深圳最著名的宾馆以"上海"命名，位于市中心繁华地段，位置极为优越，素有深圳"坐标原点"之称，朋友间约见常以上海宾馆为标志确定方位，多少上班族从这里辐射到城市的四面八方。后来一度准备拆除重建，市民闻之纷纷反对，业主尊重民意，于是这个只有 163 间房的宾馆得以保留。

83　SEZ and Features

我们的员工与众不同 023

中国第一家山姆会员店开在深圳福田，仓储式环境、着红T恤衫员工、大推车、大包装，完全颠覆了人们对超市的印象。山姆的口号响亮：第一条，顾客永远是对的；第二条，如果顾客错了，请看第一条。这条口号后来被中国服务业广为运用。永远服务至上、提供高质货品，可能从山姆开始启蒙。

Our Workers Are Different

China's first Sam's Club is in Shenzhen's Futian district, a warehouse-like environment where the workers wear red T-shirts, with forklifts and large packages everywhere, a totally different kind of supermarket. The corporate platitudes are classic. Rule one: the customer is always right. Rule two: if the customer is wrong, see rule one. These sayings have spread through the Chinese service industry. Always prioritising service and providing high-quality products may have started with Sam.

时间就是金钱 024

在大南山脚下的时间广场上，一块石碑在风雨中屹立不倒，上面的"时间就是金钱，效率就是生命"曾经名动天下。当年提出这句口号的袁庚先生，斯人已逝，风范犹存。而这句口号冲破思想禁锢，刷新了多少人的观念。踏足蛇口的土地，仿佛感受到当年走在石子路上的老人怀揣的梦想。

Time Is Money

At Time Square, at the foot of Mount Danan, a stone stele stands through the wind and rain, upon it the words "Time is money, efficiency is life". These are the words of Yuan Geng, Secretary of the Party Committee of Shekou Industrial Zone, which remain even after his passing. This slogan has opened many minds and changed perceptions. Walking around Shekou, you can almost feel the dreams of this old man who walked the stone streets in years past.

不慕虚荣的深圳人 025

深圳人如果有淘汰的东西，大到家私、电器，小到衣服、童车，在扔之前都会先问问身边的同事和朋友有无需要。送的人心情愉快，收的人感激满怀，没谁觉得有损面子。因为大家都厌恶浪费，物尽其用的理念已经越来越得到深圳年轻人的认同，社会普遍以环保、节约为时尚，以浪费、虚荣为不齿。

Shenzhen Talent Day 026

Shenzhen is a city of talented people which continues to attract more of them. The *Regulations on Talented Work of Shenzhen Special Economic Zone* were created for this reason, establishing a system for the protection of talented labour. November 1st of every year is the "Shenzhen Talent Day". At the Shenzhen Science and Technology Park, there is the only "Talent Park" in China, which includes the Shangxian Pavilion, Qunying Garden, and has Wi-Fi coverage.

深圳人才日 026

深圳是一座因人才而兴、人才而盛的新城，始终吸引人才、呵护人才。《深圳经济特区人才工作条例》在这里因时而生、应势而为，它为天下英才提供了制度保障。每年11月1日是"深圳人才日"，在深圳科技园的绿荫碧水之中，环抱着全国唯一的"人才公园"，这里有尚贤阁和群英荟，实现了Wi-Fi全覆盖。

Don't Call Me Mr. Vain 025

If people in Shenzhen have something they're going to discard, from furniture and white goods to clothing, or a pram, before getting rid of it they ask their coworkers and friends whether they are in need of such an item. The givers are happy to do so and the receivers are grateful; nobody feels without face. Because everyone dislikes waste, full use of resources is more and more popular among the youth of Shenzhen. The society tends towards environmental protection and efficiency, with waste and vanity looked down upon.

深圳手信 027

"千里送鹅毛，物轻人意重。"古人唤"贽"，今人称"手信"，在粤地十分流行。一包点心、一盒茶叶，是粤人外出归来捎带给亲友的手信。而出差带给外地朋友的深圳手信可能是：一个硬盘、一本电子书。深圳本土电子类、时尚类、文创类、食品类的礼品，正在成为深圳新的城市文化名片。

Hand Letters in Shenzhen 027

A small gift sent from far away can have a great impact; these gestures are known as "hand letters" in modern times, and are quite popular among Cantonese people. A package of dim sum, or a box of tea are common gifts for Cantonese people to give to friends when they travel. For people from Shenzhen, these gifts can be a hard drive, or an e-book, or some local electronic goods, fashionable item, literary article, or foodstuff; these are the marks of modern Shenzhen.

早产的共享单车 028

20多年前,深圳就有了共享单车"奔喜客"。开发者想借特区二线关卡,让车在特区内自由流动,没想到惊世骇俗的商业模式几年后烟消云散,据称很多车骑到了珠三角其他城市。如今共享单车遍地开花,但难免残枝败叶。共享梦想的背后,是现实的一地鸡毛。如果出行思维不变,什么"人间骑迹"都会发生。

Early Bicycle Sharing 028

More than 20 years ago, Shenzhen saw the creation of a ride sharing scheme—the creators wanted to make movement around the SEZ easier for all. Shockingly, the scheme and the bikes evaporated quickly, with most of the cycles ending up in other cities in the Pearl River Delta area. Bicycle sharing schemes are flourishing now, but the bikes still take a beating. If people don't change their ways of thinking, it will continue to be a wild ride.

Shenzhen Blue 029

There is a kind of weather called "Shenzhen Blue", a pure blue sky that serves as the face of the city, a point of pride for the metropolis. Shenzhen is also green city, with large forests in fields of grass. Shenzhen is also golden, with nearly one hundred yellow-sand beaches at the banks of the ocean. Out of all these colours, blue is the most important for Shenzhen.

深圳蓝 029

有一种天气叫"深圳蓝"。湛蓝通透的天空,清新纯净的空气,这一切成为这座城市的颜值,也成为这座城市的骄傲。深圳还是绿色的,在不太大的面积里,它拥有大块的森林草坪;深圳也是金色的,在修长的海岸线上,它拥有近百个黄金沙滩。而在这些色彩之上,蓝色是深圳的本色。

深圳,你被谁抛弃? 030

2002年,深圳的空气里充满了担忧和焦虑,一个网民在强国论坛发表了《深圳,你被谁抛弃?》一文,很快就点燃了深圳乃至全国的舆情。深圳市市长约见作者,就深圳的问题与未来,进行了理性对话。盛世危言之下,深圳并未被抛弃,而是在包容试错和不断自省中继续向上。

Shenzhen, Who Forsook You? 030

In 2002, the air of Shenzhen was full of worry and anxiety. Someone posted in the BBS of *People's Daily Online* an essay: "Shenzhen, Who Forsook You?" It quickly gained popularity nationwide. The mayor of Shenzhen met with the author and had a dialogue about the problems and future of Shenzhen. In the end, Shenzhen was not forsaken, but rather recovered from errors and continued to improve.

山就在那里

深圳登山爱好者众多，最出名的除了登顶珠峰的王石，要算银行职员张梁。他已成功登顶世界14座8000米以上山峰，并徒步到达南极和北极，成为首位完成"14+2"的中国人。为什么登山？因为山就在那里。他说："每次攀登都是与生命对话，于我是最难得的历练。"登山也许是深圳人爱冒险的实证。

That's Where the Mountain Is

Shenzhen has many hiking enthusiasts. After Wang Shi, who summited Mount Everest, the most famous climber is probably bank employee Zhang Liang. He has already climbed 14 peaks higher than 8,000 metres, and has reached both the north and south poles, making him the first Chinese to complete the "14+2". Why does he climb mountains? Because they are there. He says: "Every time I climb a mountain, it's like a dialogue with life, one of the most real things out there." The behaviour of climbing mountains may be a testament to how the people of Shenzhen like to take risks.

赠人玫瑰，手有余香

一根电话线，一份善念，成为深圳义工联与需要帮助的人群之间的桥梁。每位义工都是一个种植玫瑰的园丁，他们开通热线，答疑解惑，慰藉求助者的心理和情感。深圳义工联是中国境内的第一个义工团体，拥有义工140万。已故歌手丛飞曾经是义工联艺术团团长。"赠人玫瑰，手有余香"，是义工不变的信念。

Give Someone a Rose

Telephone lines and kind feelings connect volunteers in Shenzhen with those who need assistance. Each volunteer is like a gardener in a rose garden; they've set up a hotline and answer questions and assuage worries, comforting those who seek help. The Shenzhen Volunteer Union is the first of its kind in the mainland of China, with 1.4 million volunteers. The late singer Cong Fei used to be the head of the Volunteer Union Art Troupe. "Give someone a rose and you'll still have the fragrance upon your hand" is the unchanging belief of the group.

"三自"精神源出深大

深圳大学创办之初,即在办公楼下竖立一面石墙,刻上"自立、自律、自强"几个醒目大字,勉励学生经济自立、严于律己、自强不息,在全国首创激励大学生独立自主的"三自"精神。后来深大又创出学生勤工俭学、参与学校管理、开办学生银行等新生事物,皆源于"三自"精神。

4分钱的故事

4分钱不值钱。但在1979年蛇口工业区建设中,施工方为激发工人运泥的积极性,规定完成定额每车奖励2分钱,超过定额每车奖励4分钱。这是中国第一次推行定额超产奖。一个月后,完成最好的司机收入超过中层干部,工程也提前完工。此举惊动了中央高层,获批文支持,平均主义工资体制终被打破。

舌尖上的深圳

深圳的美食和深圳人一样汇自全国各地,有人戏称:"深圳没有自己的菜系,但有中华菜系。"无论你来自何方,在这里都能找到适合自己的口味。踏遍深圳的每一个角落,天上飞的,地上走的,土里爬的,水里游的,只有你想不到的,没有你吃不到的。深圳人是有福之人,口福不浅,幸福很深。

The "Three-Self" Spirit

When Shenzhen University was built, a stone wall in front of the administrative building had a phrase carved into it: "Self-reliance, Self-discipline, Self-strengthening", encouraging students to be economically independent, strictly discipline themselves, and continually improve themselves, making the university the pioneer in the promoting of the "three-self" spirit. The students took to working as they studied, participating in the administration of the university, and operating programs like a student bank, all originating from this "three-self" spirit.

A Story of 4 Pence

4 Chinese pence (0.04 yuan) is hardly anything. However, in 1979 when the Shekou Industrial Zone was being built, in order to motivate the workers to move more earth, it was put up a reward of 2p per truck load, and 4p per load over quota. This was the first time bonuses were given out in China. A month later, the best driver earned more in salary than a mid-level cadre, and the work was finished ahead of schedule. This surprised the central higher-ups, who issued an official document supporting it, and egalitarian salary was no more.

Shenzhen on the Tip of the Tongue

Just like the people in Shenzhen, the food in Shenzhen come from all over the country. Somebody said: "Shenzhen doesn't have its own cuisine, but it does have Chinese cuisine." No matter where you come from, you can find something that suits your taste here. Everywhere in Shenzhen you can find things that fly, walk, burrow and swim to eat—if you can think of it, you can eat it here. This is a prosperous place with plentiful food.

深圳考证的外国人 036

中澳合资的乌石古采石场派来的洋司机无中国驾照，在深圳不能开车上路，市领导一商量，特事特办，便让澳洲司机去考中国驾照，成了第一批有了中国驾照的外国司机。继而，这些外国司机第一次在深圳取得运送炸药的通行证。过去都是中国人去外国考证，现在外国人在中国考证，深圳开了先河。

Taking Tests 036

The foreign operators of equipment at the China-Australian joint venture Wushigu Quarry didn't have Chinese driving licenses, and were thus unable to drive on public roads. The leaders of the city had a discussion and held a meeting, making a special provision to allow these foreign operators to sit examinations for a Chinese driving license, making them the first group of foreigners to obtain them. Later, these operators also became the first foreigners to obtain hazardous materials transportation licenses in China. In the past Chinese went abroad to obtain licenses, and now the trend has reversed, with Shenzhen at the forefront.

乌石古的外籍员工 037

1979年，深圳和澳大利亚合作经营乌石古采石场，澳方派驻人员成为深圳最早的外籍员工。虽然是住在侨社总统套房的贵宾，但每天回来都是一身泥水，成为侨社接待过的最"脏"的外国友人；还曾外出寻找水源却误入旁边的军事禁区，差点引发外交风波。前几年他们重返深圳，深圳的变化，令他们惊讶得目瞪口呆。

Foreign Workers in Wushigu 037

In 1979, Shenzhen and Australia worked together to operate the Wushigu Quarry, with Australia sending workers over to be the first foreign workers in China. Although they lived in the president suites, every day they came back covered in mud, becoming the "dirtiest" foreigners in China. Once when looking for water resources they strayed into a military-controlled zone, almost causing a diplomatic incident. A few years ago, they came back to Shenzhen to visit. They were simply shocked when they saw the changes to the city.

无偿献血 038

国内无偿献血始于深圳。1996年11月24日，一辆捐血车旁人头攒动，"无偿献血，奉献爱心"的横幅颇为新鲜。黎明亦加入献血行列，200毫升B型血缓缓流入血袋，他从医生手中接过红色的献血证。几年后，路边的捐血车越来越多，车身广告语换成了"我不认识您，但我谢谢您"。目前无偿献血已成国人常态。

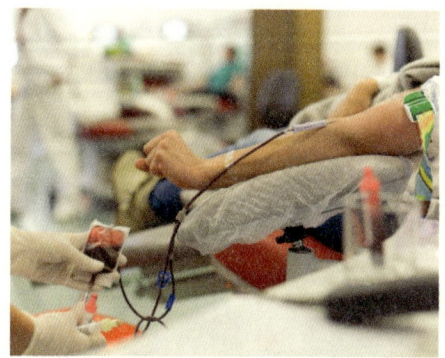

Voluntary Blood Donation

Voluntary blood donation in China started in Shenzhen. On November 24, 1996, a blood donation van rolled out a banner reading "Donate blood, show your love". Singer and actor Li Ming participated, donating 200ml of type B blood, and receiving a donation badge from the doctor. In the subsequent years, more and more people donated, and the banner was changed to read "I don't know you, but I thank you". Donating blood has now become a national habit.

Appointments Required

"Set up a time beforehand, and be on time." This is the norm for people in Shenzhen, and it's been written into the *Morality Guidelines for Shenzhen Residents*. When visiting others, you must set up a time beforehand; you can't just show up. If you don't show up at the appointed time, it's considered a lack of respect for the person you are visiting. This practice of valuing time and respecting others has progressed with the internationalisation of Shenzhen, and makes life nicer here.

无约不访，有约守时 039

"无约不访，有约守时"是深圳人公认的生活习惯，并被写进《深圳市民行为道德规范》。造访他人必须事先预约，不能贸然登门。预约后不准时到达就是对他人的不尊重。这种珍惜时间、尊重他人的现代观念，与深圳国际化的程度同步，也让深圳人活得自在。

Driving Limitations

Starting in August 2017, Shenzhen limited the movements of vehicles registered in other cities, with fines being issued to those that entered the city on workdays during rush hour. The city resisted Beijing and Shanghai-style limitations, but as traffic congestion became more serious, it took a page from their playbook. Officials explain it's about combating pollution, congestion, and promoting cars that use new resources. Yue-B license plates, those of Shenzhen, are still quite hard to come by.

外地车限行令 040

2017年8月起，深圳已将非深号牌汽车限行区域扩大至全市。外地车如在工作日早、晚高峰进入，将扣分罚款。虽然深圳一直避免与京沪一样限外，但严重的拥堵最终促使交通部门痛下决心，向京沪看齐。官方解释，一是治污染、治拥堵，二是推广新能源汽车。本地粤B车牌如今一牌难求。

人与城的交集

1994 年是深圳城市史上的重要节点。这一年，华强北从工业区成为新的商业区，世界之窗开业、广深高速通车、盐田港集团成立。今天深圳的大动脉北环大道在这一年建成通车，另一条大动脉滨海大道在这一年动工。而对于工科生姜禹安来说，初来深圳的这一年充满新鲜感，他决定扎根这里，随遇而安。

People and City

1994 was an important year in Shenzhen's history. This year, Huaqiang North became a new commercial district, the Window of the World opened, the Guangzhou-Shenzhen expressway came into service, and the Yantian Port Group was established. Today's Beihuan Boulevard also was constructed and opened this year, and work on Binhai Boulevard also began this year. For engineering graduate Jiang Yu'an, when he came to Shenzhen this year it felt very fresh, and he decided to stay.

亲嘴楼

闯深圳的年轻人大多住过"握手楼",还有个更刺激的名字"亲嘴楼"。顾名思义,是指楼与楼的间距过于狭窄,对面的人打开窗户就能握手,甚至接吻。"亲嘴楼"多属城中村,采光不佳。居于其中的年轻人迷茫的青春和闪烁的希望,混合成生活的味道。他们在梦中也在唱:"跟着感觉走,紧抓住梦的手,希望就在不远处等着我。"

Kissing Buildings

Many young people that come to Shenzhen have lived in "handshake buildings" that are very close together, but the area is also called "kissing buildings". These buildings are even closer together, so close that if you were to open your window, you could almost kiss the person in the building across from you. These buildings are mostly downtown, and have poor light exposure. The young people who live in them are grinders, with hopes and dreams, following their feelings as they chase them.

抑郁症更需要关爱

这几年,李兰妮的长篇小说《旷野无人》一直热销。她是深圳市作家协会主席,毫不避讳自己是抑郁症患者,最终她走出来了,她要帮助其他人走出来。胡纪泽曾是深圳康宁医院院长,被视为中国式焦虑文化研究第一人。他认为抑郁症的激增与"中国式焦虑心态"有关,患者更需要关注和包容。

Love for the Depressed

A few years ago, Li Lanni wrote the novel *Nobody in the Wilderness*, which sold quite well. She is the head of the Shenzhen Writers Association, and doesn't deny that she suffers from depression. In the end she came out and revealed that she wanted to help others do the same. Hu Jize is the former head of the Shenzhen Kangning Hospital, and is seen as the premier researcher into Chinese-style anxiety culture. He believes that depression is tied to the Chinese culture of anxiety, and that sufferers need attention and compassion.

一个人的长征

深圳摄影家、纪录片导演左力,用一年时间重走红军长征路。一度在都市中迷茫的他,认为长征改变了他,他说:"树立一个单一而坚定的目标,反而能够成就一段幸福的旅程。我们现在有很多的痛苦,都来自于选择太多。"一个人的长征,让左力有了新的体会:幸福绝对不在终点,幸福永远在路上。

Long March

Shenzhen photographer and documentarian Zuo Li spent a year walking the path of the Red Army's Long March, and over the process felt it became a part of him. He said: "When you set up a unique goal like this, it can become a nice journey. These days we have so much struggle, because we have too many choices." A one-man Long March gave a new experience to Zuo Li. Happiness wasn't the end point, but rather the journey itself.

休憩的"绿美人"

这是一片很强势的绿地，硬生生地在大片的钢筋水泥的高楼大厦之间顽强地铺了下来，悠然地横躺在福田中心区，像一个休憩的"绿美人"。"绿美人"的头朝南枕着笔架山，脚在北抵着皇岗口岸，此美人占地面积1.47平方千米，长约2.5千米，东西最宽处约800米，让市民在闹市中寻得一方宁静。

Resting "Green Beauty"

Here there is a strong green area, growing between concrete-and-rebar structures, calmly in the centre of Futian District, just like a resting "Green Beauty". At the head is the Bijia Hill in the south, and at the foot is the Huanggang Checkpoint in the north. The total area is 1.47 square kilometres, the plot being about 2.5 kilometres long and 800 metres at the widest part. It allows the city residents to enjoy some quiet amidst the clamour of the city.

诗意的居住证

海德格尔提出了"诗意地栖居"。特区政府为了严格地管理暂住人口,在1985年开始推行深圳经济特区暂住证,让怀揣梦想的外来深圳人总有一丝不便。20多年后,暂住证退出历史舞台,深圳成为我国首个全面推行"居住证"制度的城市。仔细想来,只要梦想不灭,暂时的栖居也能充满诗意。

最小的超大城市

深圳有多小?首先是地方小,客家话里它是"深深的小水沟";其次是年龄小,相对历史悠久的古城它还是个少年。但深圳又很大:它的人口密度很大,它的"心"也很大,包容着来自四面八方的不同语言、民族、文化的人。正如歌中所唱:"小城故事多,充满喜和乐。若是你到小城来,收获特别多。"

Poetic Residence Permit

Martin Heidegger introduced the concept of "poetic dwelling"; in order to strictly regulate the population, the SEZ government rolled out a temporary residence permit scheme in 1985, making things inconvenient for those who wished to come from elsewhere. 20 years later the scheme was recalled, and Shenzhen became the first city to have permanent residence permit scheme in China. Looking at the situation, one sees that as long as one's hope isn't extinguished, poetic living is possible.

The Smallest Supercity

How small is Shenzhen? The geographic area is small, the scope of history is small as it's a young city. How large is Shenzhen? The population density is a large figure, its "heart" is large. It is home to dialects, ethnicities and cultures from all over China. Just like stated in a Chinese songs: "This small city has many stories and is full of joy; when you visit it you'll gain a lot."

Migration and Feelings

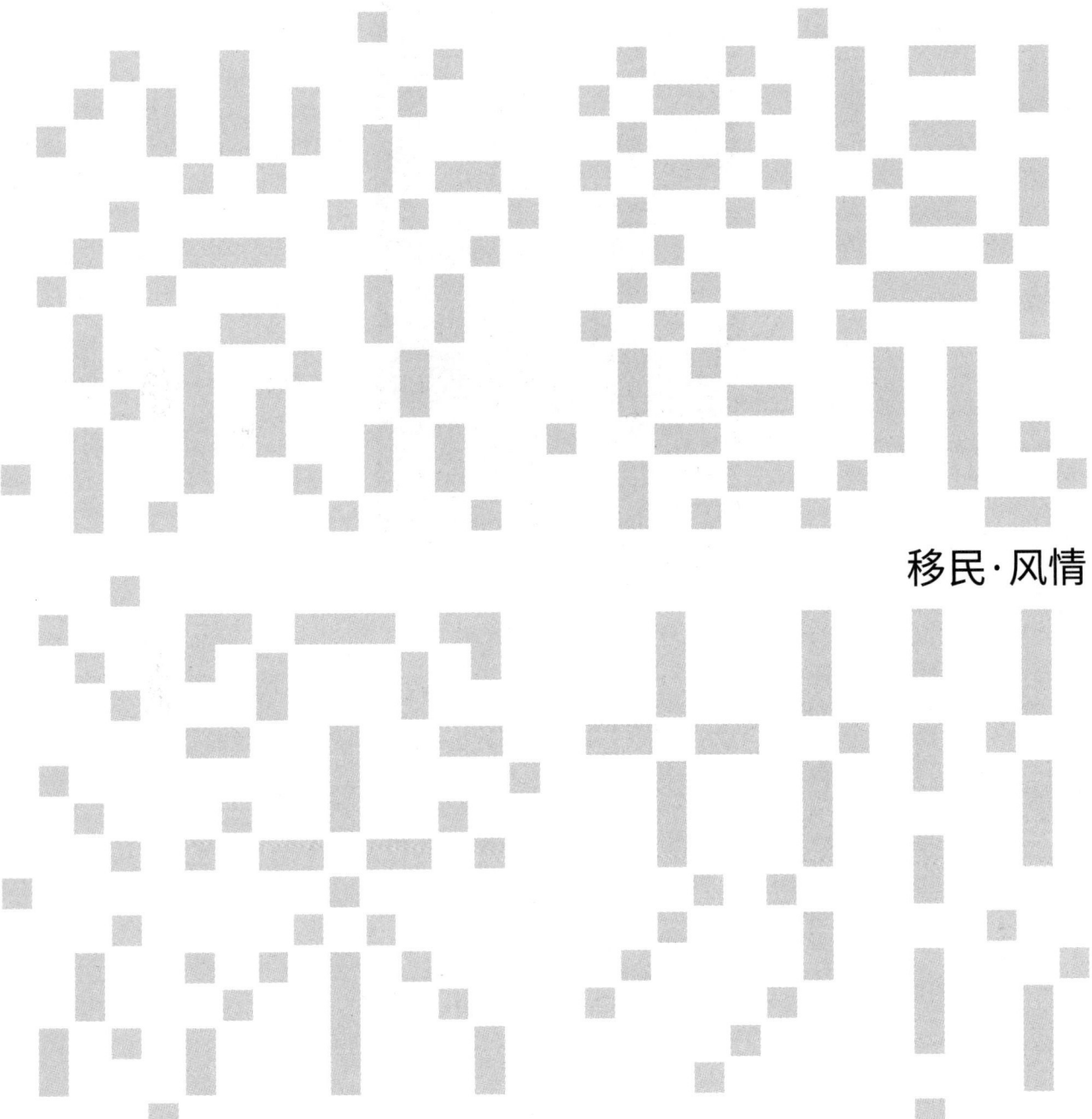

移民·风情

你在深圳还好吗？ 001

没有搬过三次家的人绝不算深圳人。原住民从低矮的瓦房搬进小洋楼；"拓荒牛"从工棚搬进过渡房，从过渡房再搬进新楼房；后来居上的年轻创业者从狭窄的出租屋搬进宽敞的小区、公寓之"家"。城中村见证了无数的人生百态、悲欢离合。面对追问，你在深圳还好吗？如人饮水，冷暖自知。

Are You Doing Well in Shenzhen? 001

If you haven't moved house at least three times you're not a Shenzhen local. Original residents moved from low tile structures to small foreign-style buildings. Those pioneers moved from sheds into makeshift shelters, and then into newer structures. Young innovators later moved from cramped rented flats to spacious communities, and high-rise buildings. The people of the villages have seen countless changes in their lives, both happy and sad. So are you doing well in Shenzhen? This is something you'll feel naturally.

Does Love Last a Lifetime? 002

On the one hand, older unmarried women are increasingly common in Shenzhen—finding love isn't easy. On the other hand, couples are also parting ways. Government statistics show that the divorce rate in Shenzhen is the highest in Guangdong Province, 10 times higher than the city in the province with the lowest rate, Shantou. Pressure is intense in Shenzhen, and in a world where virtual and real intertwine, the divorce rate continues to climb, as couple's personalities clash. Hopefully those in love can be tolerant and grow old together.

爱，会不会是一辈子？ 002

一面是深圳大龄剩女越来越多，相爱不易；另一面却是同甘共苦的夫妻分道扬镳。民政部发布的统计公报显示，深圳为广东省内离婚率最高的城市，其离婚率竟是最低的汕头市的10倍。在高压力的深圳，虚拟现实交织的世界，离婚率始终上涨，性格不合是主因。爱了就请包容一下，与子偕老。

Girls in *Time* 003

In December 2009, the USA's *Time* Magazine revealed its people of the year, with Chinese workers in the second place, the only group entity in the ranking. The women representing Chinese workers all came from a LED company in Shiyan Sub-district, Bao'an District. The workers' names were Xiao Hongxia, Huang Dongyan, Qiu Xiaoyuan, and Peng Chunxia. They come from Shaoyang in Hunan and Meizhou in Guangdong, and have middle school educations. They're practical, hardworking and optimistic.

登上《时代》周刊的女工 003

2009年12月，美国《时代》周刊揭晓年度人物，中国工人登上亚军位置，成为榜单上唯一的群体。而代表中国工人登上《时代》的女工们，全部来自宝安区石岩街道的一家LED企业。女工们的名字是肖红霞、黄冬艳、邱小院、彭春霞。她们分别来自湖南邵阳和广东梅州，初中学历，踏实、勤奋、乐观。

长粽长有 004

因为块头巨大，用冬粽叶包扎得结结实实的大粽子又叫作枕头粽。客家人口味重，爱吃咸，粽子里除了雪白的糯米、绿豆蓉，又放了腌好的五花肉，用柴火煮10个小时，糯米染成了绿色，猪油渗透在糯米和豆蓉里，五花肉入口即融。若是切片煎着吃，则是松脆酥香，此乃"长粽长有"，和幸福一样。

Long Zongzi 004

As zongzi, or glutinous rice creation wrapped in bamboo leaves, made here is quite big and long, it is called "pillow zongzi". Hakka people have strong tastes, and like the savoury taste of these snacks. They're made with rice and green bean paste, stuffed with pork, and then boiled for about 10 hours. The rice is dyed green, and the pork fat leaks into the rice and beans, with the meat inside melting in the mouth. If cut into slices and fried, it's crisp and crunchy.

梦里依稀当当糖 005

逝者如斯夫。生活中有很多烂熟于耳的声音会消失，当当糖的叫卖声亦是。当当糖就是麦芽糖，小何做糖的手艺传自他的父亲老何，老何已经在深圳卖了30年的当当糖，他熟知深圳的大街小巷，如今小何也和他一样。子承父业，挑着担子当当地敲着切糖刀走街串巷的声音，唤起了很多人童年的记忆。

麦当劳叔叔来了 006

中国境内第一家麦当劳开在深圳东门，那是1990年10月8日。红黄相间的小丑叔叔端坐在解放路光华楼顶，笑容可掬地俯瞰着人山人海，队伍从一楼排到二楼，再绕着整个光华楼转了一圈。餐厅第一批员工多达400人，还是忙不过来，不得不从香港临时调来500名员工相助。如今麦当劳遍布中国，改名"金拱门"。

Boom Boom Sweet 005

As time goes by, many of the familiar sounds in one's life vanish, just like that of the "boom boom sweet" known for its sound. It is formed of malt sugar. Mr. He's craft is one he inherited from his father, who sold the sweet in Shenzhen for 30 years. He was familiar with the large thoroughfares and small alleys of Shenzhen, and Mr. He today is like him. The son inheriting his father's craft carries a pole with him, smacking it on the sweet-cutting knife to make the "boom boom" sound that echoes throughout the alleyways as he walks them.

Uncle McDonald Is Coming 006

The first McDonald's in the mainland of China opened in Dongmen on October 8, 1990. Ronald McDonald sited upon the Guanghua Building on Jiefang Road, smiling as he looked over the sea of people. The queue lined up from ground to first floor, and then all the way around, and then circled around the Guanghua Building. The first round of workers for the restaurant numbered 400 people, and was still stretched thin; 500 temporary workers had to be sourced from Hong Kong. Today McDonalds is all over China, where it has changed its official name to "Golden Arch".

600 年的大盆菜

下沙是一个村，他们吃"大盆菜"已历600 年。相传宋少帝赵昺仓皇逃入岭南时，乡人慌忙把各家各户的菜集中倒在军用大盆里煮，慰劳饥肠辘辘的宋军。后来逐渐发展成一种民间饮食形式，将五花肉、鸭肉、蚝等15 种主材分别加工，再按一定顺序盛入木盆。这种壮观的饮食已入选非物质文化遗产。

让天下不再有孤独的老人

在年轻人的世界，深圳数量渐多的老人怎样安享晚年？深圳的很多大厦，都有一个近千平方米的地方，一群老人在享受着充实的生活。每天在这里唱歌、跳舞、练字、弹琴、读书，颐养天年，这是公益的天年之家，是老年人健康、文化的社区养老所。让天下不再有孤独的老人，是城市的初心。

Six Centuries of Poon Choi

Xiasha is a village where poon choi has been eaten for more than 600 years. It's said that when the Song Emperor Zhao Bing fled to Lingnan, the people of the village hurried to gather up whatever food they had and put it into a big military basin to cook to sustain the hungry Song army. Later, this gradually evolved into a folk culinary custom, in which 15 kinds of meats including fatty pork, duck meat, oyster, etc., were specially processed and then placed in a wooden basin in a certain order. This grand tradition has been listed as an intangible cultural heritage.

Underground Workers

The Shenzhen underground system goes all over, and requires constant maintenance, a hard job. Underneath the city, there are these workers who run around deep underground, working until 4 in the morning, sometimes climbing into shafts 5 metres deep. Day after day, they maintain the order of the system, unseen by most. We should respect these hard workers!

No Lonely Elders

In the world of young people, how can the increasing number of old people in Shenzhen enjoy their later years in peace? Shenzhen has many buildings that have an area of almost 1,000 square metres where groups of elderly people enjoy a full life. Every day together they sing, dance, practice calligraphy, play instruments, read, and enjoy themselves. These are public spaces for the elderly, places for the health and cultural enjoyment of the older generations. It's nice that the city makes sure they aren't left all alone.

地下工作者

地铁在深圳四通八达，不可须臾离开，维护保养是一件艰苦的事情。在城市之下，有这样一群地下劳动者，他们奔赴在地底深处，见过凌晨4 点的地下隧道，爬过5 米多的深井，日复一日，维护着地下地上的秩序，却很少为人所知。致敬地下工作者！

福永醒狮

福永醒狮可上溯到清嘉庆年间,

作为一种民间传统喜庆和祈福的活动,

绵延至今。

醒狮为舞狮流派之一,集舞与武于一身。

凡新狮初舞,都要举行"开光点睛"仪式。

舞前礼毕,狮子返回原地继续睡觉,

待鼓声五响,酣睡的狮子伸懒腰,忽睁眼,

一只威猛的"百兽之王"跃然起舞,

遂称醒狮,已入非遗名录。

Fuyong Dancing Lion

The Fuyong Dancing Lion can be traced back to the Jiaqing Emperor's reign in the Qing Dynasty, a customary folk celebration and ceremony to court prosperity, continuing to the present day. This's a specific type of lion dance, called "Awakening Lion" that combines dance and martial arts. Initiating a new dancing lion starts with a ceremony in which its eyes are painted. When the ceremony concludes, and before the dance starts, the lion returns to its place of origin to sleep, and waits for the drum to sound five times before it awakens, stretches, opens its eyes and then begins its dance as the king of beasts. The Awakening Lion has been listed as an intangible cultural heritage.

既不凉也非茶

走到路边，5块钱买一杯凉茶，饮罢神清气爽，这一定是广东人。其实凉茶既不凉，也非茶。它是粤港澳地区民间常用草药煎熬而成的饮料，被列入国家级非物质文化遗产。数百年来，林立于粤港的凉茶铺，形成了一道岭南文化的独特风景线。购物中心里是茶咖的世界，街头巷尾间是凉茶铺的江湖。

Neither Cold Nor Tea

Walking over to the side of the road, he buys a cup of "cold tea" or herbal tea, for 5 yuan. He drinks it down, cool and refreshing; this is a Cantonese guy. It's actually neither cold nor tea, but a rather common drink popular in Guangdong, Hong Kong and Macao made from medicinal herbs, which has been listed as a national intangible cultural heritage. For centuries, there have been herbal tea stalls all around Hong Kong and Guangdong, forming a cultural component of the Lingnan culture. Shopping malls have tea and coffee, but the streets and alleys are the domain of "cold tea".

港式月饼需要品

北方人在深圳过的第一个中秋节想必都会印象深刻，第一次吃月饼的记忆还有吗？深圳人喜欢港式月饼，美心冰皮、荣华双黄莲蓉都是最爱。当你去亲戚家过节，迫不及待地拿起一块月饼大快朵颐时，忽然发现，人家吃月饼是一分为四，用牙签扎着吃。一头雾水的你回家一查，才知道那块月饼有多贵。

过番转来的唐人

客家话把"回来"叫"转来"，非常形象。深圳当年出去的客家人多，有的漂洋过海到"金山"等地，有的在外娶了洋人妻子，生下"半唐番"的小孩，后来领着转来，回乡拜山，百感交集。就像他们改的诗："幼小离乡为异客，每逢佳节倍伤神。遥知兄弟祭祖处，遍燃爆竹少一人。"

Hong Kong-style Moon Cakes: Essential

When people from the north spend their first Moon Festival in Shenzhen, they're left with a deep impression—think about the first moon cake. People of Shenzhen like Hong Kong-style moon cakes, such as the iced ones from the chain Maxim's, and the double egg yolk variety from Wing Wah. When you go to Shenzhen for the Moon Festival, you'll be eager to pick up a moon cake. You'll see that the people of the city quarter the cakes, and pick the pieces up with a toothpick. Head misty, you'll head home and looking it up, be surprised to see how expensive these moon cakes are.

Hakka People "Turning Back"

In the Hakka dialect, they say "turn back" when they mean "come back". Previously many Hakka people came to Shenzhen, with some continuing on to San Francisco and other cities, marrying foreign ladies, having mixed-race children, and then bringing them back to visit. Emotions flow as they see their greatly changed places of birth. One always feels the distance of a relative who has left.

尴尬的玩具店

聪明的深圳孩子，不去玩具店买玩具。现在购物中心里到处都有潮品生活馆，展示琳琅满目、稀奇古怪的玩具，可是深三代在这里往往只看不买。他们会偷偷用手机拍下来，然后去淘宝选择性价比最高的玩具，快递到家。小朋友说，店里10块钱的公仔在网上只要1块钱。实体店主们面对马云无可奈何。

Toy Shop

The clever children of Shenzhen don't go to toy shops to buy toys. Now the shopping centres of Shenzhen are full of stores with innovative and fashionable items, whereas the random toy store doesn't get much love from recent generations of residents. Shoppers will sneakily snap a picture of something they like with a phone and then find the best deal for the same item on Taobao, having it delivered to their home. The kids say that what costs 10 yuan in the store only costs 1 yuan online. Jack Ma is really messing with these brick-and-mortar stores.

Farmed Shrimp

Farming fish in walled plots is common in China; those that partake in this activity are "plot lords". They have come down from the sea, constructing plots via a series of dykes near the sea in which they farm crabs and shrimp. These "farmed shrimp" are quite good, especially those from the Xixiang Town; in the city of Shenzhen they are popular, with their thin shells, tender meat, and nourishing properties. Tasty, and healthy.

基围人的基围虾

人们养殖鱼虾蟹的"基堤鱼水围"，简称"基围"，基围人就是住在"基围"上的人。他们从海上"漂移"而来，上了岸仍不离海，在浅海滩涂上筑起土堤，养殖鱼虾蟹，"基围虾"由此得名。深圳是一座不折不扣的"吃货城"，西乡的基围虾，虾皮极薄，肉质鲜嫩，常食有明目洁齿、养颜健身之功效。

Orchids at Home

Liu Qinxian, originally from Zhejiang, is 80 years old, and has lived in Shenzhen for 15 years already. She goes to the park every day to walk, and like to look at the bougainvillea and peach flowers on Lianhua Hill, but what she loves the most are the orchids of her hometown. Her brother over 70 years old comes from Yunhe County, bringing an orchid. When it blooms, Ms. Liu smells the fragrance of her home. Her son records her sentiments: the smell of the orchid floats through the summer air, and feelings for my hometown bloom in my heart.

家乡的兰花

居住深圳已15年的浙江人柳琴仙已经80岁，每天去公园散步。她喜欢看莲花山的簕杜鹃、桃花林中的桃花，可最惦记的还是家乡的兰花。70多岁的弟弟从老家云和带来一株兰花。兰花开了，柳奶奶又闻到了家乡的花香。儿子记录下老母赏兰的心情："兰草香夏日，摇曳醉花丛。乡关千万里，心意自可通。"

红红火火客家年

客家人的新年很隆重也很简单。"花灯照不夜,歌声喜欲狂。人人争买花,忙煞卖花郎",逛花市买花回家装饰是必不可少的。光明新区最重要的年俗活动是舞麒麟和醒狮,从大年初一开始,街上便能不断地听到锣鼓震天响,浩浩荡荡的队伍从村头舞到村尾,村民们也从村头看到村尾,老少乐不可支。

Hakka New Year

The Hakka new year is grand yet simple. Lanterns shine as bright as day, and songs are everywhere. Flowers and gaiety are everywhere. Walking around the flower market, one must pick up some decorations for the house. In the Guangming New District, the most important activities are the kylin dance and awakening lion dance. From the first day, you can continuously hear the booming sound of drums, the procession running through the entire village, everyone lining the streets, young and old, all enjoying themselves.

"四头四尾"的客家女子

客家女子的勤劳、朴实、善良和美貌在华人世界里闻名,俗话云"娶妻当娶客家女"。旧时把客家女子的美德概括为"四头四尾",即"田头地尾、针头线尾、灶头锅尾和家头教尾",改革开放后的富裕生活,没有改变她们的这种优秀品质。在客家人眼里,母亲在家庭中的主体地位难以撼动。

Hakka Women

Hakka women are hardworking, practical, kind and beautiful; these characteristics of theirs are famous throughout China. Classically, they were known for excelling in four areas: working in the field, sewing, cooking, and raising children. After opening up and reform, living conditions improved but they retained their excellent character. In the eyes of the Hakka people, the mother is the centre of the family.

一条界河波浪宽

一条深圳河,两道铁丝网,隔开了深港两地。北边是深圳的罗芳村,"握手楼"云集;对面的香港新界,亦有罗芳村,依旧保持着岭南水乡的原始风貌。从前深圳罗芳村的村民,每天前往香港那边种地,也有村民偷渡过去后不愿回来。至今,不少罗芳村村民仍过着"双城"生活:在深圳收租,到对岸养老。

Water Works

The Shenzhen River and two fences separate Shenzhen and Hong Kong. To the north is Luofang Village, heavily built up, and on the other side is the New Territories District of Hong Kong, where there is also a Lo Fong Village, which retains the original appearance of a Cantonese village. Previously, the residents of Luofang in Shenzhen would come to Hong Kong every day to work the land, with some illegally crossing and staying. Today, a number of residents of the village live a "two cities" life, collecting rent in Shenzhen and relaxing in Hong Kong.

逗利市

广东人把红包称作"利市",过年要派利市,婚丧嫁娶皆如此。起初派个5块10块,逗孩子高兴,可后来就演变成了成百上千的大利市,更有让人咋舌的超大利市。凡未婚青年均可向成家者讨利市。春节后开工大吉,"开工利市"更成惯例,笑逐颜开"逗利市"是朋友圈里不倦的游戏。

深二代夏春秋

春夏秋冬,和于天时;深圳无冬,隐于小名。夏春秋是个很有深圳文化味儿的名字。小夏同学在小学是大队长、三好学生,朝气蓬勃、品学兼优、健康阳光。其父为其起名的潜台词是"春秋在南方,深圳无冬天"。夏春秋父亲是资深咨询师,腹有诗书,为了平衡,为爱子起小名为冬冬。

Tribute Item—Lychee

In *The Chronicles of Xin'an County*, it's recorded that when the lychee trees are three or four metres high, the green leaves dense, the flowers blooming brightly and the lychees the size of eggs, that is the best time to harvest them, as they'll have wonderful white, juicy flesh. From the time of the Tang and Song Dynasties, the "Nanshan lychee" has been an article of tribute. Representative strains of the Nanshan lychee have names like "Smile of the Princess" and "Sticky Rice", with protected geographical origins; they are famous products with enshrine cultural significance.

Lai See

The people of Cantonese refer to red pockets as "lai see", giving them out at Lunar New Year, weddings, and other occasions. Small denominations of 5 or 10 yuan are given out to children for fun, which later turn into hundreds or thousands of yuan. Unmarried youths can all ask for lai see from their married relatives. When the lunar new year rolls around, and the fun starts, with everyone clamouring for lai see.

Shenzhen Boy Xia Chunqiu

Shenzhen is a city that doesn't have a real winter. Xia Chunqiu is a Shenzhen boy, with the three Chinese characters in his name respectively referring to summer, spring and autumn. He is an elementary school student, head of his class. He excels in his studies, works hard, and is healthy and bright. His father thus named him, with the understood following words to his name being "spring and autumn are in the south; Shenzhen has no winter". His father likes to read books of poetry; for balance, his nickname is Dongdong ("little winter").

一骑红尘妃子笑

《新安县志》记载:"荔枝树高丈余或三四丈,绿叶蓬蓬,青花朱实,实大如卵,肉白如脂,甘而多汁,乃果中之最珍者。"从唐宋开始,"南山荔枝"便是贡品。国家对以妃子笑、糯米糍等品种为代表的南山荔枝,实施地理标志产品保护。"一骑红尘妃子笑,无人知是荔枝来",荔枝里啖出了文化。

南粤婚俗重上头

传统的南粤婚礼仪式里，定亲、过大礼、上头、搬嫁妆、跨火盆，这些仪式一样也不能少。经过百余年的变迁，仪式化繁为简，但在迎亲前一晚，男女双方"上头"的仪式却保留了下来。上头就是帮新人梳头，"一梳梳到尾，二梳白发齐眉……"，"好命佬"或"好命婆"的祝福很重要。

Cantonese Wedding

There are a number of essential steps to a traditional Cantonese wedding, such as engagement, betrothal, dowry, changing hairstyle, etc. Over the centuries, these traditions have been simplified but on the night before meeting relatives, the male and female must participate in the "hairstyle" ceremony, which is combing each other's hair by a married man or woman who has good fortune. It is still considered very important.

南澳鲍鱼在险处

素有"食海鲜，到南澳"美誉的南澳街道，是全国最大规模的陆地养鲍基地之一。鲍鱼古称"石蝮""石决明"，又称"九孔螺"，肉质滑爽脆嫩，营养丰富，自古便被视为"鲍、参、翅、肚"四海味之首。南澳鲍鱼主要产于南澳海湾悬崖险要处，尤以东涌的鹿嘴为最。为了口舌之欲，冒点儿风险也值。

Nan'ao Abalone

Nan'ao Sub-district has always been famous for its seafood. It is one of the largest-scale abalone operation in the country. The abalone has smooth flesh and nutritious properties, and along with sea cucumber, shark's fin, and fish maw, are considered four of the classical seafood delicacies. The best of the Nan'ao abalone lives around the dangerous cliffs of Nan'ao Bay, especially in the Luzui area of Dongchong Town. For such a flavour, it's worth a little risk.

葬我于大海 025

海葬在深圳逐渐兴起。3月的深圳，海风有点儿刺骨，安徽人李程和姐姐扶着父亲站在船尾送别母亲，看海水泛起的浪花，卷着刚刚抛撒的玫瑰花瓣，慢慢远去，也慢慢平静。父亲轻声道："你会游泳，在这里你会开心的。"李程母亲生前对儿女叮嘱："我走后，把我的骨灰撒到海里，来海边就能看到妈。"

Bury Me at Sea

Sea burials are becoming more common in Shenzhen. In March, the wind is a bit sharp, and Li Cheng alongside his father and his sister, Anhui natives, stand at the stern of the boat, bidding farewell to their mother. Looking at the spray on the waves as the rose petals they have just scattered float away, the scene is calm and quiet. The father speaks quietly: "You can swim, so you'll be happy here." Before she died Li Cheng's mother said to her children: "When I die bury me at sea. That way, when you look upon the ocean, you can see me."

年桔橙黄 026

深圳的客家人爱讲好意头。逢年过节，鲜花水果必不可少，每年大年三十的年花、年桔就显得格外重要。普通人家一般也都会摆放发财树、富贵竹之类的常绿植物，预示着欣欣向荣。"年桔"，也叫"大桔"（大吉）。除夕，人们用一对桔子放在床头、桌面，有大吉大利、吉到运到的寓意，是应节必备果品。

New-Year Oranges

The Hakka people of Shenzhen like auspicious phrases. When the lunar new year rolls around, there must be fresh flowers and fruits around. Every year on the eve of the new year, new-year oranges (Citrus oleocarpa) are quite important. People will place lucky trees (Pachira aquatica), lucky bamboo (Dracaena sanderiana) and other evergreen plants outside their doors as a prediction of prosperity. At night, people will place two new-year oranges at the head of their beds and on tables to court luck and prosperity—it's viewed as an essential step.

平民自助餐 027

正如时装界的潮流一样，美食界也有食物流行期。20世纪90年代中后期自助餐风靡一时，传统的中西餐馆都纷纷推出，在燕南路上还有低至28元的海鲜自助餐，饮料任饮，啤酒要钱。琳琅满目的食物，随心所欲地选择，食客们都吃得"扶墙而出"。如今除了星级酒店百元以上的自助餐外，平价盛况不再。

Cheap Buffets

Just like the fashion industry, cuisine also has its trends. In the middle and late 1990s, buffets became popular, and were rolled out in all kinds of Western and Chinese restaurants. On Yannan Road there was even a 28 yuan seafood buffet. Soft drinks were free, but beer costed extra. There was wonderful food everywhere, which you could select as much of as you wanted. Everyone ate until they were very full. Nowadays aside from the buffets above 100 yuan at various starred hotels, cheap buffets are no longer around.

亲切的"阿"

无论称呼老幼,深圳人都喜欢加个"阿"字。"阿"字为汉语名词词头,盛行于魏晋以后,加在亲朋好友称呼前面有亲昵的意味。老者如阿伯、阿叔、阿公、阿婆,非常亲切。称呼年轻人也如此,要么加在姓前:阿张、阿李;要么加在名前:阿元、阿香。久而久之,从北方来深圳的人也习惯这种称谓。

The Prefix of "A"

Whether young or old, people in Shenzhen like to add "a" to the start of names. This is a prefix that came about after the Wei and Jin Dynasties, which adds an element of sincerity or familiarity to a name. Names for family relations can contain this like, "A Bo" (father's elder brother) and "A Shu" (father's younger brother), "A Gong" (grandfather), and "A Po" (grandmother) are all very intimate. Younger people can be thus called by prefixing "a" to their surname, such as "A Zhang", "A Li", and the prefix can also be used with given names, such as "A Yuan" and "A Xiang". Even northerners who come to Shenzhen get used to being thus called.

Weird Food

There's a saying about Cantonese people: "The only thing they don't eat in the air is an airplane, the only thing they don't eat on the ground is a car, and the only thing they don't eat in the water is a boat." When a friend from out of town came by, in a Cantonese restaurant the waitress asked: "Can we get the human head rice?" My friend looked shocked, saying we really were too extreme in what we ate. Only when the white rice came did he understand the phrase meant a bowl of rice per head (person). After the meal, we had "raw fruit" which was, well, just fruit.

人头饭与生果

粤人敢吃,传说"天上飞的飞机不吃,地上跑的汽车不吃,水里游的舰艇不吃,其他见啥吃啥"。外地朋友来深圳去吃粤菜,末了服务员问:"上人头饭?"朋友大惊失色,都说这里什么都敢吃,真够狠的。待到白饭上桌,才明白"人头"指的是人数。饭后还要上"生果",端上西瓜才知道,生果就是水果。

深圳才有家的感觉

文艺女青年苇公子,金陵人氏,1994年夏天来深,阳光满街流淌,青春灼热,这一印象多年未变。有几年她离深在外,无论在哪个城市停留,只有飞机降落深圳机场,才令她有家的感觉。她有个"四季"微信朋友圈,圈内女友或单身,或离异,或在婚内平静而波澜壮阔地活着,十分深圳。

Shenzhen Feels Like Home

The intellectual "Princess Wei" of Nanjing, capital city of Jiangsu Province came to Shenzhen in the summer of 1994 when the streets were full of sunshine and she was full of passion; this impression still hasn't changed. She left Shenzhen for a few years, but no matter where she stayed, whenever the flight touched down at Shenzhen, only then did she feel at home. She has a "four seasons" chat group in her chat app full of women single, divorced, or in a rocky marriage—typical Shenzhen.

文豪也喜沙井蚝 031

皆知苏东坡嗜肉，自己发明了东坡肘子，殊不知苏东坡亦嗜蚝，在惠州任职时吃了新安蚝，挥毫写下《食蚝》一文。新安蚝产区便在今日的沙井，《新安县志》介绍："壳可以砌墙，可烧灰，肉最甘美，晒干目蚝豉。"沙井蚝油的名声在海内外食客中也是响亮得很。因其独特魅力，沙井有了金蚝节。

蛇口老街 032

古老的石板路和现代的高压线令人恍惚，无数弄潮儿曾在此大显身手：蛇口老街是当之无愧的中国改革开放的缩影。如今这里的慢节奏，在高速发展的深圳看来，已显得"格格不入"。老街日渐冷落，淡出了大家的视线，甚至被遗忘。只有街道两旁既土又豪的农民房和大排档，还在默默诉说当年的繁华景象。

Oysters of Shajing Town 031

It's widely known that Song-dynasty poet Su Dongpo was a fan of meat, and developed the famous dish of Dongpo stewed pork joint, but it's less commonly known that he was also a fan of oysters, and when stationed in Huizhou even wrote an essay about eating the Xin'an oysters. Xin'an oysters are still produced in Shajing Sub-district. *The Chronicles of Xin'an County* says: "The shells can be used to build walls, and can be burnt into ash. The meat is sweet and delicious, and can be dried." The oysters of Shajing Sub-district are famous both in China and abroad, and the Sub-district even has a festival dedicated to them.

Shekou Laojie Street 032

The old stone street of Shekou contrasts with the modern high-tension cables in startling way. These used to be a real thoroughfare. Shekou Laojie Street is a typical reflections of the time of opening up and reform, but now the pace here seems out of sync with the quickly developing city. The street seems quieter by the day, and is fading out of view, almost forgotten. Only those residences and restaurants of rustic style on the sides of the small streets reflect the past glory of these avenues.

So Smart 033

More than ten years ago there were a group of "rebellious" youths who appeared online, with long, dyed hair and crazy makeup and accessories. They called themselves the "Shamate Clan", in an approximation of the English word "smart", thinking themselves intelligent and fashionable. Luo Fuxing, the "Father of Shamate Clan" lives today in Baishitang Village, Longgang District. His days of online popularity are over, and all he is left with is a tattoo that he can't wash off.

"杀马特" 033

10多年前网络上突然出现一批离经叛道的青少年，留着五彩长发、化着刺目浓妆、佩戴奇怪首饰。他们自称为"杀马特家族"，这个词源于英语smart，原义是聪明、时尚。号称"杀马特之父"的罗福兴，如今租住在龙岗区白石塘村，这位当年一呼百应的网红领袖，风光不再，只留下遍体文身无法洗去。

松岗赛龙舟

与其他地方端午祭屈原不同，松岗赛龙舟的习俗，与文氏家族纪念民族英雄文天祥有着密切的关系。义氏家族为松岗龙舟赋予了独特的家族祭拜先祖的宗族色彩，并形成一套完整、规范、严谨的仪式，松岗也便成为粤港澳端午节赛龙舟的主场。茅洲河上，鼓声震天，百船齐发，天地间充盈浩荡之气。

生命在于折腾

深圳有一批爱折腾的人，阿林乃其一。他坐着绿皮火车来深，在东门老街租下一间店铺，蚂蚁搬家一般，一趟趟地把沙头角的港货运回东门加价售出。数年之后，阿林的店开得满大街都是，当初帮阿林运货的香港女店员成了阿林的老板娘，阿林的生意也折腾到了香港。生意和生命都在折腾中红火。

Dragon Boat Races

Unlike the Dragon Boat Festival in other places, the races in Songgang Town have different customs, which are intimately connected with the national hero Wen Tianxiang. The Wen family contributed special characteristics to ancestor worship in the festival, and formulated a complete, regular and strict ceremony. Songgang is the chief location for dragon boat races for Guangdong, Hong Kong and Macao. On the Maozhou River, the beat of the drums rises to the sky as many boats set out in the vibrant atmosphere.

Life Is a Grind

Shenzhen has people who like to grind; A Lin is one of them. He rode in a slow train to Shenzhen and rented a shop in Dongmen Laojie Street, and continually moved goods from Shatoujiao to his store in Shenzhen, padding the price and selling them off. A number of years later, the shop girl from Hong Kong who helped send him goods became his wife, and his business expanded to Hong Kong. Business and life are both achieved through the grind.

深圳舞麒麟

200多年前，新安县的观澜、龙岗等地风行舞麒麟。深圳舞麒麟已入选非物质文化遗产。表演分为麒麟舞、武术两部分，透出岭南民间喜庆的民俗特征和崇尚礼义谦让的文化传统，是客家移民精神的传承。喜庆之日，麒麟队各司其职：扮麒麟、唱麒麟歌、撑罗伞、举彩牌、司鼓乐。老少皆爱，其乐融融。

添丁点灯

自古客家人重男丁，家中生了男孩，要到祠堂去祭拜祖先报告家中添丁，告知男丁家长的姓名、男丁的姓名及出生日期。添丁的人家必须要在正月初四这天开灯，求祖先保佑家中财丁两旺。开灯要点亮灯，直到正月十五元宵节前，每天都要到祠堂上香添油，十五当天必须挂上彩灯，此时男丁才能记入族谱。

Shenzhen Kylin Dance

More than 200 years ago, places in Xin'an County such as Guanlan and Longgang held kylin dances. The dance has already been listed as an intangible cultural heritage. There are both dance and martial arts components, which show the special characteristics of celebration among the people of the Lingnan area, as well as the cultural custom of polite declining, traditions from the spirit of the Hakka people. On days of celebration, the members of the kylin team all perform their own functions: acting as the kylin, singing the kylin song, holding the umbrellas, raising the coloured cards, playing the drums. Everyone young and old loves to view this spectacle.

Light the Lantern

Hakka families favour the males, and when a son is born one goes to the ancestral hall to report the birth, report the name of the head of household, as well as the son's name and date of birth. Those who have a son born this year must light a lantern on the fourth day of the first lunar month, and pray to the ancestors to protect him and ensure prosperity. The lantern must burn until the fifteenth, and during this period one must go to the ancestral hall every day to burn incense and add fragrant oil, and a coloured lantern must be hung on the fifteenth day; only then can the son be entered into the family register.

Lard Cakes

Shenzhen doesn't just have seafood, it also has the lard cake. Maybe as it's produced in the SEZ, the lard cakes in Shenzhen are especially big and thick, golden in colour and shining like amber. The glassine under the wax paper is especially thin, and as you bite into it, it almost dances as it melts on your tongue, fragrant and not cloying. If you want to experience this flavour, you'll have to put in a bit of work and search around the old streets.

特区猪油糕的特别之处

深圳不只有海鲜，还有猪油糕。或许因为产在特区，深圳的猪油糕个头特别大、特别厚，金黄的糕体像一块晶亮的琥珀，包裹在油纸下的那层玻璃纸特别薄，一口咬下，玻璃纸仿佛在舌尖滋滋起舞，满口的香甜韧而不腻……如今要想吃到，恐怕还得花费一番工夫，去老街的巷子深处寻觅。

外来工

从来没有一个城市像深圳这样，聚集着如此众多的来自全国各地的打工者。作为建设者和追梦者，关于外来工的种种记忆已经纳入这座由无数外来工缔造出的城市的历史。有作家感叹说："人活一世，从生命的起点走到终点，劳劳碌碌，营营役役，其实我们每一个人都是这个世界的外来工。"

Come Here to Work

There's never been another city like Shenzhen, with so many workers from all over the country. As builders and pursuers of dreams, the histories of these workers are integrated into the fabric of the city. An author remarks, sighing: "In a life, from its beginning to its end, working hard, fulfilling your duties; in the end we all come here to labour."

Parental Melancholy

The "matchmaking corner" is something familiar to the residents of the large cities in China. At the park, the people who come to the corner aren't unmarried youths, but rather anxious parents. There is a matchmaking corner in the palm grove in Shenzhen's Lianhuashan Park, near the south gate, upon which there are all kinds of personal ads hung upon the trunks of the trees, with personal details, incomes, property holdings, educational history, and the like in bold print. The parents posting these ads are really losing it.

父母亲的"情愁"

大城市的居民对"相亲角"都不陌生，公园草地上，前来"相亲"的都不是适婚的青年男女，而是心急如焚的父母们。深圳的"相亲角"在莲花山公园南大门后的棕榈树林里，高大的棕榈树上挂着写有基本资料的征婚启事，收入、房产、学历等为加粗字体，同时挂着的是父母亲们的满怀"情愁"。

深圳十大观念

一座城市的根和魂，就是观念与精神。2010年深圳启动了"最有影响力十大观念"评选活动，"时间就是金钱，效率就是生命""空谈误国，实干兴邦""敢为天下先""让城市因热爱读书而受人尊重""来了，就是深圳人"等入选。支撑了深圳从小渔村到大都市的正是这些观念，真理是朴素的。

Ten Views of Shenzhen

The roots and soul of a city are in its views and spirit. In 2010, Shenzhen started a voting activity for the "Ten Most Influential Views of Shenzhen". "Time is money, and efficiency is life", "talk doesn't built a nation; get things done", "let's get to it", "let's give respect to our city's book lovers", "ah, this is Shenzhen life" and others were selected. These are the views that took Shenzhen from a small fishing village to a huge city.

Drink Tea and Chat

Cantonese people like to drink tea and chat, especially the older generation, sitting in a restaurant, drinking a good fill of tea. It's frequent to see scenes in Hong Kong films of people talking through differences over tea. So for those Cantonese, drinking tea is not simply for the tea, but to have a good talk and sometimes dispel some misunderstandings.

饮茶倾解

倾解,在粤语中是聊天儿的意思。广东人喜欢饮茶倾解,尤其是老人,上酒楼一坐,"一盅两件",饮一肚子茶水,心满意足地打道回府。他们的重点是"倾",倾诉心事。香港的影视剧里经常看到"和事佬"对有误会的两家说去饮茶倾解,他们的重点是"解",解释误会。饮茶倾解是一种文化内涵。

粤之糖水

主持人孟非曾经在电视节目中点评道:"广东人最怕上火,所以爱喝糖水。"其实"糖水"就是甜品,大多是以清润、清热为主的甜羹,如绿豆粥、红豆粥、番薯粥;也会融入奶的元素,如双皮奶、姜汁撞奶等。粤语一般称"食糖水"而不会称"饮糖水"。情侣喜欢食糖水,大抵因为糖水能增加爱情的甜蜜。

Sweet Water

A famous TV host, Meng Fei, noted that Cantonese people liked to drink "sweet water" to stay healthy from the hot weather. The "sweet water" is actually sweet stews such as those made from green beans, red beans, and sweet potatoes, sometimes with dairy, ginger, and the like added in. So in Cantonese dialect it is called to "eat" instead of to "drink" sweet water. Couples like to enjoy this stuff together, as it's said to strengthen the relationship.

一碗靓汤

"宁可食无馐,不可饮无汤。"广东人爱喝汤,饭前必喝一碗老火靓汤,与北方人程序相反。传统的广东女人都是煲汤的高手,她们深谙煲汤的学问,把普通食材放在砂煲里,煲出来的不单是美味的汤,更有对丈夫和亲人浓稠的深刻的爱。广东母亲给外地的孩子打电话通常都会问上一句:"今日饮汤了吗?"

One Bowl of Soup

It's OK to have no side dishes, but not OK to have no soup. Cantonese people love soup, and it's essential to have a bowl before the meal, opposite to the course of things in the north. Traditional Cantonese women are experts at making soup, able to put a combination of normal ingredients into a pot and produce a delicious creation. When mothers call their children in other cities, they may open the conversation by asking them if they've had soup yet that day.

早熟的孩子

一样的年龄,不一样的孩子。深三代对各种信息的掌握,远超出家长和老师的想象。当年我们还在跳皮筋、玩泥巴,如今他们已拿着平板电脑心鹜八极;当年我们对青春期话题还在羞羞答答,如今他们早已洞察玄机;当我们对社会还混混沌沌,他们已经懂得了人情世故、成本利润。如此,不知是喜是忧?

Precocious Children

Same age, different children. Children in Shenzhen have great grasp of information. Kids these days, at the age when we were still cheeky little things, have a familiarity with tablet computers and the like; at the age when we were shy to talk about certain topics, they already have a familiarity with certain mysteries; at the age when we were still silly and clumsy, they understand love, capital, and profit. Is this good or bad?

Tech and Finance

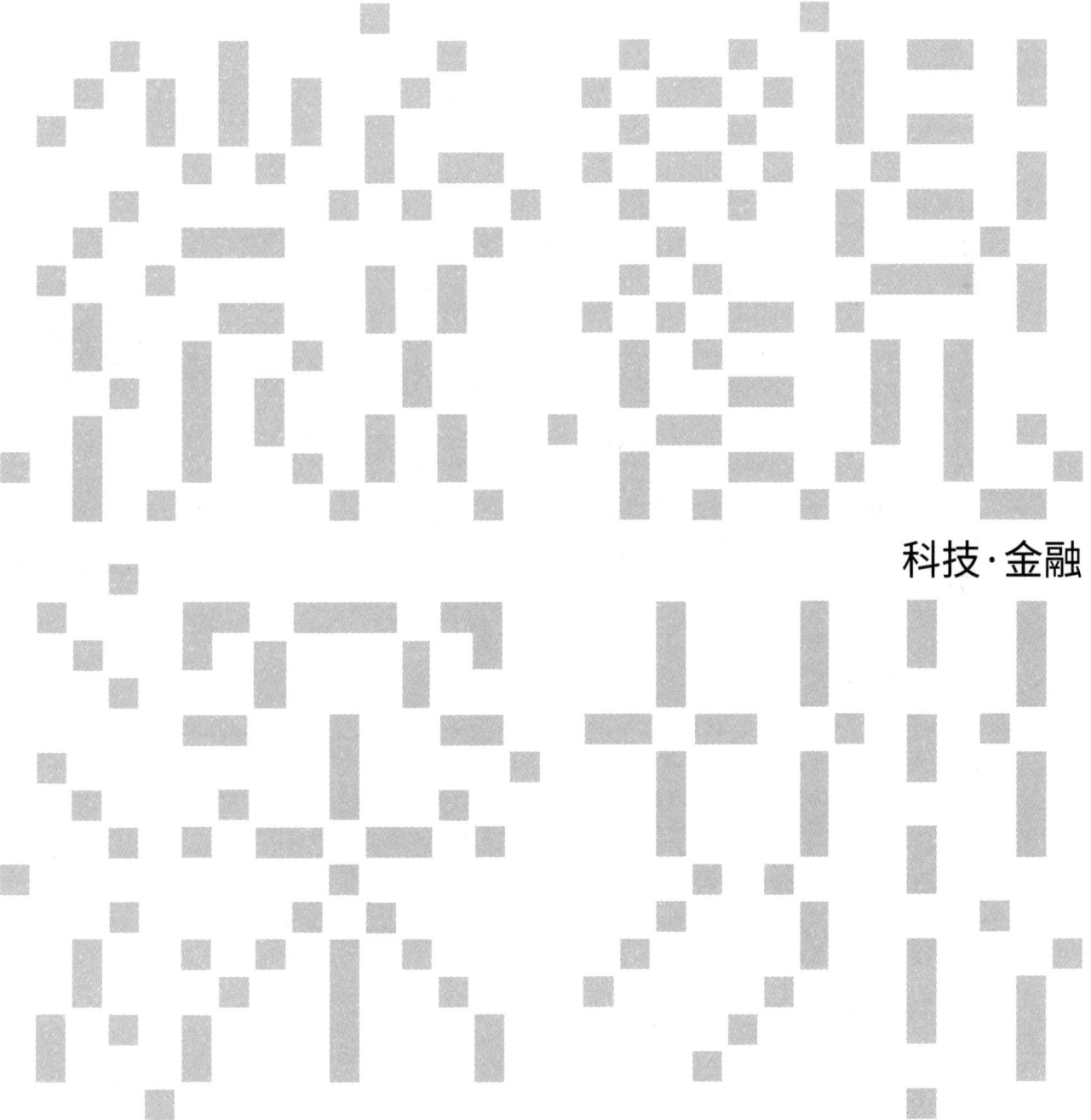

科技・金融

梦想在钟声中醒来 001

创业板被称为"中国的纳斯达克",深圳甫出,凤凰齐聚。创业板是造富板,上市公司富豪辈出,创投企业盆满钵溢;创业板也是造梦板,全国创业者的梦想激荡于此。创业板落户深圳,成为"中国梦"的一只翅膀,深交所功不可没。开板10年,钟声敲响了一些人的梦,又敲碎了另一些人的梦。

Dreams Awaken with the Bell 001

The Growth Enterprise Market is like China's NASDAQ. It's an avenue towards wealth, with public companies coming forth in large numbers, and venture capital enterprises making huge amounts of money; it's an avenue towards dreams, sparking the hopes of entrepreneurs from across the country. This market serves as a wing for the "Chinese dream"; the contribution of the Shenzhen Stock Exchange cannot be ignored. Open for ten years, the ring of the bell awakens the dreams of some, and crushes the dreams of others.

最佳试验场 002

追求没有止境,上市只是开始。大族激光创始人高云峰毕业于北航,靠着拿下了一位香港客户订购激光打标机的业务,获得40万预付款,开始创业。从小作坊,到中小板首批上市的"新八股"之一,再到市值500多亿的激光业龙头,高云峰感恩深圳,他说,这座城市是把想法变成产品的最佳试验场。

只为遇见你 003

成为"创投之都",是深圳的理想,更是深圳人的心声。每一个不眠的夜晚,每一个看得到星星的早晨,深圳的空气里都有资金和项目在寻找彼此,创业和投资已是生活的一部分。这里有全国最大的创投机构,还有市场化程度高、聚集度高和活跃度高的"三高"创投业。过尽千帆皆不是,一切只为遇见你。

The Best Testing Ground 002

To strive is an activity with no limit, and going public is only the start. A graduate of the Beijing University of Aeronautics and Astronautics, Gao Yunfeng, is the founder of Han's Laser; he took the deposits for orders for laser marking machines, 400,000 yuan in total, and started the business. From a small workshop, to one of the first eight companies listed in Small and Medium Enterprise Board, to the laser industry leader with a huge valuation of 50 billion yuan, Gao Yunfeng thanks Shenzhen. He says that the city was the ideal testing ground to turn his ideas into products.

Just to See You 003

To be known as the "Capital of Venture Capital" is Shenzhen's wish, and the song of the hearts of the people of the city. Every sleepless night, every starry morning, the air of Shenzhen is full of capital and projects searching for each other; innovation and venture capital activity is a part of life. There is where the largest venture capital entities are in the country, and is also the most marketized, concentrated and active location for investment.

Penguin Bank

WeBank is China's first internet bank, established by Tencent and some other companies. Its symbol is a penguin; it evokes the grandeur of the Emperor Penguin which is the traditional symbol of Tencent, and also is a nod to the nature of the internet bank as a new organism, just as penguins huddle together for warmth. Internet banks have neither traditional branches nor counters; loans require neither guarantors nor collateral. When Premier Li Keqiang was researching the bank, he tapped the enter key on his keyboard and lorry driver Xu Jun immediately received his loan of 35,000 yuan.

New King's Flag

Each age brings forth new genius on this noble land, and each will rule its own domain for years to come. In the incredibly profitable property sphere, a decade ago the four big players where the China Merchants, Poly, Vanke and Gemdale, three of which were registered in Shenzhen. Times and fortunes change, however, and besides Vanke retaining its place on the through, the other three players were replaced by Country Garden, Evergrande and Sunac. As the country develops, those that profit most are real estate companies. When rulership changes and the new king's flag is raised, some companies rejoice, whilst others panic.

企鹅银行

微众银行是中国第一家互联网银行，由腾讯等发起成立。其标识也是企鹅，既表明帝企鹅的血统，又寓意互联网银行是新生事物，要像企鹅一样抱团取暖。互联网银行没有传统的网点和柜台，贷款不需要担保和抵押。李克强总理调研微众时，敲下电脑回车键，卡车司机徐军立刻就拿到了3.5万元贷款。

城头变幻地王旗

江山代有才人出。在富可敌国的地产圈，10年前的四大天王是"招保万金"，即招商、保利、万科、金地，其中三家注册在深圳。岁月流金，各有各命，除了万科仍保有王座，另三家已换为碧桂园、恒大和融创，"碧恒万融"。城市化进程中，房地产公司受益最多，王旗易主一瞬间，几家欢乐几家愁。

独角兽的阴影 006

短短数月,13 名富士康员工跳楼自杀,郭台铭在深圳新闻发布会上鞠躬致歉。年轻鲜活的生命逝去,引发了全社会关注。连续加班、严苛管理,人沦为赚钱工具,成为流水线上的一个零配件。富士康创造了神话,被视为制造业和资本市场的"独角兽"。面对生命的消逝,"独角兽"收敛兽性,最终回归正途。

"8·10" 股疯 007

1992 年牛市行情后,股票风行全国,股市沸腾又疯狂。深圳定于当年 8 月 9 — 11 日发售新股认购抽签表,争购者从全国各地潮水般涌来,买不到抽签表的就到市政府示威,发生了"8·10"股市风波。多年之后,经过股市涨跌起伏历练的股民,懂得不再找市长,而去找市场。避免股市风险,需要练就一双火眼金睛。

一步之遥 008

恒大在广州起家,完成金融产业的核心布局后,又剑指金融全牌照。金融是深圳的支柱产业,优势远超广州;恒大欲和深房洽谈借壳回归 A 股,这两点促使恒大把总部迁到深圳。许家印离他的全牌照梦想又近一步,深圳的世界 500 强企业也由此增至七家,距"打造八家世界 500 强"的目标,只有一步之遥。

Shadow of the Unicorn

In just a few months, 13 workers at Foxconn committed suicide, jumping to their deaths. Terry Guo bowed and expressed apologies at a press conference in Shenzhen. The loss of these young lives attracted national attention. Extreme overtime and harsh management debased the status of these workers, turning them into tools for profit, another piece in a chain. Foxconn was a legend, seen as a unicorn in the production industry and capital market. Watching its reputation wither, it had to restrain its brutish behaviour and return to the proper path.

One Step Away

Evergrande was started in Guangzhou, and after completing its core economic arrangement, set its sights on a full financial license. Finance is a pillar industry in Shenzhen, where it is far stronger than that in Guangzhou. Evergrande wanted to borrow the Shenzhen Properties Group for a regression to A shares. These two points motivated Evergrande to move its headquarters to Shenzhen. Xu Jiayin became one step closer to his dream of a full license, and Shenzhen's number of world's top 500 companies increased to 7, bringing it one step closer and just one step away from having 8 top 500 companies headquartered there.

The 8 / 10 Disturbance

After a bull market in 1992, stocks were all the rage across China, and the market was shipped into a frenzy. From August 9th to 11th, a draw was held for the purchase rights for new stocks, which led to people from all over the country flooding in. Those who weren't able to buy went to the city government to protest, which led to the 8/10 Stock Market Disturbance. A number of years later, as the market rose and fell, and people who played the market learned that they needed to not go after the mayor, but rather the market. In order to avoid risk on the market, one needs sharp eyes.

鼓励创新，宽容失败

1992年小平同志视察深圳，东方风来满眼春，股市却备受争议，他一锤定音：世上哪有百分之百正确的事，上海和深圳的实践证明，资本主义的东西社会主义也可以拿来用，错了不要紧，关闭就是，以后再开。没有宽容失败和失败后的从头再来，哪有成功的春暖花开。

Encourage Innovation, Forgive Failure

In 1992, Deng Xiaoping came to Shenzhen to check it out. Oriental flavour abounded, but the stock market was the subject of controversy. He made a statement, giving the effective final word on the project: nothing in the world is 100% correct; Shanghai and Shenzhen are practical proof that capitalist elements can exist in a socialist system. If mistakes are made, it's no reason for worry; what's important is to try again. Without the ability to forgive mistakes or try again after they happen, there's no way to achieve true growth.

1997 年，深圳的长途电话全价每分钟约 1.35 元，邮电局排队打长途的人和现在去医院看病的人一样多。于是，不少人拿着 IC 电话卡，就近去公共电话亭"煲粥"，尤其深夜优惠时段，更是恋人倾诉衷肠时。现已绝迹的电话卡，曾是乡愁的味道：你在青春和奋斗的深圳这头，故乡和恋人在温暖和回忆的那头。

说吧，乡愁 010

Feelings for Home

010

In 1997, a long-distance call in Shenzhen cost 1.35 yuan a minute. Queues of people at the post and telegraph office resembled the jammed crowds at Chinese hospitals today. For this reason, a number of people bought prepaid IC telephone cards and went to payphones that accepted them, especially in the middle of the night when the rates were lower; it was the perfect time for spilling one's feelings to a lover. These telephone cards are a thing of the past now, but they used to be a ticket to the flavour of one's hometown. If you were a young person grinding in the city back then, they're still a market of these memories of your lover and hometown.

金"基"唱晓

中国基金业的半壁江山曾在深圳，现在也是深圳和京沪共执牛耳。深圳曾公开表态要打造"基金之都"，也保持了多个业内第一：第一只封闭基金、第一只公募 REITs、第一届中国基金论坛、第一家外资控股基金公司等。从投资和研发，到产品和人才等，深圳都在第一阵营。鹏城花艳，金"基"唱晓。

Fund Fun

A large portion of the Chinese fund industry is located in Shenzhen, which along with Beijing and Shanghai almost completely controls the industry. Shenzhen previously publicly positioned itself as wanting to become the "Fund Capital", and has stayed at the forefront of firsts: the first closed-end fund, the first publicly issued REITs, the first Chinese fund forum, the first foreign capital holding fund, and more. From investment and research and development to products and human talent, Shenzhen is number one in this field.

巨大中华

九万里风鹏正举，开放和充分竞争的行业，风景最美。电信市场最初开放时，路长日暮，国际巨头横行。20 世纪 90 年代，以巨龙通信、大唐电信、中兴通讯、华为为代表的本土通信制造厂商崛起，"巨大中华"由此诞生，寓意强大的中国电信产业整体崛起。

The Four Dragons

An open and competitive market where everyone strives to fly high is a beautiful scene. When the telecommunications market first opened up, it was dominated by big international players. In the 1990s, GDT, DTT, ZTE and Huawei bust onto the scene, representing domestic manufactures of equipment; the "Four Dragons" were thus born. This marked the beginning to the giant Chinese telecommunications industry.

激浊扬清

杨柳堆烟，帘幕无重数，震惊全国的基金黑幕，由《财经》杂志 2000 年的一期封面文章揭开。文中机构交易行为的报告，暴露了制造虚假成交量、利用倒仓操纵市场等问题，多家在深注册的基金公司卷入其中。行业声誉跌到谷底。问题推动了日后的制度建设，基金业今逢 20 华诞，野蛮少年已长大成人。

Cleaning House

Sometimes things aren't always as clean as they appear to be—in 2000, *Caijing* Magazine blew the lid off a scandal which shocked the nation—shady funds. In a report on transaction activity, the magazine revealed funds falsifying transactions, shuffling assets, and using other methods to manipulate the market. Many registered funds in Shenzhen were revealed to be involved, and the reputation of the industry hit rock-bottom. The problem led to later stronger regulatory mechanisms, and with the industry now being two decades old, these savage youths have hopefully grown into responsible adults.

没有悠闲的树叶

深圳没有悠闲的树叶，只有开花的梦想。通宵亮灯的腾讯大厦，是照亮科技园区的灯塔。这座城，承载小公司的渴望，收获大公司的荣光。随着深圳总部经济的崛起，阿里中心来了，百度国际总部也来了。2018 年世界 500 强中，华为、万科、平安、腾讯、招行、正威、恒大等七家落户深圳。

Leaves that Don't Rest

Shenzhen has no resting leaves on trees, only blossoms jonesing to bloom. The Tencent Building, lit day and night, is like a beacon that illuminates the science park. In this city, small enterprises sparkle and large enterprises blaze. As the headquarters economy has risen, the Ali Centre and Baidu's international headquarters have both come here. In 2018, of the world's top 500 companies, Huawei, Vanke, Ping An, Tencent, China Merchants, Evergrande and Amer are all here.

家里的大户室

每个深圳人都有股票情结，在必须电话委托交易的时代，通过电脑接收无线信号、在家炒股，无疑要靠彼时的高科技产品。"每日商情"股市台找到痛点，让散户在家炒股。这款名为"金牛股市"的信息系统曾风靡深圳，一卡难求。广告语是："大户室的行情，中文机的价格。"

VIP Room at Home

Everyone in Shenzhen is into stocks. In the era when there was no internet and one had to entrust trades only through the phone, computers could receive wireless signals, and people could trade stocks at home, these supporting technologies were essential. Distributors of financial news had found that a key service people wanted was the ability to gain relevant news on markets from their homes. Such an information software named "Golden Bull Market" was quite popular in Shenzhen: it was like having a VIP room at the exchange in your own house, and for a low price, too.

告别航母明斯克

明斯克，这艘陪伴了深二代成长的苏联航母，是深圳记忆及合影里的温暖背景，也是"德隆系"资本乱象的历史配角。2000 年 5 月，航母落户沙头角，开幕式上，深圳队对俄罗斯队，在甲板上踢了一场足球，航母之巨令人惊叹。2004 年，"德隆系"崩溃，申请破产。此后，明斯克虽继续运营，但风光不再，2016 年正式告别深圳。

Goodbye Minsk

The Soviet aircraft carrier Minsk accompanied Shenzhen in its growing-up phase, and was a nice background for many group photographs. It also played a role in the scandal of the collapse of Delong Group. In May 2000, the Minsk arrived at Shatoujiao. At the opening ceremony, a Russian and a Chinese team played football against each other, showing off the size of the vessel. In 2004, Delong Group collapsed, and applied for bankruptcy. After this, although the Minsk World military theme park continued to operate, it was past its prime, and in 2016 the ship said farewell to the city.

《市场快报》周刊

信息流带来人流，信息就是可以变现的资源。深圳人需要最新最精准的商业信息，《市场快报》周刊应运而生。市场化运作的这本信息周刊，内容涉及市场评述、法规、商贸信息等。读者最关心的供需桥，就是买卖双方直接对接，很多小企业常年订阅多份，为的是可以免费在上面发布商业信息。

先出生，再拿证

深圳证券交易所试营业的钟声，在1990年12月1日早晨敲响。但其"准生证"，直到四个月后才由中国人民银行正式下发。当时流行一句话："深圳试试再开业。"深圳是改革试验田，创新是深交所与生俱来的使命。特区的发展，离不开深交所的运转。灵魂要找到栖息的肉体，深圳是深交所可依傍的强健体魄。

Market Express

The flow of information brings about the flow of people; information is a resource that can be converted into money. The people of Shenzhen have a constant need for the newest and most accurate business information—*Market Express*, a weekly publication, was born out of this need. This market-operated weekly publication covers market commentary, legal regulations, business information, and the like. Readers are most concerned with the column of "Supply-demand Bridge", which connects buyers and sellers to each other; many small businesses have a number of subscriptions, each of which allows them to publish some business information in the publication for free.

Birth Before Certificate

The bell for the Shenzhen Stock Exchange first rang on the morning of December 1, 1990, during the exchange's test run. However, it's "pregnancy certificate" was only formally signed four months later by the People's Bank of China. At the time, there was a popular phrase: "Try it in Shenzhen before starting business." Shenzhen is a revolutionary test field. Innovation has been the innate mission of Shenzhen Stock Exchange since its birth. Development of the SEZ is intimately connect to the exchange. A soul needs to find a body to live in; Shenzhen is the strong and healthy body for the soul that is the Shenzhen Stock Exchange.

Air-supported Structures

Air-supported structures use a special air film for their outer shell to create a living space. Broadwell, a public company that originated in Shenzhen, is the world's leader in the air-supported structure industry. Within the structure, air pressure, temperature, humidity and other factures can all be controlled in accordance with needs; they are currently used for many athletic stadiums. NBA star LeBron James says: "Winter is long and cold, so I'm thankful we have these structures so I can continue to train normally."

神奇的气膜建筑

气膜建筑用特殊的气膜做外壳，构建生活空间。诞生在深圳的上市公司博德维，是全球领先的气膜建筑商。气膜建筑的内部空间中，气压、温度、湿度等所有因素，皆可按需控制，目前广泛运用于各种场馆的建设。NBA巨星詹姆斯说："这个冬天很漫长，感谢气膜建筑可以让我照常进行训练。"

一念之差

2006 年，马乐从清华大学毕业，过关斩将入职深圳一家基金公司。其后他担任了基金经理，通过自己掌控的账户买卖股票，非法获利近 1900 万元，成为史上最大"老鼠仓"案的主角。他在法庭上自陈，17 年寒窗苦读，7 年辛苦工作，身体透支严重，不到 30 岁就腰椎间盘突出，痛得整夜无法入睡。一念之差，人生崩塌。

Whoops

In 2006, Ma Le graduated from Tsinghua University and went through many difficulties to join a fund in Shenzhen. Later, he became the fund manager, and through his own account bought and sold stocks, gaining almost 19 million yuan in illegal profits, making him the key player in the largest case of front-running in history. In court, he talked about how he studied as a poor student for 17 years, and worked hard for 7 years, greatly taxing his body; he experienced a herniated intervertebral disk before he was 30, and was unable to sleep at night. With just a few mistakes he managed to destroy his life.

First Self-driving Car Plate

In May 2018, Shenzhen issued its first car plate for an experimental self-driving car, and Tencent's test vehicle was able to get on the road. To test these cars in Shenzhen, one needs to designate a route, and get a license for each test. Currently, Shenzhen has only applied for this license for one vehicle, Yue B9K60 Shi. If the fairy tale of self-driving cars becomes a reality, would you dare to ride in one?

无人驾驶首发牌

2018 年 5 月，深圳发出首个无人驾驶测试牌照，腾讯自动驾驶汽车将上路。在深圳开展无人驾驶测试，需要在指定路段，一车一个测试牌照。目前，腾讯申请测试的车辆只有一台，测试号牌为"粤 B9K60 试"。无人驾驶曾是神话故事里的场景，如今已成为现实，你有没有胆量试乘呢？

一旦拥有，别无所求

2003年，中国首次载人飞船"神舟五号"遨游太空，杨利伟就戴着飞亚达极限系列航天表。征战太空的飞亚达，从深圳一间20平方米厂房和9名员工起步，如今已是中国境内唯一一家表业上市公司。演绎钟表文化，传达对时间的认知、对生活的主张。其广告语"一旦拥有，别无所求"，风靡大江南北。

Fiyta Watch

In 2003, China sent its first manned craft into space, Shenzhou 5. Yang Liwei wore a Fiyta watch on the expedition. The first Chinese company to have its watch taken into space, Fiyta started in a 20-square metre workshop with nine employees. Today it is the only listed watch company in the mainland of China. Its slogan translates to "With one of these, you won't desire anything else". The brand is quite popular throughout China.

魔高一尺，道高一丈

一连10个跌停板，大半市值化为泡影，这就是中国证券市场头号大案"中科创业股票操纵案"。中科创业的前身是康达尔，主营饲料的一家深企，被庄家吕梁包装成"高科技+金融"公司，股价从17元涨到80元。股价一日崩盘，无数眼泪在飞。魔高一尺，道高一丈。法治日益严明，庄家必付代价。

蹒跚的第一次

先驱已成先烈，勇者踏浪前行。1985年1月，中国第一家券商"特区证券"在深圳试运营。没有电子显示屏，股票价格就写在黑板上；营业场所太小，渴望财富的人们用麻袋背着现金到对面的荔枝公园"黑市交易"。特区证券后更名为巨田证券，取"巨大的试验田"之意，却一直步履蹒跚，2006年黯然离场。

As Vice Rises One Foot, Virtue Rises Ten

With a series of 10 limit-downs, most of the market value was a bubble—this is what happened in the first big incident in the Chinese security market, the "CVC (China Venture Capital) Stock Manipulation Case". CVC known as Kondarl, a company involved in livestock feed; player Lv Liang packaged it as a "hi-tech + finance" company, and the price soared from 17 to 80 yuan. The stock collapsed in a single day, crushing many people. Still, as vice rises one foot, virtue rises ten—legal regulation becomes stricter by the day, and manipulators pay the price.

Staggering Along

Pioneers are the first to become martyrs, but the show goes on. In January 1985, China's first securities company—Shenzhen Special Economic Zone Securities Ltd, began test operations in Shenzhen. It had no electronic display, with stock prices written on a blackboard. The operating site was too small, and people looking to make money took gunnysacks of cash to the Lychee Park across the street to participate in the stock trades. The company was later renamed Jutian ("Giant Field") Securities, as it originated as a giant test field, but it staggered along, and quietly exited the scene in 2006.

一呼天下应

润迅创立于深圳，进入传呼市场时江山已定，其突围一靠技术优势，二靠服务品牌。20世纪90年代中后期，润迅举办演出《红色娘子军》，并组建了国内第一支职业化篮球俱乐部，提高了市场知名度。"润迅，一呼天下应"，成为传呼机时代最响亮的记忆。随着手机的入场，传呼机销声匿迹，成为历史名词。

CMT, a Call to the World

China Motion Telecom was established in Shenzhen. The paging market was already established when entered, so to break in it relied on technological superiority and a brand with good service. At the end of the 1990s, it produced the play *Red Detachment of Women*, and also established the first Chinese professional basketball club, increasing its market recognition. "CMT, a Call to the World" became its slogan, known to all. As mobile phones entered the market, pagers disappeared, becoming history.

外来和尚会念经

曾任美国副财长的法兰克·纽曼，挽救过三家美国亏损银行，后被请来挽救2004年商业银行中排名倒数第一的深圳发展银行。深发展是深圳首家上市公司、中国首家上市银行。"万千宠爱在一身，一朝梨花深闭门"，只好请来外援帮忙。在深发展大厦那间充满东方色彩的办公室里，纽曼又一次救活银行，再创奇迹。

中国科技第一展

高交会是深圳倾心打造了20年的名片，是中国科技创新的缩影。1999年起，高交会每年11月在深圳举办，每届参会人数超过50万，交易额超过130亿美元，是公认的中国科技第一展。高交会发挥着全球创新的主场作用，微软等巨头云来，400多名诺贝尔奖得主和跨国公司总裁先后在高交会发表演讲。

A Monk from Afar Reads the Scriptures

Former United States Deputy Secretary of the Treasury Frank Newman saved three American banks from collapse, and then was invited in 2004 to Shenzhen to save the dead-last Shenzhen Development Bank. SDB was the first company in Shenzhen to go public, and was China's first listed bank. It was deemed necessary to enlist foreign help to help the beloved bank. In the office full of oriental colour, Newman worked hard and managed to pull off a miracle, saving the institution.

China Hi-Tech Fair

The China Hi-Tech Fair, or CHTF, has been held for 20 years in Shenzhen, showcasing all the country has to offer in the field. Since 1999, the fair has been held in November every year in Shenzhen; more than 500,000 attendees visit each year, and the transaction volume reaches 13 billion USD; it's recognized as the first technical fair in China. It promotes innovation worldwide, and is attended by giants such as Microsoft. 400 Nobel laureates and presidents of multinational corporations have visited the fair over the years, participating in fora and giving speeches.

Creation and Design

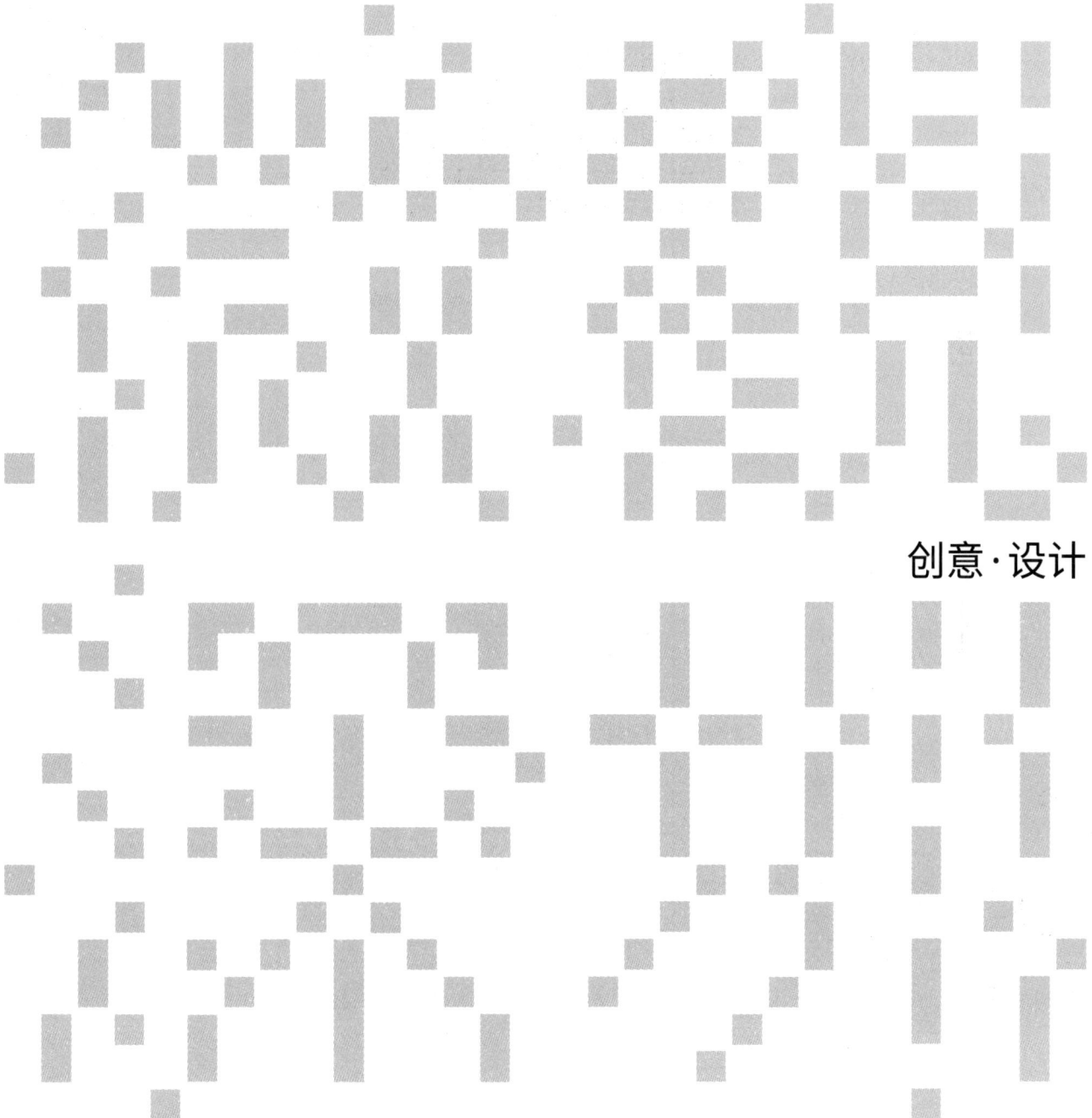

创意·设计

创客之城 001

创客的聚集和创客文化的兴起正成为这座"创新之城"的先锋标志。Fab Lab 创始人尼尔·哥申菲尔德教授评价道:"全球再也找不出第二个城市能够有这么全的创客产业链,深圳是不可复制的城市!"2016年,全国"双创"活动周在深圳举行,马云、马化腾、任正非都来了,"大众创业、万众创新"在深圳全城绽放。

Maker City

Makers gather and the Maker culture flourishes in Shenzhen. Fab Lab founder professor Neil Gershenfeld thus appraised it: "There's no other city that has such a complete Maker industry chain. The success of the city is unique." In 2016, the "Mass Entrepreneurship and Innovation week" was held in Shenzhen; attended by the likes of Jack Ma, Pony Ma and Ren Zhengfei. The city found itself flooded with creators and creative enterprises; it was a week to remember.

"沟通" 002

与"平面设计在中国1996"同步,"沟通"海报邀请展盛大开幕,邀请海峡两岸暨香港、澳门的设计师创作以"沟通"为主题的系列海报。"沟通"的题旨,在于通过视觉语言实现不同人群、不同社会制度、不同地域文化之间的沟通。设计界通过沟通,找到了中华文化共同背景下的设计理念。

Communication

Along with the "Graphic Design in China 1996 Exhibition", "Communication" Poster Exhibition was revealed, inviting designers from the mainland and Taiwan, Hong Kong and Macao regions to make posters with the theme of "Communication". The aim of this theme was to enable communication between different groups of people under different societal structures in different places with different cultures via graphic language. Communication through the world of design yielded evidence of design concepts against the backdrop of a common Chinese culture.

平面设计在中国 003

1992年,"平面设计在中国"于深圳启幕,这是中国首个面向全球的设计竞赛,王粤飞、王序、陈绍华等为策划者。这次比赛创造了很多第一:明确使用"平面设计"词汇、采用国际化评审规范、邀请外国评委。比赛对中国平面设计的发展起到了至关重要的作用,并在日后催生了深圳成为"设计之都"。

Graphic Design in China

The Graphic Design in China took off in 1992 in Shenzhen. This was the site of the first Chinese globally-oriented design competition, planned by Wang Yuefei, Wang Xu and Chen Shaohua, among others. The competition yielded many firsts: it clearly used the word "graphic design", used international judging rules and invited foreign judges. The design had a great effect on the development of the industry in the country, and played a part in Shenzhen becoming the "City of Design".

"融合"

深港一衣带水，因此深圳香港设计邀请展共结连理。有意思的是，2009年首届展览在关山月美术馆举行时，两地的设计作品被分至两厅，创作意念各自表述。而第三届在香港会展中心展出时，两地作品被合为一厅，表现了深港两地设计师"和而不同"的创作理念。这种融合逐年递增，如今已不分彼此。

Merging

Shenzhen and Hong Kong are separated by a narrow strip of water, and connected by the SZ-HK Design Exposition. In 2009 at the Guan Shanyue Art Museum, the first exposition was held, with the design works from the two cities split between two halls, each showing their own styles. When the third expo was held in Hong Kong, the two halls were merged into ones, showing the harmonious contrast between the different works. This kind of merging has increased over the years, with a distinction no longer made.

中国境内首个平面设计组织

深圳平面设计协会，成立于1995年，是中国境内首个平面设计协会，旨在展现杰出的设计成就，鼓励和促进专业创作和探索的学术精神，推动社会对设计的关注和平面设计行业发展，促进协会和国际专业机构的学术交流。协会成立后，深圳平面设计师组团出击，不断获得国际设计顶级大奖。

Shenzhen Graphic Design Association

The Shenzhen Graphic Design Association was founded in 1995 to become the first graphic design organisation in the mainland of China. It aims towards great publishing accomplishments and encourages and promotes professional creativity and a spirit of academic exploration. It promotes societal attention towards design and the development of the graphic design industry, and encourages academic interchange with international professional organisations. After its establishment, the association's members bust up onto the scene, continually winning important international awards.

实至名归设计之都

其他城市是在漫长积淀中发展而来的,深圳却是一座被设计出来的城市。2008年,它被联合国授予了中国第一个"设计之都"称号。设计师都把这里当作事业的福地,商业和制造业高速发展,为设计产业提供了得天独厚的土壤。从建筑到街道,无处不设计,在这座城市散步,你常会与雕塑大师的作品不期而遇。

A Famous City of Design

Other cities develop through slow accumulation, whereas Shenzhen was designed. In 2008 it was designated as the first UNESCO City of Design in China. It's a great place for designers, with rapid business and production development, making it very fertile ground for those in the design industry. From architecture to roads, thought has been put into their design everywhere. No matter where you walk in the city you'll frequently see works sculpted by masters.

文字设计在中国

"文字设计在中国"是继"平面设计在中国"之后的又一国际性设计盛会,它的成功举办,宣告全球首个立足中国、面向全球的文字设计盛会正式诞生。它探讨文字设计与城市、文化、生活的关系,通过多种形式推动国际设计界及华人社会对视觉艺术、信息传达与文字设计的沟通交流。

Typographic Design in China

Typographic Design in China is a continuation of the major international awards event, GDC, Graphic Design in China. It marks the birth of the first Chinese text design awards event that faces the world. It explores the relationship between text design and the city, culture and life, and encourages communication about how the international design work and Chinese society influence graphic art, the transmission of information and text design.

设计让生活更美好

深圳设计周于2017年初试啼声,便得到全球数十个国家和地区设计界的响应。活动覆盖平面、工业、建筑、时尚等领域。一年一度的盛会将国际一流的设计师和设计作品引入深圳,同时培养了公众对设计的认知和审美能力,让设计真正融入市民的日常生活。人们开始懂得:设计可以让生活更美好。

Designing a Better Life

The Shenzhen Design Week began in 2017, seeing involvement of dozens of countries and regions. The activities include graphic, industrial, architecture and fashion design. Ever year top international designers and works travel to Shenzhen. The exhibition encourages people to appreciate and enjoy these works, and brings design into the lives of everyday people. People thus realise that design can make all aspects of one's life nicer.

Shenzhen Fashion Week

Shenzhen is a young city of young people, and thus it is easy for a culture of fashion to flourish there. As the most important site of origin for Chinese fashion brands, the city is home to thousands of individual labels, with a large group of new and vigorous designers cutting striking figures on the international stage. It's a natural course of development in a place like this. Starting in 2015, all manner of rich attire has appeared on the scene, exhibited at the Shenzhen Fashion Week at the start of March. It aims to match the top four international fashion weeks.

深圳时装周

深圳因为年轻,所以包容,时尚文化易于开花结果。作为中国最重要的服装品牌发源地,深圳本土服装品牌企业有几千家,一批新锐服装设计师在国际舞台崭露头角,深圳时装周可谓是水到渠成。自2015年起,这一秀场林立、衣香鬓影的时尚嘉年华便和阳春三月一道来临,形式格局瞄准"四大国际时装周"。

问鼎"金顶"的深圳人

"金顶奖"是中国最高的时装设计奖项,一年只有一位得主,2006 年罗峥成为第一个获奖的深圳人。她毕业于深圳大学国际经济与贸易专业,从小怀有时尚梦,10 岁就给自己设计过裙子。她曾获美国 Nautica 创意基金白金大奖,担纲 APEC 会议领导人服装设计,并第一批赴卢浮宫举行时装发布。逐梦路上,向美而行。

匠心之悟

秋冬"匠心系列"发布会圆满落幕后,设计总监李东站在公司静态展厅中央,眼前错落有致的当季新品,呈现出艺术品般创意、手作之美,服饰的每处细节无不体现着设计师的匠心笃定和初心执着,仿佛清风拂面,夜静春山。深圳作为巴黎、米兰时尚展的常客,众多服饰公司的梦想,也承载了设计之都的梦想。

设计业的"黄埔军校"

深圳国际企业服务公司是国内首家合资广告公司。中国设计界领军人物之一的陈绍华,1988 年来深圳后便进入"国企",在这里发掘、培养了很多设计方面的人才,特区很多设计公司和广告公司的创始人都有过"国企"从业的经历,被誉为深圳广告设计业的"黄埔军校"。"设计深军"从这里出发。

I Wanna Be the Very Best

The "China Fashion Designer Top Award" is the highest-level fashion design prize in China, with only one winner per year. In 2006, Luo Zheng became the first person from Shenzhen to win. She graduated from International Economics and Trade from Shenzhen University. She was into fashion since she was 10, and had designed her own dresses. She previously received the Platinum Prize from the Nautica Innovation Fund, and was responsible for the outfits of the leaders at the APEC Summit, and one of the first round of individuals to a fashion show at the Louvre. Her life has been a journey to beauty and dreams.

Masterpiece

After the "Masterpiece" Autumn/Winter Launch Event successfully concluded, head of design Li Dong stood quietly on the centre of the stage, looking at the various arranged products for the seasons, full of artistic innovation and fine crafting. Every single article of clothing displayed masterful design and thought, like a clear breeze over the mountains on a quiet spring night. For Shenzhen as a frequent guest at fashion exhibitions in Paris and Milan, the dream of the clothing companies and designers is the dream of the city.

Whampoa Military Academy of Design

The Shenzhen International Enterprise Service Company is the first joint-venture advertising company in China. One of the leaders in Chinese design, Chen Shaohua came to Shenzhen in 1988 and started working in SIESC. Here he developed and trained many talented designers. Many of the design companies in the SEZ and their founders have experience originating in SIESC, which have become known as the "design equivalent of the Whampoa Military Academy".

Working Hard for the Public Good

In the Autumn of 2006, Shenzhen organised an advertisement competition with the theme of public service announcements. The UNESCO City of Design (Shenzhen, China) Public Service Advertising Competition show the values of the city. By 2018, it has been held thirteen years consecutively, and more than 150,000 works have been submitted from China, the USA, the UK, France, and other countries. Excellent works have been shown in Cannes and Brussels, exhibiting the creative culture and spirit of working hard for the public good to the world.

设计之都的公益精神

2006年金秋，深圳举办了全国第一个以公益广告为主题的广告大赛——设计之都（中国·深圳）公益广告大赛，这座城市的人文价值观由此可见。截至2018年，大赛已连续举办13届，作品征集数量超过15万件。参赛作品来自中、美、英、法等国家。优秀作品曾赴戛纳、布鲁塞尔展出，向世界展现了中国深圳的创意文化和公益精神。

全球唯一的"建筑双年展"

"深港城市/建筑双城双年展"由深圳2005年创办，2007年香港受邀加入，展览演变为双城互动、一展两地的独特类型。这是全球唯一关于城市固定主题的双年展。每年主题均引发热议：城中村与自发城市、城市过期与再生、公共空间、城乡关系与农业、边缘等。人们开始反思城市化的另一面。

The Only Biennale

The "Bi-city Biennale of Urbanism / Architecture" was first started in 2005 in Shenzhen and joined in 2007 by Hong Kong, evolving into a two-city interactive exhibition. It's the only biennial two-city exhibition focused on the city in the world. Ever year's theme is the topic of hot discussion: urban villages and self-development, urban expiration and rebirth, public spaces, city-town relationships and agriculture, borders, etc. People here have started to think about the other side of urbanisation.

The First Industrial Design Park

The Tian Mian Creative Industrial Estate, known as simply the land mark of the Shenzhen design industry, is the largest industrial design park in China with the highest number of creative industry districts. It's been named "The First Industrial Design Park" by some. It's a major channel for China's "going out" strategy, and is a platform that unifies service operation for the entire industry chain. Many domestic design firms connect with the international market here; one will see foreigners of all kinds walking about.

中国工业设计第一园

田面创意产业园是深圳设计产业地标，是中国工业设计企业规模最大、龙头企业数量最多的创意产业园区，被业界誉为"中国工业设计第一园"，是中国设计"走出去"的重要通道，也是全产业链的整合运营服务平台，国内很多设计企业从这里打开国际市场，园区里不同肤色的外国人穿梭来往。

崛起的大湾区设计群

改革开放40周年，粤港澳区域正在进行一轮空前的整合，因此大湾区设计群落在深圳设计周的整体亮相，成为中国当代设计的一个标志性事件，设计与地缘之间的关系被提升到区域战略的高度。地域文化的相似性，包容多元的国际性，使设计师们更容易找到亲近的设计语言。

Dawan District Designers

On the 40th anniversary of the opening up and reform, the Guangdong-Hong Kong-Macao area is undergoing unprecedented merging. "Dawan" means "greater bay area" and refers to the three locations. At the Shenzhen Design Week, these "Dawan Designers" made an amazing display, making a landmark event for design in China. The relationship between land and design was elevated to that of a regional strategy. The similarities of regional culture and acceptance of international elements make it easier for designers to find an intimate design language to share with each other.

Artworks that Display Artworks

The Shenzhen Museum of Contemporary Art is a public welfare institution; the City Planning Exhibition mainly displays the path of the development of the city. The two institutions have different functions, and have their own halls, unified under a magnificent giant shell; this is the main site of the Shenzhen Design Week. This architectural work was designed by Austrian firm Coop Himmelb(l)au, adding a splash of colour to the CBD of Futian District.

展示艺术品的艺术品

深圳当代艺术博物馆以展示当代艺术为主，是一家公益性机构；城市规划馆则以展示城市规划发展历程为主。两座功能不同、相互独立的展馆，统一于一片巨大的极具设计感的辉煌表皮之下，这里是深圳设计周的主会场。这座由奥地利蓝天组设计的独特建筑本身就是件艺术品，为福田中心区增色不少。

Global Angle of View

Facing the Shenzhen Bay, with views of city, mountains and ocean, the Sea World Culture and Arts Centre was Japanese architect Fumihiko Maki's first project in China. The famous V&A Museum of the UK established its overseas branch here. The overall structure looks like a giant white boat anchored at a harbour, with wonderful works from all over the world displayed throughout, a display of designs of past and future from a global angle for the masses to enjoy.

国际视角下的文艺中心

面朝深圳湾，坐拥山、海、城市三重视野，海上世界文化艺术中心是日本建筑师槇文彦在中国的首件力作。世界著名的艺术与设计博物馆V&A在这里设立了它的首个海外分馆。这座建筑的形态如停泊在港口的一艘白色大船，舶来世界各地的先锋艺术展览，为大众呈现国际视角下设计的历史和未来。

深圳湾畔育春茧

深圳湾体育中心，又称"春茧"，采用一体化设计，将体育场、体育馆、游泳馆置于一个白色的巨型屋面之下，线条柔美的屋顶犹如大鹏即将破茧而出，与北京"鸟巢"的设计异曲同工。体育场东侧被大胆地"切"出了一扇通透的"落地窗"，被称为"海之门"，坐在体育场里就可以看到大海及对面的香港。

Spring Cocoon

The Shenzhen Bay Sports Centre is also called the "Spring Cocoon". It uses an integrated design to cover the stadium, gymnasium and pool all under one giant white roof. The smooth lines and white colour of the structure make it look like a giant cocoon—similar in function but different in form to Beijing's "Birds Nest". The east side of the cocoon has been boldly "cut" to form a "floor-to-ceiling window" which is known as "the gate of the sea". Sitting in the stadium you can see the ocean, and beyond it, Hong Kong.

水晶石顾盼生辉

龙岗大运中心是第26届世界大学生夏季运动会的主场馆区，三座体育场馆颇似三块水晶巨石镶嵌在湖面上，并与周围的山体、绿地配合，形成了独特的"山水石"结构。体育场为达到"水晶石"的建筑造型，屋盖钢结构首次采用单层空间折面网格结构。每到夜晚远远看去，水晶石顾盼生辉，驱散黑暗。

Manta Ray, Bird and Beehive

Terminal 3 at Shenzhen Bao'an International Airport is made in the shape of a manta ray, as the word for this animal in Chinese, "fu fen", sounds like the word for "good luck"; it can change its form. The design also includes a bird, which symbolises the start of a beautiful flight. What's special about this building is that all the lighting during the day is from sunlight, with a double-layer beehive structure wrapping the building allowing light to pass through, for a great environmentally-friendly energy savings.

Crystal Rock

The Shenzhen Universiade Sports Centre was the main site of the Shenzhen 26th Summer Universiade. The three gymnasiums look like three giant crystal rocks embedded in the surface of a lake, and the surrounding mountains, covered in green, form a unique structure of "mountains, water, and rocks" ("mountains and water" is the Chinese word for "landscape"). The gymnasia are built in the form of "crystal rocks", the roof's steel structure using for the first time single-layer folded-plane spatial reticulated structure. Every night when you look out over the distance, you will see the crystal rocks sparkling, driving away the darkness.

蝠鲼、鸟和蜂巢

宝安国际机场T3航站楼，总让人想起"蝠鲼"的形象，这种海鱼谐音"福分"，能自由改变自己的形状。设计同时融合了一只鸟，象征着从这里开始将有一段美妙的飞行。这座建筑的奇特之处还在于，白天照明完全取自于日光，包裹着建筑的双层蜂巢结构让自然光照射进来，环保效应独步世界。

"地王"

地王大厦,设计灵感来源于西方教堂和中国古代文化中通、透、瘦的神髓,宽高比例为1:9,创造了超高层建筑"最扁""最瘦"的世界纪录。1996年建成,因其所占土地当年拍得深圳土地交易最高价格,被尊称为"地王",本名"信兴广场"已无人提及。有关地王大厦的记忆与深圳崛起的高度紧密相连。

Land King

The inspiration for the Diwang Building comes from Western churches and the classical Chinese aesthetic concepts of pass-through and thinness. With a width to height ration of 1:9, it broke world records for being "thinnest" amongst high-rise buildings. Built in 1996, as the costs of land were very high in Shenzhen, it was known as "Diwang", or "Land King". The original name, Xinxing Plaza, is never used anymore. Memories about the rise of Shenzhen and the rise of the building are closely interlinked.

Largest Art Wall in the World

The Artron Wall is located at the Artron Art Centre, and is 50 metres long and 30 metres high; equivalent to a 10-storey building. The wall is covered with tens of thousands of books, and is an impressive sight. The books include art books, sets of classical works in foreign language, valuable ancient books, publications from museums, art galleries and foundations around the world, works from world-renowned universities, and artistic series from famous Chinese artists. The wall isn't just art, but also the history of art.

全球最大的艺术书墙

Artron Wall 位于雅昌艺术中心,长50米,高30米,相当于10层楼高,一面墙容纳了上万本藏书,壮观震撼。书籍涵盖艺术图书,经典外文套书,珍贵古籍孤本,世界顶级博物馆、美术馆、基金会的权威出版物,世界权威大学、艺术院校艺术杰作,国内大师级艺术系列等。一面书墙,一部斑斓的艺术史。

无限延伸的大厦

平安金融中心是一座集办公、酒店、观光、购物功能为一体的综合性建筑。建成后成为深圳的最新地标，华南第一高楼，共有118层，主楼高600米。造型类似纽约的帝国大厦，但整体较之更圆润、线条更简洁。最初的设计理念是从地面的中心点往上拉，无限延伸，象征"未来创造无限可能"的追求和探索精神。

Limitless Building

The Ping An International Finance Centre combines office space, hotel, tourism, and shopping functionalities all in one giant complex. After it was built it became a new landmark in Shenzhen, the tallest building in south China with 118 storeys, 600 metres in height. Its style of construction is similar to that of the Empire State Building except that it is rounder, and has simpler lines. The original design concept comes from a column being pulled up from the middle of the ground, extending limitlessly, symbolising a pursuit and exploration for "a future that creates limitless possibilities".

珍珠养于水贝

深圳不产黄金珠宝，却是中国最大的黄金珠宝设计、加工基地。罗湖水贝村占据着最重要的"山头"，这里黄金珠宝的加工及批发量占国内黄金珠宝市场七成以上份额，所谓"中国珠宝看深圳，深圳珠宝看水贝"是业界共识，"水贝·中国珠宝指数"已成行业的"风向标"和"晴雨表"。珍珠养于水贝。

Shenzhen Art Design Centre

If you want to decorate and furnish your house all in one stop, a lot of people think of IKEA, but Shenzhen natives will proudly remark that they have the ADC. A designer said: "Relying only on the ADC, I can furnish and decorate a villa in just three days." This is the largest furniture platform with the widest selection of products visited the most frequently by designers in China. It transforms furniture into art, and has made a big impact on the way people live.

深圳的"潘家园"

北京有潘家园，深圳有新秀村。创建于2002年的深圳古玩城，有城门、城墙环抱，已成中国规模最大的古玩艺术品交流平台。这里推出的"文玩文创集市"，主打年轻人市场。2018年，深圳古玩城又正式开启首个"淘宝鬼市"，爱玩的深圳人又有了一个好去处，更吸引来自香港、澳门的众多淘宝者。

Pearls Grow in Oysters

Shenzhen doesn't produce gold jewellery, but is the largest site in China for the design and processing of gold jewellery. Shuibei ("oyster shell") in Luohu is the biggest site for this activity; more than 70% of gold jewellery worked in China passes through this market. People say if you're looking for jewellery in China, look at Shenzhen, and if you're looking for jewellery in Shenzhen, look at Shuibei. The "China Shuibei Jewellery Index" is both the weather vane and barometer for the industry in China—pearls grow in oysters, after all.

深圳艺展中心

Shenzhen's "Panjiayuan"

Beijing has the Panjiayuan Antiques Market and Shenzhen has Xinxiucun. Founded as a curio market in 2002, it has a city gate and wall, and is by this point the largest antiques and curios exchange platform in China. The "Curio and Creative" market is focused at the youth market. In 2018, the market formally started the first "Night Market" for hunters, adding to the scene for the people of Shenzhen and attracting customers from Hong Kong and Macao.

如果希望一站买齐所有家居物品，很多人能想到的只有宜家，但是深圳人可以自豪地说：我们有艺展中心！一位设计师说："只要有艺展中心，我三天就可以布置好一栋别墅。"这里是中国规模最大、品类最全、设计师采购频次最高的家居平台。它让家居产品艺术化，登堂入室地改变着人们的生活方式。

华侨城创意市集 028

这是全国历史最悠久、频率最密的街区型创意市集。从 2008 年起，定期在华侨城创意文化园北区开集。届时整条街鳞次栉比摆满摊位，售卖原创手作或从各地搜集来的工艺品。这里成为摊主们碰撞灵感的平台，也成为热爱生活的青年的淘货胜地，享受有偶遇、有惊喜的周末。

OCT LOFT Creative Market 028

This is the nation's oldest and most frequently held creative market. Starting in 2008, the market has been held at the northern zone of the OCT LOFT creative complex. Each time the venue is packed with rows upon rows of booths, sellers peddling their own crafts or those they've sourced from all over. This is a place where the booth owners can collide with inspiration, and is also a great shopping spot for youths who love life, one where one can enjoy encounters and wonderful surprises on the weekend.

枯燥的畅销书 029

很难想象，枯燥的《深沪股市上市公司年度报告大全》会成为畅销书。这本海天出版社出版的大部头，把上市公司的年报汇编成册，印了 1 万册，三个月就被一抢而空。枯燥的内容却被设计得华丽、美艳，有些人冲着封面设计而买。如果当初认真研读，买了排在最前面的深发展、深万科，到今天会是怎样？

A Dry Book that Sells Well 029

It's hard to imagine that the dry *Annual Report of Shenzhen and Shanghai Listed Companies* would be a best-seller. This large volume from Haitian Publishing House compiled the annual reports of these companies into a single volume, and printed 10,000 copies, which were sold out in just 3 months. The dry contents are displayed with beautiful design, making some people snatch the book up just looking at its cover. If you read this book diligently when it first came out and bought stock in the top-ranked Shenzhen Development Bank or Vanke, how would things be today?

创意园的前世今生 030

华侨城创意文化园由工业区的旧厂房改造而成，园内建筑具有鲜明的工业风格，人们习惯称之为 LOFT，很多艺术家工作室和创意公司集中在这里，书店、咖啡馆、酒吧、餐厅、工艺品店更是星罗棋布。文艺青年们大都喜欢来此度过休闲时光。这里已经成为深圳最具人气和创意氛围的都市文化生活"聚点"。

Creative Park, Past and Present 030

The Huaqiaocheng Creative Cultural Park, known as the OCT LOFT in English, is built on the site of a former factory. There is a clear industrial vibe within; many artists' workshops and creative companies are located here, as well as bookstores, cafes, bars, restaurants, and shops selling artworks. Cultured youths like to walk around and spend time here; the site is one of the major aggregation points for creative culture in Shenzhen.

"创意中国"走出国门 031

"创意中国"2008年在英国V&A博物馆举办,这是英国首次举办关于当代中国设计的大型展览。展览聚焦中国设计业发展最迅速的三个城市——北京、深圳、上海。深圳展区以"前沿城市"为名,凸显其作为中国平面设计发源地的地位,全方位地呈现了平面设计与视觉文化,先锋城市海外亮相获得喝彩。

虚拟动漫,活力中国 032

深圳是中国最具活力的动漫之都,承接了迪士尼三分之一的动画片制作,深圳动漫交易会风生水起地举办了八届。与其他动漫展会不同,这是个以投融资和版权交易为核心的国家级行业盛会,并诞生了一批具有国际竞争力的动漫、游戏产品与企业。每届展会全城布满卡通人物,成为欢乐嘉年华。

Going Out 031

"Creative China" as held in 2008 at the UK's V&A Museum; it was the first time an English museum held a large-scale exhibition of modern Chinese design. The exhibition focused on the three cities developing most rapidly in the field of Chinese design—Beijing, Shenzhen, and Shanghai. The Shenzhen area was named "Forefront City", shown as the point of origin for graphic design in China. A full presentation of the city's graphic design and visual culture gained cheers from overseas viewers.

Virtual Cartoons 032

Shenzhen is the most active city in the anime industry in China, and is responsible for a third of Disney's cartoon production. The Shenzhen Annual Animation Fair is already in its eighth year. Other like other animation fairs, this one mainly concentrates upon investment and copyright transactions, and has seen the birth of internationally competitive products and enterprises in the fields of anime and games. Every year when it takes place it's full of cartoon characters of all kinds, like a great carnival.

Jiamei Printing Creates Classics

In the 1980s, Shenzhen's printing industry was second to none. Orders for printing of publications and packages came in from every region. In order to satisfy clients' needs for design, the Shenzhen Jiamei Design Company was created by Wang Yuefei. The logos for Taita Beauty Essence and other popular brands at the time all came from Jiamei. Their designs and printed products are classics of the industry, and many later core characters in the Chinese graphic design industry come from this company.

Creative December

Shenzhen's December is steeped in creativity and creation. Starting in 2005, "Creative December" has gathered together hundreds of individual creative cultural activities, with the people of the city experiencing first-hand the fun that creativity brings, artists mingling with the people. The events include design, art, performances, anime, games, and more. The whole city gets wrapped up in the spirit, and the value of creative culture is recognised by the people of the city as they share it; the creative strength and imaginative strength of the whole affair explode like year-end fireworks.

嘉美印刷 典范制造

20世纪80年代，深圳的印刷业在全国首屈一指，各地出版和包装印刷的订单云集于此，为解决客户找不到设计师的问题，深圳嘉美设计有限公司应运而生，创建者是王粤飞。太太口服液等当时知名品牌的包装设计都出自嘉美，在业界嘉美印刷等于典范制造，后来国内平面设计界的许多核心人物也出自嘉美。

创意十二月

深圳的12月，属于创意。自2005年始，"创意十二月"便汇聚了数百项创意文化活动，市民们亲身体验创意带来的乐趣，艺术家们也走进民间。活动涵盖创意设计、工艺美术、文艺表演、动漫游戏等。整个城市弥漫着浓郁的创意氛围，创意文化被市民认可，分享、裂变出的创造力、想象力，如岁末烟花随处绽放。

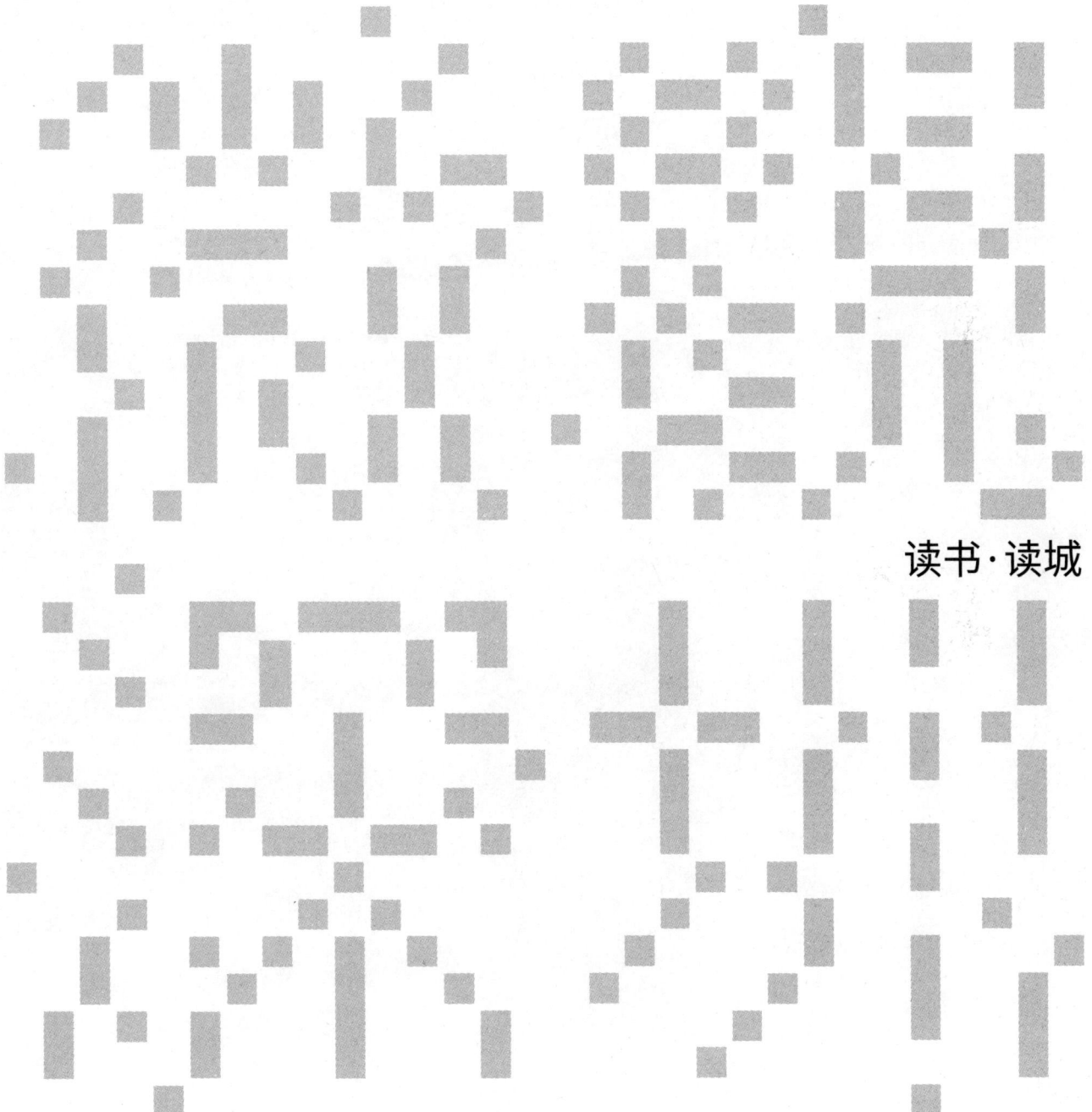

Books and Reading

读书·读城

八卦岭的阅读记忆 001

那时候，没有当当、亚马逊，更没有智能手机、电子书。那时候，深圳人读的是有墨香的纸质书，读《哈佛中国史》《万历十五年》……仿佛每打开一本书，就打开一扇看世界的窗户。八卦岭的书刊批发市场，是读书人的精神乐园，这里的书一律七折以下，让穷书生们尽享推着购物车淘书的快乐。

并非一座城的《命运》 002

《命运》以深圳为焦点，书写改革开放历史。陆天明用"命运"点明小说的主题：命运不仅是小说中人物的命运，更是中国"大历史"的命运。它表现深圳的成长，也由深圳的成长看到了中国发展轨迹，看到了"中国梦"的成长。同名电视剧在央视播出时，特区全城追剧，家家户户都锁定频道。

Memories at Bagualing 001

At that time, there were no online merchants, smartphones, or e-books. Back then, everyone read ink on paper. Books like *History of Imperial China*, and *1587, A Year of No Significance* were quite popular. Each time you opened a book, it was like opening a window into the world. The Bagualing Book Wholesale Market was a playground for readers; books here are all at least 30% off cover price, which makes for a fun shopping experience for poor students pushing trolleys around.

A City's *Fate* 002

Fate for Shenzhen is a focal point; it tells the story of the city during opening up and reform. Lu Tianming used *Fate* as the title of his book, not talking about the fate of his characters, but rather the fate of the "grand history" of China overall. He tells the tale of the growth of Shenzhen, and from this angle explores the development of China, and the growth of the "Chinese dream". When a television show of the same name was broadcast, people in the SEZ were all over it.

"第五项修炼"和"六顶思考帽"

进入21世纪,深圳最流行的四个字是"知识经济"。各种成功学的讲座、培训铺天盖地,成功学书籍大行其道,求知青年趋之若鹜。据说各大企业面试,能熟读励志、鸡汤的求职者,立被录取。一时间,"第五项修炼""六顶思考帽"等概念书脱销。一些出版界人士认为,深圳陷入了实用阅读的泥淖。

从"烫手山芋"到"香饽饽"

1996年11月,第七届全国书市在深圳举行,门票5元一张,这个曾被认为是亏本买卖的"烫手山芋",在深圳变成了"香饽饽"。书市当天前来参观购书的市民多达10万人!短短10天,深圳书城销售额高达2117万元,创5项全国纪录。时隔22年,全国书市已更名"全国图书交易博览会",书博会2018年再度花落深圳。

The Fifth Discipline and Six Thinking Hats

In the 21st century, a popular phrase is "knowledge economy". All kinds of motivational and "success" gurus give lectures, training centres are everywhere, and self-improvement books are extremely popular with younger people seeking employment. Some people say that when interviewing at a large enterprise, being able to spout off the self-help and "chicken soup" kind content will land you a job immediately. Borrowing phrases from Taoism and other classical schools of thought such as "the fifth discipline" and "the six thinking hats", books of this variety sell quite well. Some people in the publishing industry believe that Shenzhen has become mired in the bog of these "practical" books.

From "Tricky" to "Beloved"

The 7th National Book Fair was held in Shenzhen in November 1996. The entry price was 5 yuan, the event was believed to be a money-losing venture that still had some value, but in Shenzhen it became universally liked. More than 100,000 people showed up when it opened. In just 10 days, 21.17 million yuan in book sales took place, breaking five national records. Twenty-two years later, the fair goes on, as the National Book Exposition, and returned to the city this year.

15次来深圳的莫言

第十八届深圳读书月论坛上，诺贝尔文学奖得主莫言受邀开讲，活动现场人山人海，"莫氏效应"可见一斑。莫言先生沉着、平和、睿智、幽默，尽显长者风范。他说："文学的无用，就是它的有用。"这是莫言第15次来深圳了，他称，"深圳是我除了家乡山东和居住地北京之外来得最多的城市"。

The Fifteenth Visit

At a forum at the 18th Shenzhen Reading Month, Nobel Laureate Mo Yan was invited to give a speech. Masses of people showed up for the event, evidence of the "Mo effect". The man is reserved, calm, sharp and humorous. He remarked: "The lack of a practical application is precisely wherein the application of literature lies." This was the fifteenth time he visited Shenzhen. He said that it was the city he had visited the most after his hometown in Shandong and his city of residence, Beijing.

"门可罗雀"的免费博物馆

20年前的深圳博物馆小得可怜。冷冷清清，没几个参观的人。谁会到特区参观博物馆呢？只有博物馆门口"壮汉推开大门"的名为《闯》的雕塑，吸引些许游客合影留念。如今的新博物馆则大有看头。有古代深圳、近代深圳、深圳民俗、走进野生动物的情感世界等展厅，并成为全国第一座免费开放的博物馆。

深圳中心论

陈海滨著《深圳古代史》，从先秦写到清朝，他将古代深圳迈向文明时代、融入华夏家族、打造军事重镇、扼守经贸咽喉、铸就海防要塞和屹立抗英前线这一发展脉络清晰地勾勒出来。书中首次提出"深圳中心论"的概念。作者是平湖中学80后历史老师，他用史实否定了深圳"文化沙漠"的论调。

Nobody Here Knocking on My Door

The Shenzhen Museum was pathetically small 20 years ago, with almost nobody visiting. Why would someone visit a museum for the SEZ? The only popular point was a statue of "a strong man pushing open the gate" at the museum entrance, which was popular for taking photos with. The new museum is much larger. There are exhibits on Shenzhen's ancient history, modern history, cultural customs, and wildlife. It feels like a real world-class venue, and what's best is that it's the first museum in China open free to the public.

Shenzhen Centrality

A History of Ancient Shenzhen by Chen Haibin describes the city from the Pre-Qin to the Qing Dynasty, talking about the progression of the city into the modern era, from very early China to its presence as a military site to an economic corridor and naval defence site to a barrier against English incursion. The book proposes a theory of the centrality of Shenzhen for the first time. The author is a history teacher at the Pinghu Middle School born in the 1980s, who refutes the idea that Shenzhen is a "cultural desert".

因阅读而受人尊重

这座城市在国内第一个为阅读立法——《深圳经济特区全民阅读促进条例》，并被联合国授予"全球全民阅读典范城市"。从2000年开始，声势浩大又扎实推进的"深圳读书月"横空出世，王京生先生倡导的"让城市因热爱读书而受人尊重"终于落地。中心书城是目前世界最大的单体书店，它也成了市民老幼假日休闲之地，也是文化旅游必到景点。

Shenzhen is the first city in China to pass a reading law—*Regulations of Shenzhen Special Economic Zone on Civil Reading Promotion*, and has also been awarded a "Worldwide All-Citizen Reading Model City". Starting in 2000, a major campaign for a "Shenzhen Reading Month" came into effect. Wang Jingsheng supported "let's give respect to our city's book lovers". The Shenzhen Book City is currently the largest bookstore in the world, and has become a place for citizens of the city young and old to relax, as well as a site for cultured tourists to visit.

外文书店的清凉 009

深南中路的深圳外文书店是20年前的一道风景。对面是深圳特区报,旁边是劳动局,后面是巴丁街城中村。外文书店里,英文书籍并不多。炎热的夏天,求职者躲进书店,既为读书,也为享受那一份清凉。每天午饭时分,从窗外可见书店里神情专注的年轻人,他们捧着心爱的书,面色安详,若有所思。

随处借阅 随处还书 010

社区图书馆深受深圳市民喜爱,它们之间互相联网,家门口就可以方便地借阅书籍,读完了可以在任何地方还书,这是市民的一大福利。社区图书馆一般面积都不大,仅仅一两百平方米,几万本藏书,但是足够社区里面的老人跟孩子借阅。去社区图书馆的人越来越多,用书籍和电视、手机争夺时间,是一大善举。

Cool Foreign Bookstore

The foreign-language bookstore on Shennan Middle Road was a site more than 20 years ago. Across from it was the Shenzhen Special Zone Daily Building, and to its side was the Labour Bureau. Behind it lied the Badingjie Urban Village. Within the store, there weren't many English-language books. On hot summer days, job-seekers entered the store to read and also enjoyed some cool air. Every day at lunch time, one could look in through the windows and see a number of young people, carrying books they love with peaceful expressions on their faces.

Read Anywhere

Community libraries are quite popular in Shenzhen. They form a network, where people can borrow books and publications in their residential compounds, and when finished reading then return them at any other point in the network. This is a great convenience. These community libraries are usually quite small, only one or two hundred square metres in size, with only a few tens of thousands of books each, but they satisfy the needs of the young and old people in these communities. They're increasing in popularity, and visited more and more.

读书·读城

人生如书 后院读过

学哲学的王绍培和几个书友，一时兴起组了个后院读书会，有着各自职业的读书人，在工作之余，以书为媒，找到和自己性情相投的人。他们实践着一种叫"席明纳"的读书方式，"席明纳"是 seminar 的音译，其实就是书友之间的对话。读什么已然不重要，喜欢阅读的人聚在一起便是乐趣。

Life Is Like a Book

Student of philosophy Wang Shaopei and a few friends have started a group, where readers from various walks of life come together to interact through the medium of books in their free time, finding people they can exchange sentiments with. They call it "Ximingna", an approximation of the English word "seminar"; it's essentially a book club. It doesn't matter what everyone reads; as long as people can read and gather together, it's a good time.

书店里的购书车

外地人来深圳书城，看到很多市民都推着小推车买书，大为惊讶。原本以为深圳人赚钱的时间都不够，哪里还会读书？殊不知，深圳的年人均购书量常年稳居全国第一，究其原因，是因为深圳人都面临着"充电"的压力，一日不学习，就有被淘汰的危险。他们认为在物价高昂的深圳，买书性价比最高。

文学博士的"深圳梦"

北京大学文学博士尹昌龙，在关于深圳人身份的讨论中提出："深圳的命运最终取决于深圳人，有什么样的深圳人就有什么样的深圳。"当年在毕业时，他被招聘者告知，在深圳一个月工资可以买一大包书，他打起行装就来了。如今他身为深圳出版发行集团的掌门人，是深圳全民阅读的重要操盘手。

Trolleys in the Bookstore

When people from elsewhere come to Shenzhen, they are surprised to see citizens of the city pushing about trolleys buying books; thinking that everyone is busy earning money—how could they have time to read books. They don't know that Shenzhen is by far the first in the country in readership rates every year; for that reason, the people here face a kind of pressure—if you don't study every day, you'll fall behind. They believe that in a city with such high commodity prices, books yield the most bang for your buck.

Literati Shenzhen Dream

Yin Changlong, a PhD in literature from Peking University, speaks on the identity of the people of Shenzhen: "Shenzhen's fate is decided by its people; what kind of people are there will determine what kind of city it is." When he graduated, he received a hiring notice, and figured out that with the salary offered he could buy a big stack of books each month. He packed his bags and headed out. He now works as the general manager of the Shenzhen Publishing and Distribution Group, and is a key figure in the book trade for all of Shenzhen's residents.

"查理九世"和"朱佩琪"

你听不懂深圳小学生的流行语是很正常的，因为它实在是太新了。小朋友对新话题的习惯和喜爱匪夷所思。2010年是"查理九世"，你以为是一位国王吧？你错了，是一条狗。2018年最火的网红是只小猪，它叫佩奇。当孩子回家念念有词时，爸爸还以为新来一个叫"朱佩琪"的同学，是孩子新交的好朋友。

Charlie IX and Zhu Pei Qi

It's nothing to be concerned about if you can't understand the slang of elementary school students here—it's normal in fact, as it changes so quickly. The children think up all kinds of weird phrasings. In 2010, it was Charlie IX—you might think this is some kind of king, but it was actually a dog. In 2018, the most popular is a pig, called Peppa, or "Pei Qi" in Chinese. When you hear your kids prattling on about "Zhu Pei Qi", you might think it's a classmate, maybe a new friend.

小区里的午托班

绝大多数中小学生吃午饭是件大事。学校的食堂名额有限，催生出小区里的午托班。这些午托班大都是以家庭为单位开设，作坊式管理，三两个人，接送、买菜、做饭、午休、辅导功课一条龙服务。深圳家长离不开午托班，但监管是个大问题。食品安全、卫生条件，关乎孩子身心健康，这是个良心活儿。

Lunch Care

Lunchtime is a big deal for younger students. Space in the canteen at school is limited, and thus administrators encourage students to attend "lunchtime day care" or "lunch care". Most of these are operated out of private residences, in a workshop-type format, with two or three people picking up and dropping off children, buying ingredients, cooking, supervising nap time and helping with homework. These are essential services to the heads of household in Shenzhen, but oversight is a problem. Food safety, sanitation, the health of the children, and other things must all be considered.

上帝也无法阻止

传说上帝为了阻止人跟人之间的交流，便让人类说不同的语言。结果聪明的人类学会了普遍用英语沟通，各国学生皆学习英语。深圳毗邻香港，教学方式也开放。刘亚男老师教学生时，把自己在国外旅途中拍摄的照片、精彩的故事和学生分享，激发学习兴趣，让孩子渴望上英语课，连上帝也无法阻止。

God Can't Stop Us

In the traditions of some religions, "God" made the peoples of the world speak different languages to hinder communication between them. However, clever humans developed the concept of a lingua franca, which is nowadays English. Shenzhen borders Hong Kong, and education is open. Teacher Liu Yanan shows pictures of her travels abroad to her students, as well as exciting stories, sparking their interest, encouraging them to learn English. What now, God?

An Immaterial Bookstore

People can exist without a fixed residence, but the heart must always have somewhere to reside. The people of Shenzhen love to browse bookstores. Aside from the Shenzhen Book City, the people of Shenzhen also have a fondness for a bookstore on Baihua'er Road styled "La Vie matěrielle". Walking around the location, sipping coffee, and chatting with owner Xiao Yu, a former TV hostess, makes for a nice time. Although the name of the store makes a reference to the material, it is a place that is filled in all corners with spirit.

并不物质的小书吧

人可以居无定所，但一定要心有定所。爱读书的深圳人自然爱逛书店。除深圳书城外，老深圳们对百花二路的物质生活书吧情有独钟。漫步其中，随心所欲地翻书、喝咖啡，和店主晓昱聊天儿也是很开心的事情。这位曾经的电台女主持，情迷小书店，虽然用"物质"命名，实际上到处皆见精神。

Book Meeting

Running into a book is a nice twist of fate for a reader, but running into the author of that book is a small miracle. This happens often in Shenzhen. Reader Yu An was looking at books in a small bookshop in Shenzhen, when he spotted the book *Troubled Times for the Country*. He remarked on its quality to the owner, who smiled as she told him that the author Xia Shuangren was right in the store to visit. The two of them met, and had a great conversation.

因书偶遇

读者与一本书的偶遇是一种奇妙的缘分，读者与作者的偶遇更是一种奇妙的缘分。在深圳的书店，这种偶遇常常有。读者禹安在一家小书店里看书，随手拿起一本写民国大总统历史的《乱世掌国》，对书店老板赞赏其书，老板笑言作者夏双刃先生此刻就在书店。二人有缘一见，马上相约小聚。

邓一光的深圳

2009年，小说家邓一光作为特殊人才引进深圳。九年间，在这座被公认为"没有过去"的城市富矿里，他以敏锐的触觉和积极的创作力，挖掘出一部部厚重的作品。他的"深圳人系列小说"《你可以让百合生长》《深圳在北纬22°27′～22°52′》等，总是在这个城市引起一场又一场文学风暴。

Deng Yiguang's Shenzhen

In 2009, novelist Deng Yiguang became a talent of Shenzhen. Over the course of nine years, in this rich city that's believed by many to "have no past", his sharp senses and enthusiastic writing have produced great works. His "People of Shenzhen" series of novels, such as *You Can Let the Lily Grow* and *Shenzhen at 22°27′-22°52′* have provoked literary storms one after another in the city.

打工文学

深圳的文学品牌之一是"打工文学"。30年前，怀揣梦想的文学青年涌入深圳，他们催生了一个特有的文学群落：打工作家。北京大学谢冕教授曾说："打工文学的写作者和倡导者给我们提供了一个可贵的情怀，文学的悲悯精神在这里得到了重视。"盛可以、王十月等目前都是国内文坛的实力派作家。

Literature on Labourers

A major theme in the literature of Shenzhen is the lives of migrant labourers. 30 years ago, when literate youths full of dreams flooded into Shenzhen, they sparked off the creation of a literary group: labourer literati. Peking University professor Xie Mian once said: "The authors of the literature of the labourers and their exponents have given us valuable feelings; the sympathetic spirit of literature has come into focus here." Sheng Keyi and Wang Shiyue, along with others in this crowd, have become influential writers on the national literary landscape.

Poetic Ears

She founded a website—"Poem Life" which has become a major forum for poetry discussion nationwide. She didn't want to write over-the-top essays or break some kind of convention, she just cared about beautiful things and soft hearts. "Apple flowers bloom in spring, and when you hear the sound of the bubbling spring, you'll wake up earliest of everyone. When you sit upon the white carpet, you'll resemble a queen." During the CCTV Mid-Autumn Festival Gala, Zhou Tao read her poem, Lai'er, which moved many people's hearts.

诗意的耳朵——莱耳

她创办了一个网站"诗生活"，成为国内诗坛的重要据点。她既不想作锦绣文章，也不想上马杀贼，她只关心人柔软的内心以及美好的事物。"苹果花在春天开放，你听见泉水的声音，你比任何人起得早。你坐在白色的地毯上，像一个女王。"央视中秋晚会上，周涛也在朗诵着她的诗，莱耳，打动了许多人。

高贵的生活方式

文化学者大漠飞狐说："我们要从追求富贵的生活方式向追求高贵的生活方式转变，当我们在物质生活上吃得饱、穿得暖的时候，我们的精神生活同样需要吃得好、吃得饱。而读书是一种高贵的生活方式。"在深圳，节假日的书城和图书馆总是人头涌动。深圳人在物质之外，追求着另一种高贵的生活方式。

图书馆之城

如果说文化是一座城市的灵魂，那么图书馆大抵就是灵魂的栖身地。如果说灵魂有香气的话，那么，在清新的海风包围下的深圳便是处处弥漫着浓郁的书香。高楼大厦之间，街道社区里面，甚至马路边的树荫下，深圳的土地上处处可见图书馆，借、还皆方便，阅读便成了深圳人的一种习惯。

A City of Libraries

If culture is the soul of a city, then libraries are where the soul resides. If one says that souls have a fragrance, then it makes sense that the city of Shenzhen, surrounded by the ocean, has the scent of books all about. Between the high-rise buildings, in the streets and compounds, in the shade under the trees, everywhere in Shenzhen can one see libraries where one can freely borrow and return books. Reading is an ingrained habit for the people of Shenzhen.

小津书房的光影生活

当今人类的危机在于无法安静地在房间里待着，但小津书房会让你安静地在那里待着。他们主要经营电影书，店面极小，唯有一墙书，却被电影书籍以及海报充满。在这里当然不止读书，每晚都会有书友和影迷沙龙，你可以享受电影和书籍带给你的乐趣，当然还有很多冷门电影，让你避开人间烦忧。

Ozubook's Light and Shadow

In an area where people can't stay still in a single room, the Ozubook bookstore quietly rests in its place. They mainly sell books relating to films. The store is quite small, with only one wall of books, but is covered with these film-related books and posters throughout. One comes here not just to read, but also to participate in book and film salons, interacting with others, watching obscure films, and forgetting worries.

A Noble Lifestyle

A cultural scholar calling himself "the Flying Fox of the Great Desert" remarked: "We need to convert from a life of prosperity to a life of nobility. When our basic needs are satisfied, we need to satisfy our spiritual needs. Reading is a kind of activity in that vein." In Shenzhen, bookstores are jam packed with people on holidays. Aside from pursuing the material, they also pursue that which is noble.

Commerce and Change

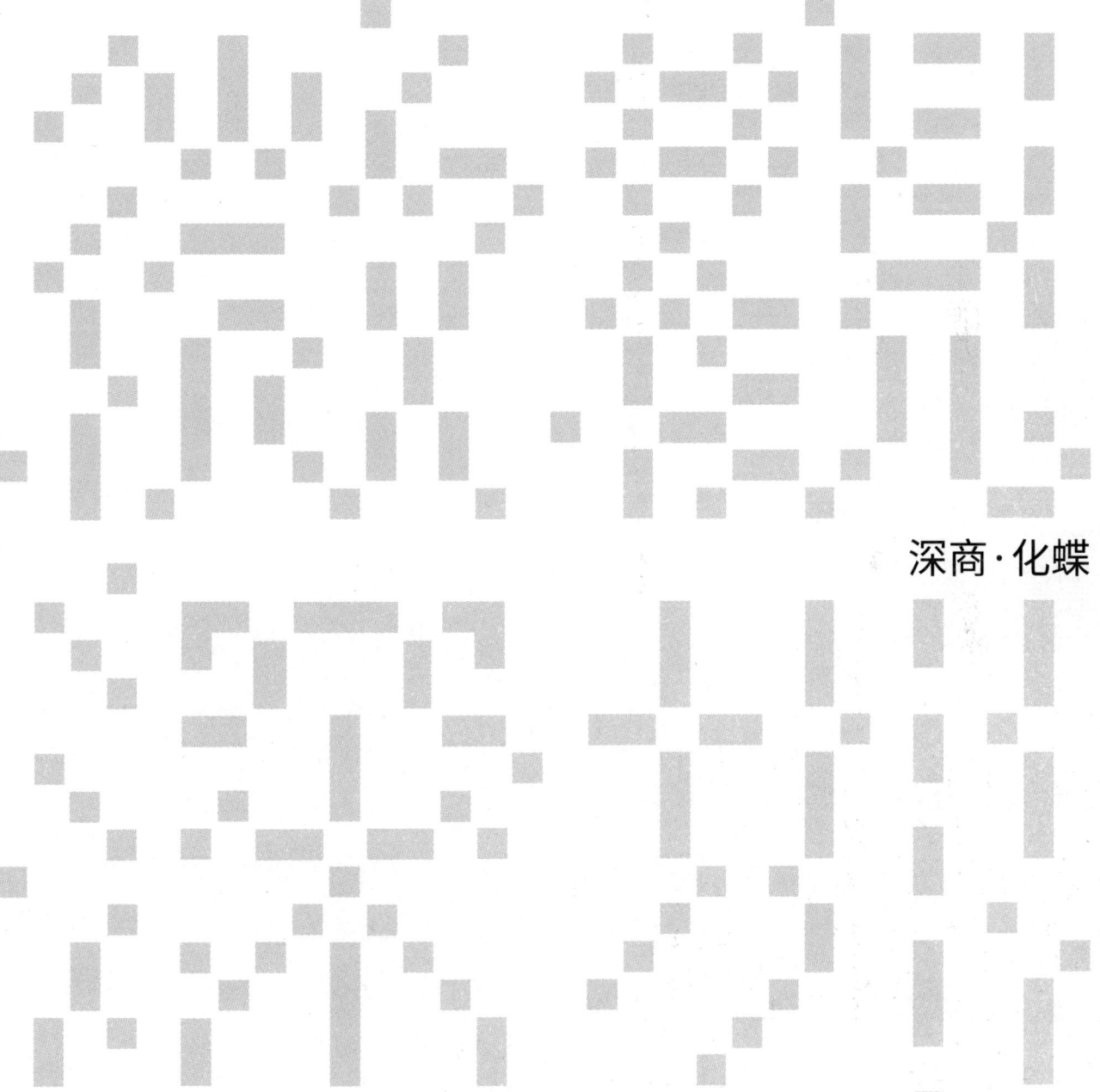

深商·化蝶

深商的"头啖汤" 001

粤商历来分两支——平民商人和买办商人,深圳商人则是吃"第一只螃蟹"的新粤商,与前二者均不同。用粤语说他们饮了"三来一补"的"头啖汤",20世纪八九十年代,靠来料加工、来料装配、来样加工和补偿贸易赢得了巨大的商机。商海沉浮,喝"头啖汤"需要发现的眼光,更需要尝试的勇气。

The First Soup

Cantonese merchants were historically of two classes—civilian merchants, and compradors. Those in Shenzhen are a new breed. The Cantonese locals, say they drink "the first soup", made of the ingredients of incoming materials processing, incoming materials packaging, incoming sample processing, and compensatory trade: these four areas were huge businesses in Shenzhen in the 1980s and 1990s. The business world has ups and downs, and those people who want to drink the soup need to have an eye for opportunities, and a stomach for risks.

Founder of Business in Shenzhen 002

If one knows of Shenzhen, one must know of Shekou, and if one knows of Shekou, one must know of Yuan Geng. He was born in Shenzhen and revived the China Merchants Group and created great enterprises such as Ping An Insurance and China Merchants Bank. The "Father of Shekou" left behind the "Shenzhen Spirit". He was previously doubted, and left behind these words: "If we fail, I'll be the first to jump into the sea." On the day he died, chrysanthemums sold out, and many huge merchants penned elegiac couplets, paying respect to the "Founder of Business in Shenzhen".

深商教主 002

大抵知深圳者必知蛇口,知蛇口者必知袁庚。他生于深圳大鹏,缔造了百年招商局的二次辉煌,创办了平安保险和招商银行等一批优秀企业。"蛇口之父"留下"蛇口精神",但也曾受质疑。他留下名言:"要是失败了,我领头跳海去。"袁庚逝世当天,菊花一度卖光,诸多商界巨子敬献挽联,致敬"深商教主"。

国企改革的"深圳模式"

Shenzhen Model

深圳最大的国企深圳市投资控股有限公司，2004年10月组建，旗下全资和控股公司60多家，参股20多家，遍及房地产、金融、高新技术和公用事业等领域。其以世界500强为目标，资产规模将超3万亿。主业有三块：产权管理、资本运作和投融资，对标新加坡淡马锡控股，不断探索国企改革的"深圳模式"。

Shenzhen's largest state-owned enterprise is the Shenzhen Investment Holdings Company, organised in October 2004. It controls more than 60 companies, and participates in the shares of over 20 companies, with activities in fields such as real estate, finance, new high technology, utilities, and more. It aims to be a world top 500, and has more than 3000 billion yuan in assets. Its three main areas of operation are asset management, capital operations and investment. It benchmarks the Singapore-based Temasek Holdings, and continually explores the "Shenzhen Model" to revolutionise state-owned enterprises.

让世界造起来 004

李克强总理 2015 年考察深圳柴火创客空间，创始人潘昊一夜成名。他来自四川，痴迷硬件技术，除柴火创客空间外，还创办了全球第三大开源硬件设备生产商 Seeed Studio，入选福布斯"中国 30 位 30 岁以下创业者"。他认为 Maker 就是创造风口的人，有意促进 Maker 创意的实现以至产品化，让整个世界造起来。

Let's Make Things

When Chinese Premier Li Keqiang visited the Chaihuo Makers in 2015, founder Pan Hao became famous overnight. A native of Sichuan, he's obsessed with hardware technology and aside from Chaihuo also established the world's third-largest open-source hardware device producer, Seeed Studio, and was listed by Forbes as one of the "30 under 30 China". He believes Makers are people who fill in gaps, and wants to help them make their ideas into actual products.

中国第一家股份制企业 005

中国宝安集团成立于 1983 年，是中国第一家股份制企业，发行了中国第一张股票、第一张可转债、第一批中长期认股权证等，创下九项第一，赢得资本市场万千关注。2011 年因石墨矿风波引发炮轰。多年入围世界品牌实验室百强，目前以高科技产业为主，兼顾股权投资、生物科技和城市运营开发。

深港通 006

深港通指深港股市交易互联互通机制，使股民的投资渠道得以拓宽。李克强总理 2015 年在深圳考察时表示，沪港通后应有深港通。次年，深港通正式启动，深市 881 只股票和香港联交所 417 只股票纳入交易范围，首个交易日成交额超过 35 亿元。尤其是香港博彩股等稀缺项目，对内地投资者颇具吸引。

China's First Share Issuing Enterprise

China Bao'an Group was established in 1983, making it the first share issuing enterprise in China. It issued China's first stock, first convertible bord, first medium and long term equity warrant… it's responsible for nine firsts in total, and is widely paid attention to in the capital market. In 2011 it suffered a scandal due to contradictory statements about its ownership of graphite mines. It's been included by the World Brand Lab in its list of top 100 companies for many years, and currently focuses on high technology, while also conducting investment, having ventures in biotechnology, and carrying out urban operation development.

Shenzhen-Hong Kong Stock Connect

The Shenzhen-Hong Kong Stock Connect is an interconnection and internetworking mechanism for the Shenzhen and Hong Kong Stock Exchanges, allowing traders to enjoy a broader investment channel. When Chinese Premier Li Keqiang visited Shenzhen in 2015, he announced that after the Shanghai-Hong Kong Stock Connect, there would be a program for Shenzhen. The next year, the Connect was officially initiated, with 881 Shenzhen stocks and 417 Hong Kong stocks brought into the scheme. The first day of trading saw 3.5 billion yuan in volume. Hong Kong gambling stocks and other rare items were especially attractive to mainland traders.

滚石不生苔

50后企业家王石,从在深圳倒卖玉米赚到第一桶金,到创立万科,一直特立独行。他带领万科披荆斩棘,杀入世界500强,又在镁光灯下交棒后任,酿成佳话;还代言摩托罗拉,登顶珠峰,游学哈佛,同时拥有了诗歌和远方。滚石不生苔,上下求索,灵魂才能跟上脚步。

Rolling Stone Gathers No Moss

Wang Shi, born in the 1950s, earned his first fortune scalping corn in Shenzhen, and later founded Vanke. He's always had his own way of doing things. He pushed through all kinds of obstacles to get into the world top 500. The story of him handing over the reins to his successor has become a kind of fable. He's been a spokesperson for Motorola, climbed Mount Everest, studied at Harvard… A rolling stone gathers no moss; only with continuous efforts can one's soul keep pace.

Ever Grand

The Evergrande Group's annual sales passed 500 billion yuan in 2017. The creator of this towering empire, Xu Jiayin, comes from Henan. His mother died when he was one year old, and his family was poor. In 1992, when looking for a job in Shenzhen, he slept in the hallway of his friend's house. He got things really started in Guangzhou, making a huge success with his first building. In 2017 he moved the headquarters of Evergrande back to Shenzhen; he is the richest individual in China. The Chinese name of the group, Hengda, "stable and grand" comes from a classical phrase: "Continuing from past to present in an unbroken succession is called stable; the continuous development of the heaven, earth and all things is called grand."

有恒乃大

恒大集团2017年销售额超过5000亿元,帝国巍峨。帝国缔造者许家印来自河南,1岁丧母,家境清贫,1992年求职深圳时睡过朋友家的走廊。他真正起家在广州,首个楼盘一炮打响,到2017年把恒大总部迁回深圳时已是中国首富,他为企业取名恒大,因为"古往今来连绵不绝,曰恒;天地万物增益发展,曰大"。

Penguin Empire

Tencent's penguin mascot made its first appearance at the 1999 China Hi-Tech Fair; at the time the number of QQ users just passed 1 million. Today, that number is 780 million, and the WeChat application has more than one billion active monthly users. The giant penguin empire was formed by the shy technologist Ma Huateng. When he was 13 he moved with his parents to Shenzhen, and graduated from Shenzhen University. The 39-storey Tencent Building is right to the north of the campus of the university. Study hard, and this could be you—a world class spokesperson for the business world of Shenzhen.

Glory of Kings

Glory of Kings is a first-rate game made by Tencent, jokingly termed "pesticide" by gamers. It's first in both popularity and income. The statistics are shocking: three billion yuan a month in cash flow, and 150 million yuan a day in decorative skins. This is a champion in the Chinese game industry with a currently unshakable position. Players range from small porters to high-powered business elites. Some sociologists are worried, however—could this be the new "mental crack"? The line between splendour and shade is razor-thin.

企鹅帝国

1999年第一届高交会上，腾讯的企鹅形象第一次亮相，其时QQ用户注册数100万。现在，这个数字是7.8亿，而微信的月活跃用户更已逼近10亿。庞大的企鹅帝国由羞涩的技术男马化腾一手缔造。他13岁时随父母迁居深圳，毕业于深圳大学，39层高的腾讯大厦就建在深大北面。小马哥，已是深商的世界级代言人。

王者荣耀

腾讯的一款游戏产品，玩家戏称"农药"，连续霸榜，是收入和热度的双料冠军。有着令人尖叫的数据：30亿元的月流水，一款皮肤的日流水1.5亿。它是中国手游的翘楚，其王者地位难以撼动。玩家从商界精英到贩夫走卒皆有。但有社会学家担忧，它会否成为新时代的"精神鸦片"？荣耀与阴影，只在毫厘间。

创投大佬 011

深创投是中国最大的创业投资公司，截至2014年年底，投资了500多家企业，其中94家上市。军人出身的靳海涛2004—2015年担任董事长。他是央视年度经济人物，上榜各类中国最佳创投家榜单。他61岁时在深圳设立前海母基金，商业巨头马蔚华、沈南鹏、熊晓鸽、厉伟等为联合合伙人，阵容豪华。

区块链布道者 012

1998年4月，37岁的肖风负责筹建老五家公募基金之一的博时基金。他是南开大学经济学博士，有着丰富的资产管理经验。2001年博时总部南迁深圳，肖风带团队在鹏城继续奋斗，2011年他离开时，博时的资产管理规模已近2000亿。肖风现在万向集团任职，他的新征途是互联网金融，近年已是区块链的布道者。

南方有嘉木 013

作为国内最早的五家公募基金公司之一，以及最早的封闭式基金，南方的资产管理规模始终在第一阵营。南方有嘉木，执掌帅印15年的高良玉当记头功。他1998年初到南方，参加了基金开元的上市剪彩。无惧于嘉木风催的挫折和艰辛，他创造并见证了基金业的发展。

Venture Capital Boss 011

The Shenzhen Capital Group is China's largest venture capital company. By the end of 2014, it had invested in more than 500 enterprises, 94 of which had been listed. Jin Haitao, originally a military man, served as president from 2004 to 2015. He's a frequent guest on financial shows on CCTV, and has been all kinds of top investor lists in China. At 61 years of age he established the Qianhai FOF in Shenzhen, with famous investors such as Ma Weihua, Shen Nanpeng, Xiong Xiaoge, and Li Wei as partners—an impressive line-up.

Blockchain Evangelist 012

In April 1998, 37-year-old Xiao Feng was responsible for the establishment of one of the first five public offering of funds—the Bosera Fund. He was a PhD in Economics from Nankai University, and had extensive asset management experience. In 2001 Bosera's headquarters moved south to Shenzhen, and Xiao Feng's team went on to work hard in the city. He left in 2011, by which time Bosera's assets totalled 200 billion yuan. Xiao currently works at the Wanxiang Group, where he is working on internet finance. In recent years he has been an evangelist for blockchain technology.

China Southern Fund 013

As one of the five earliest public offering of funds in China, and the earliest closed-end fund, the China Southern Fund has always been one of China's top-tier funds by assets under management. Gao Liangyu, holding the reins for 15 years, arrived in the south in 1998, and participated in the ribbon-cutting ceremony for the fund's listing. He took the fund through all kinds of difficulties, having it succeed and develop.

门口的野蛮人

门口的野蛮人，原指华尔街的恶意收购基金，"宝万之争"使这个词成为特指。万科的优质资产，使得包括宝能在内的众多险企破门而入，资本逐利本无可厚非，是否合法合规才是关键。高调的王石和低调的姚振华，经过较量，结果是王石退位、姚振华被罚。有人认为是双输，是非输赢，留待后人评说。

Barbarians

"Barbarians" originally refers to hostile takeover funds on Wall Street. The "Baoneng-Vanke War" is an example of this phenomenon. Vanke has excellent resources, which has allowed a number of risk enterprises to break into, including Baoneng. Seeking profit is no grounds for blame, but what's key is whether it is done in a manner that is legal. The high-key Wang Shi and low-key Yao Zhenhua went toe to toe, the result being that Wang Shi left his position and Yao Zhenhua was fined. Some people believe this was a lose-lose situation; whether anyone won at all will be decided by later commentators.

数月亮的大佬

2008年A股低迷，华尔街对冲基金合伙人邱国鹭回国，带领千亿规模的南方基金交出了漂亮答卷。其后他"下海"创业，打造了私募基金——高毅资产。他信奉价值投资，并以此扬名。他认为投资不要数星星，要数月亮，即要投行业里最好的公司。他天生属于投资，19岁时就靠股票认购证赚到了第一桶金。

Counting Moons

A-shares hit a low in 2008, and Glen Qiu, a partner at a hedge fund on Wall Street, returned to China, bringing wonderful answers for the China Southern Asset Management, with assets in the 100-billion range. Later, he joined the fray and started his own private fund—Perseverance Asset Management. He embraces and promotes value investment. He believes that when investing, one shouldn't count stars, but rather count moons, investing in only the best companies in each industry. He's always been into investment, having earned his first fortune buying stocks when he was 19.

券业"黄埔军校"

1992年,军人出身的湖北人张国庆在深圳成立了君安证券,五年后就做到了全国券业第一。当年的君安帝国如日中天,中国股市的这段时期甚至被命名为"君安时代"。1998年他因MBO入狱,君安终遭国泰合并。君安旧部虽然星散,但投资名家辈出,券业"黄埔军校"果然名不虚传。

老帅出山

一张天价美元罚单,令76岁中兴老帅侯为贵夜航赴美,刷屏的背影温和又坚毅。他生于西安,43岁时被派往深圳创业。他首创"国有控股,授权经营"机制,抓住了CDMA、小灵通和手机的发展机遇,带领中兴通讯风雨30年,成为商海传奇人物,获选"中国十大科技领袖"。风浪中老帅出山,结果已不重要。

马行长

从1999年起,马蔚华当了近15年招商银行行长,率领招行成功转型,使之从地方小行变身为仅次于中农工建交的第六大银行,以及最成功的零售银行。马蔚华知青出身,曾在中国人民银行任职,受命解决过海南发展银行的破产清理,这些人生积淀使他在复杂的金融市场游刃有余,成为英国《银行家》杂志的年度银行家。

Whampoa Military Academy of the Securities Industry

In 1992, Hubei native Zhang Guoqing established Junan Securities in Shenzhen; five years later it was first in securities in the nation. At that time it shined as bright as the sun in the noonday sky, and this period in the history of the Chinese securities industry is known as the "Junan Age". He was imprisoned during a management buyout in 1998, and Junan was merged with Guotai. The old components of Junan have scattered about, but the people involved are still around, making Junan deserve the reputation of being the "Whampoa Military Academy of the securities industry".

Here Comes the General

Drama with the USA caused the "general" of ZTE, 76-year-old Hou Weigui to board a flight bound for the country in the middle of the night. Kind and strong in appearance, he was born in Xi'an, and at 43 years of age was sent to Shenzhen to engage in enterprise. He created the model of a civilian operator being licensed to run a company the shares of which were owned by the state. He seized the opportunities of CDMA, Personal Handphone System, and mobile phones, and carried ZTE through wind and rain over the course of 30 years, making him a business legend. He's been selected as one of the top ten leaders in technology in China.

Bank Boss Ma

Starting in 1999, Ma Weihua served as head of the China Merchants Bank for 15 years. He led a successful transformation of the bank from a small operation to the sixth-largest in China, after BOC, ABC, ICBC, CCB, and BOCOM, and the biggest retail bank. Ma used to be sent to the countryside in the Cultural Revolution, and work at the People's Bank of China, where he was ordered to carry out the administration of the bankruptcy of the Hainan Development Bank. With a huge amount of accumulated financial knowledge and skill, he was named "Banker of the Year" by the UK's *Banker* magazine.

神秘的头狼

1987年，43岁的任正非因工作不顺利，集资2万元创办了华为。华为2014年国际专利申请数全球第一；2017年成为全球最大通信设备生产商，营收785.1亿美元，位列中国民营公司之首。军人出身的任正非极其低调，他的"狼性文化"和"梨子理论"却广为人知。在冬天的危机感驱使下，他带领华为走向了春天。

The Lead Wolf

In 1987, 43-year-old Ren Zhengfei's job wasn't going well, and thus he collected 20,000 yuan to found Huawei. In 2014, Huawei became first worldwide in patent applications. In 2017, Huawei became the world's largest telecommunications device producer, and it had an income of 78.51 billion USD, making it the largest private company in China. Originally a military man, Ren is very low key; his "Wolf Culture" and "Pear Theory" have become widely known. During the cold winter, he drives his team to run towards the spring.

最大的风险就是不敢冒险

王文银是安徽农民的儿子，闯深圳最窘迫时身上只有10元钱。他从仓库管理员起步，用20年时间孕育了世界500强企业——正威国际集团。他认为"最大的风险就是不敢冒险"，在"非典"和全球金融危机时，他大胆收购矿产资源，垂直整合产业链，实现了产值蝶变，成为执掌5300亿江山的世界铜王。

The Biggest Risk Is Not Daring to Take a Risk

Wang Wenyin is the son of farmers from Anhui; he arrived in Shenzhen with just 10 yuan. He started out as a warehouse keeper, and over 20 years managed to build up a world top 500—the Amer International Group. He believes the biggest risk is not daring to take a risk. During the SARS outbreak and the global financial crisis, he boldly bought up mineral resources, and formed a fully vertically-integrated chain, bringing about a metamorphosis that turned his company into the world copper king, worth 530 billion yuan.

深二代创业家

PC时代和腾讯齐名的迅雷，曾拥有4亿注册用户，2002年由邹胜龙和程浩始创于硅谷。2003年邹胜龙回国，在深圳市留学生创业园起步，带领迅雷成为中国最大的下载服务提供商。他是深二代，父亲是发明家邹德骏。迅雷2014年在美上市，上市前引入的小米几年后入主迅雷，邹胜龙卸任董事长。

Shenzhen Second Generation Entrepreneurs

In the PC Era, Xunlei was as famous as Tencent, having 400 million registered users. It was founded in 2002 by Zou Shenglong and Cheng Hao in Silicon Valley. In 2003, Zou returned to China, and in the Shenzhen Overseas Chinese High-Tech Venture Park started work, turning Xunlei into China's largest download service provider. He's a second-generation Shenzhen local; his father is the inventor Zou Dejun. Xunlei went public in America in 2014; Xiaomi, which it had taken in prior to going public, a few years later took Xunlei in, with Zou resigning as president.

Soul in Business

Ma Mingzhe is the founder of Ping An Insurance, and is like a god in the insurance industry. Thirty years passed like a day, with him working more than 13 hours daily, taking Ping An from a company with just 13 employees to one of the 50 wealthiest companies in the world. He passed on an opportunity to be vice mayor, and went through periods where he had to take three sleeping pills just to fall asleep. He chose to share his huge amount of shares with his team; he entered enterprise with his soul.

灵魂入股企业

马明哲是平安保险的创办人，保险圈"神一样的存在"。三十年如一日，他每天工作13个小时以上，带领平安从一个只有13名员工的公司，奋斗成为全球财富50强企业。他放弃过做副市长的机会，经历过吃三片安眠药才能入睡的煎熬。面对巨额平安股份，他选择了和团队分享，他是用灵魂入股了企业。

Trump's Friend

Foxconn founder Terry Gou was born in Taiwan. He has a forceful character; in 1988 he moved to Shenzhen to start a business. He previously collected 10 billion USD to build a factory in America. Trump has called him "my friend" and "the mightiest businessman in the world". Foxconn passed its A-share IPO audit in 36 days, and triggered the "unicorn war" in capital markets in 2018. With the smartphone market saturated, can Foxconn persist as a "unicorn"? Opinions differ.

特朗普的朋友

富士康创始人郭台铭生于台湾，作风强悍，1988年到深圳龙华创业。他曾斥资百亿美元在美设厂，特朗普称他为"我的朋友"和"世界上最伟大的商人"。富士康36天通过A股IPO审核，引发了2018年资本市场的"独角兽"之争。智能手机市场饱和，富士康是否担得起"独角兽"三个字？坊间说法不一。

财经界第一网红

李大霄是广东阳江人，毕业于华南理工大学电机系。在东莞证券开业当天，他办理了股票账户，成为东莞"1号股民"。从股民逆袭成为首席分析师后，他擅用新媒体，抛出过"钻石底"和"婴儿底"等市场观点，不惧专业同行嘲讽，逐渐炼成"财经界第一网红"。他在深圳券业谋生，称"不知道自己值多少钱"。

Financial Internet Celebrity

Li Daxiao is a native of Yangjiang, Guangdong, and a graduate of the Department of Electrical Engineering of the South China University of Technology. When Dongguan Securities open, he opened an account to become Dongguan's "Trader No.1". From a shareholder counter-attack to becoming the chief analyst, he excelled at using new media. Coming up with market viewpoints such as "Diamond Floor" and "Baby Floor", ignoring haters in the industry, he gradually became the first "financial internet celebrity". He works in the securities industry in Shenzhen, and claims to not know his own net worth.

Starting with a Plane Ticket

Founded in 1998, Shenzhen Tempus Group started with the dream of an airline ticket agency, and is now in the Chinese Top 500, with two listed companies. Tempus concentrates on tourism, logistics and investments. It has six production groups, services in 157 countries and regions, 81,000 employees, and serves 620 million people worldwide. Founder Zhong Baisheng is a huge fan of Wushu, and has practiced for three hours in the morning, without fail over a number of years.

从一张机票开始

始建于1998年的深圳腾邦，从一张张机票的代理开始逐梦，目前雄踞中国500强，拥有两家上市公司。腾邦聚焦旅游、物流和投资三大主业，旗下六个产业集团，业务遍及157个国家和地区，员工8.1万人，服务全球6.2亿人。创办人钟百胜热爱武术，每天清晨武术训练，长达三小时，多年风雨无阻。

以笔为船，横渡商海

赵先德来自山东莱芜，是农民的儿子。20多年前他孤身闯深，曾因醉酒在电梯里睡着了，半夜醒来回到租住的"握手楼"，窗内冷清如铁，窗外星河灿烂。他是二级作家，以笔为船，横渡商海，在深圳创建了崇德动漫，推出52集奥运动漫《福娃》，赢得了"奥运动漫第一人"称号，实现了"深圳梦"。

国企走出来的培训专家

儒雅俊秀的扬州人夏云平1994年赴深，曾在市政府、国有企业工作，后"下海"创办双象教育机构。其率先主讲的压力管理、阳光心态等课程幽默风趣，切中要害，令人耳目一新。在广东省公务员培训中享有美誉，被称为"把深圳管理理念和创新思想带到税务培训中的先行者"。

Enterprise Trainer

The handsome Yangzhou native Xia Yunping came to Shenzhen in 1994. He first worked in government, and then at a state-owned enterprise before "entering the fray" and founding an educational institution. He's taken the lead in talking about pressure management, positive attitude and other topics, in a style that both is humorous and hits home. He's received praise for his training courses for the civil servants, and has been called a forerunner in "taking Shenzhen management concepts and new thinking to tax administration training".

Sailing the Seas of Business

Zhao Xiande comes from Laiwu in Shandong, and is the son of farmers. About 20 years ago he went to Shenzhen on his own; he once fell asleep in the lift of his building because he was drunk. In the middle of the night he sobered and woke up, and went to his rented flat in the cramped building. Inside the window was a bleak scene, but outside there was a sea of brilliant stars. He is a second-class writer, who sails the seas of business with his pen as a boat. He founded Chongde Animation in Shenzhen, which has created a 52-part Olympic animation *Fuwa*; they have been recognised as the "best Olympic anime characters". His Shenzhen Dream came true in the end.

还在坚持

1992年，河南新乡人朱保国怀揣一张9万元买断的药方，南下深圳创业。他从保健品起家，推出的"太太口服液"等打破了"只领风骚两三年"的行业怪圈，20多年攻城略地，拥有了两家上市公司。这位圈中的传奇人物的成功秘诀就是坚持："当所有人都在说你是疯子的时候，你在坚持！"

Holding On

In 1992, Zhu Baoguo, a native of Xinxiang, Henan, bought out a pharmacy for 90,000 yuan and started his business in Shenzhen. He started with health products, and with his Taita brand managed to break free of the curse in the industry that businesses only last two or three years. He's made continual conquests for more than 20 years, and has two listed companies. This industry legend's strategy for success is persistence: "When everyone else is saying you're crazy, you keep holding on!"

就是想好好玩一把

"大疆"无人机,让80后技术男汪滔一战成名,身家超过亿万。他不懈追逐少时的"飞翔梦",读硕士期间在莲花北的民房里创办了大疆,如今其产品在全球消费级无人机市场占据了七成,成为"中国智造"的成功案例。汪滔直率而激烈,对乔布斯也只有欣赏而没有佩服,他说大疆的愿景"就是想好好玩一把"。

Desire to Play

DJI's drones have made technologist Wang Tao, in his thirties, not only famous but also a multibillionaire. He continually pursues his dream of flight from his childhood years. He founded DJI in a residence at Lianhua North when he was studying for his master's; the company now produces 70% of consumer drones in the world, making it a successful case of "made in China". Wang Tao is frank and energetic; he appreciates but does not admire Steve Jobs. He says his reason for creating DJI was that he "wanted to play".

激情的金蝶 030

金蝶是港股"内地民营软件第一股"。其创始人徐少春生于湖南，毕业于东南大学计算机专业，1991年在深圳创立爱普，两年后创立金蝶，开始了民族软件业的寻芳之旅。金蝶财务软件使1200万会计甩掉了算盘。徐少春信奉"人生所有的欢乐都是创造的欢乐"，自言是一个"热血沸腾"的人。

Passionate Kingdee

Kingdee is the "first mainland non-state-owned software company on the HKSE"; its founder Xu Shaochun was born in Hunan, and graduated from the Department of Computer Science at Southeast University. He founded Aipu in Shenzhen in 1991, and two years later founded Kingdee, and started a Chinese software odyssey. Kingdee's software led to 12 million accountants casting aside their abacuses. Xu Shaochun believes "the greatest joy in life is the joy of creation". He says that he is a person of passion.

上帝之手 031

"每个人都能活到100岁""未来可以化学合成任何生命"，这些惊人之语出自华大基因董事长汪建。这位自嘲"贪生怕死"又自信"十项全能没弱点"的基因专家，希望掌握如"上帝之手"的科学，从受精卵开始掌控生命。"基因第一股"上市后，他饱受争议。他希望活到120岁，墓碑拟定：1954—2074 精彩人生。

God's Hand

"Everyone can live to 100", "in the future we will be able to achieve life through chemosynthesis"—these are quotes from Wang Jian, head of the Beijing Genomics Institute. He jokingly describes himself as being afraid of dying from the day he was born, and believes he's a decathlete without a weak point. He hopes to create a "God's Hand", and control life through sperm-egg manipulation. After the first "genome stock" went on the market, he was the subject of controversy. He hopes to live until 120, with a gravestone that reads "1954-2074 a wonderful life".

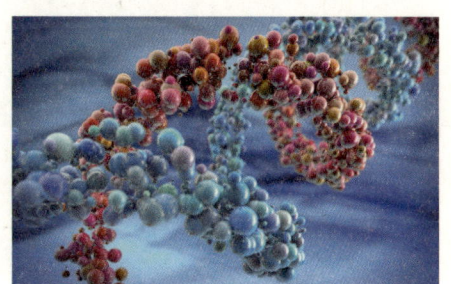

马云唯一对手 032

怡亚通是A股首家供应链上市公司，总部在深圳，1997年由周国辉创立，10年后上市。再过10年，营收年复合增长42%，业绩骄人。马云2013年成立菜鸟网络、进军供应链物流时，周国辉被看作马云"唯一竞争对手"。他有意打造一个覆盖10亿消费者的快消品直供平台，开展"深度供应链"业务。

Jack Ma's Only Opponent

Eternal Asia is the first supply chain company to go public. Headquartered in Shenzhen, it was founded in 1997 by Zhou Guohui, and went public 10 years later. 10 more years later, it had reached compound annual growth rate of 42%, an impressive achievement. When Jack Ma established Cainiao in 2013, entering the war for the supply chain and logistics market, Zhou Guohui was seen by him as his "only opponent". Zhou seeks to create a direct supply platform for FMCGs for a billion consumers, and develop "in-depth supply chain" services.

An Electric BYD

Wang Chuanfu, the founder of BYD, is the entrepreneur that Warren Buffett respects the most. He was born into a poor family, but was passionate about technology. He started making batteries, and later moved to making cars. Buffet's partner Charlie Munger believes he's a "blend of Thomas Edison and Jack Welch"—he says that he can solve technological problems like Edison and enterprise management problems like Welch. His wealth has risen continually, making him the mainland of China's wealthiest person, and investors continue to throw huge amounts of money at BYD.

Form a Respectable Enterprise

H&T is a world leader in the intelligent control industry. It is a core technical partner with BMW, Samsung, and other major players. Founded in 2000 in Shenzhen by a team from Tsinghua and the Harbin Institute of Technology; the president, Liu Jianwei is a doctoral advisor. The company has about 600 technical research engineers, the largest team of its kind in the world. With the arrival of the Internet of Things, H&T is getting in to the game. Their wish is to "form a respectable enterprise".

比亚迪带电奔驰

创办了比亚迪电动汽车的王传福,是股神巴菲特最看重的中国企业家。他出身贫寒,是技术狂人,从做电池起家,步步跨入造车。巴菲特的搭档芒格称他为"爱迪生和韦尔奇的混合体",认为他解决技术问题像爱迪生,解决企业管理问题像韦尔奇。他一度跃升中国内地首富,股神豪掷巨资投资比亚迪。

做令人尊敬的企业

和而泰是全球智能控制器行业的龙头企业,是宝马、三星等在国内的核心技术伙伴。2000年成立于深圳,由清华和哈工大共同组建,董事长刘建伟是博导。公司拥有约600名智控研发工程师,为全球最大的研发队伍。随着物联网时代的到来,和而泰全面进军物联网,他们的愿景是"做令人尊敬的企业"。

声讯电话 035

深圳是年轻的移民城市，既繁华喧嚣，又寂寞难耐，声讯电话因此在20世纪90年代大行其道，运营商数钱数到手软。声讯台有自动台和人工台，内容从生活常识到情感慰藉，应有尽有，都是靠电话语音服务收费；其中人工台的服务较人性化，更受欢迎。网络普及后，声讯台遭到较大冲击，逐渐淡出。

Telephony Services

In a young city with a large immigrant population, a noisy environment became home to many people quiet and lonely, and telephone services operators made money hand over fist in the 1990s. There were both automated platforms and those staffed by humans, which provided services from information lookup to emotional comfort—every kind of premium-rate phone number was out there; those staffed by humans were more personal, and more popular. In the internet age, these services took a big hit, and gradually faded away.

互联网拓荒者 036

拓荒是拓荒者的使命，途中不乏动人的风景。深圳市万用信息网有限公司1993年建立，比张树新创建瀛海威还早两年。1997年，公司推出门户网站"深圳热线"，1998年推出国内第一个在线新闻杂志。"深圳热线"曾获得"十佳中文网站"称号，但后来被新浪、凤凰网赶超。

Internet Pioneer

Exploring new ground is the mission of pioneers; there are always moving sights along the journey. Wanyongwang Company was established in 1993, two years earlier than Zhang Shuxin's InfoHighWay. In 1997, Wanyongwang Company rolled out its "SZOnline", and in 1998 the nation's first online new magazine. "SZOnline" was awarded the title of "Top 10 Chinese-Language Website", but later on was overtaken by Sina and Ifeng.

华强北对于深圳而言，犹如王府井之于北京，南京路之于上海。这条只有900米长的街区，集结了蜂窝般的电子商铺。它是亚洲规模最大的电子产品集散地，价格与国际市场直接接轨，堪称中国乃至东南亚和欧美地区电子配套市场的"晴雨表"，更走出了腾讯、创维等知名企业。

中国电子第一街

The Number One Chinese Electronics Street

Huaqiang North for the people of Shenzhen is like Wangfujing in Beijing, or Nanjing Road in Shanghai. This area is only 900 metres long, and has electronics shops packed in everywhere like the cells of a beehive. It's the largest-scale concentration of electronics products in Asia, with prices directly connecting with the international market. It has been called a "barometer" for prices in China, Southeast Asia, Europe and the Americas, and has produced enterprises such as Tencent and Skyworth.

Number One in Containers

With 19 product lines first in the world, 600 subsidiary companies, and a profit of 80 billion yuan, the China International Marine Containers Group, headed by Mai Boliang, first gained recognition from Yuan Geng 28 years ago. Mai was part of the first round of university students after the resumption of the National College Entrance Examination, and passed on a high-salaried job to work for 400 yuan a month at CIMC, with the dream of making it the number one containerized shipping company in the world. He said: "I fought for my dream. I wasn't afraid of difficulty or hardship or pain. There was no way I would back down."

Father of Chinese Theme Parks

Shenzhen has a phrase: "In ancient times, the First Emperor of Qin built the Great Wall. In modern times, Emperor Ma builds the Great Wall." This refers to the Splendid China amusement park built by Ma Zhimin. In the 1980s, Shenzhen Bay was barren and desolate. The State Council authorised the development of Huaqiaocheng, "Overseas Chinese Town", or OCT, in Shenzhen by the China National Travel Service (HK) Group Corporation. Ma started with the Dutch "Madurodam" to design the OCT. The theme park has all kinds of areas running now, and Ma is known as the "Father of Chinese Theme Parks".

集装箱世界第一

19条产品线世界第一，旗下600家企业，营收800亿，这是曾获袁庚赏识的麦伯良掌舵中集集团28年后的成绩单。他是恢复高考后的第一届大学生，放弃高薪到月入400元的中集集团时，就有了要让中集成为集装箱世界第一的梦想。他说："我就是为梦想而战，不畏艰难、不怕苦难、不怕折腾，绝不后退。"

中国主题公园之父

深圳有句话，"古有秦始皇修长城，今有马始皇修长城"，指的是主持修建了微缩景观"锦绣中华"的马志民。20世纪80年代的深圳湾很荒凉，国务院批准由香港中旅集团投资开发深圳华侨城，马志民从荷兰的"小人国"中受到启发，规划了华侨城景区。如今主题公园在各地盛行，马志民"中国主题公园之父"实至名归。

首家五星级酒店 040

南海酒店坐落在蛇口,是深圳首间由"中国政府评定的五星级酒店"和涉外酒店。一栋背山面海的巨帆式白色建筑,阶梯式阳台让每个房间都能充分享受海景与阳光。1986年开业后,最初只接待政要和名人,留下无数故事。时光荏苒,如今深圳五星酒店林立,南海历经30年的岁月后,洗尽铅华更显真。

First Five-Star Hotel

The Nanhai Hotel is in Shekou, and was Shenzhen's first hotel to be certified as five-star by the Chinese government, and the first for foreigners. A huge white structure shaped like a sail sits in front of a mountain, facing the sea. The terraced construction allows each room to have a full view of the sea and sky. After it opened in 1986, it received numerous officials and celebrities, and was involved in countless stories. Time flies by, and 30 years later the hotel still stands there, magnificent as ever.

Old Department Store, New Life

老牌百货的新生

1996年年初，在红岭路开业的岁宝百货共有10层，经营面积达1.8万平方米，经营品种达10多万种。成立伊始，打出"全心全意为人民"的口号，并开出了数辆免费接送顾客的岁宝购物车，引起了深圳社会的极大轰动。早期零售巨头的黄金时代已经过去，多家岁宝店将改为盒马鲜生超市，老牌百货将获新生。

连锁的魅力

1995年被称为深圳连锁经营元年。这一年，除了麦当劳、西武百货、佐丹奴等外，本地的华润、天虹、百姓、大快活、公惠、竹生、比三佳、南油百汇直销商场等连锁超市如雨后春笋般涌现，促销手段从有奖销售转向特价优惠，至今经久不衰。20多年过去，大浪淘沙，华润、天虹仍旧欣欣向荣。

Incognito OG

At the start of 1996, the 10-story Shirble Department Store opened on Hongling Road. With a total of 18,000 square metres, it stocked more than 100,000 kinds of products. At the beginning, it had the slogan "serve the people heart and soul", and had a few buses to pick up and drop off customers, which caused quite a sensation in Shenzhen. The golden age of the department store has passed, and a number of Shirble locations have changed to Freshhema-branded fresh food supermarkets—a new life for an old store.

One doesn't always have to be ostentatious. At the street-side restaurants in Shenzhen, one will frequently see a boss jump out of a Benz at night in pajamas to get some snacks. They have money and status, and live comfortable lives, but don't show up. This is "incognito OG" style. Still waters run deep—people here keep a low profile and diligently deal with work matters, making Shenzhen merchants the most open, and closest to the world.

Chain Attraction

1995 was the year of the reign of chain in Shenzhen. This year, aside from McDonald's, Seibu, and Giordano, local direct sellers and chain markets such as CR, Rainbow, Baixing, Fairwood, Gonghui, Zhusheng, Bisanjia, and Nanyou Baihui sprung up like bamboo shoots after spring rain. Sales methods shifted from prize-giving sales to discounts, a practice which continues today. Not everyone stands the test of time, but after more than two decades, CR and Rainbow are still thriving.

扮猪食老虎

大音希声，深商不深。深圳街头的大排档，常常会看到开着奔驰穿着大裤衩的大老板去消夜，他们有钱有地位，日子过得很滋润，但绝不张扬，更不扮深沉，是典型的"扮猪食老虎"作风。静水深流，低调务实，正是这种不事张扬的风格，才使得深商成为中国最开放、与国际接轨最好的群体。

抑郁的深渊 044

2015年10月23日，国信证券总裁陈鸿桥因抑郁症自缢身亡。他是寒门子弟，靠读书改变了命运，曾参与筹建创业板，走访了上千家民企，培训了上万名高管。资本圈是抑郁症重灾区，"涌金系"创始人魏东也曾在家人面前纵身跃下九楼阳台，留下了百亿资产和无解之谜。在资本面前，人们重新思索生命的价值。

做人至紧要开心 045

港产片里有一句出名的台词"做人至紧要开心"，是小张用来激励自己的"心灵鸡汤"。他20年前到深圳打工，有了积蓄后开始创业，创办了一家网站，以失败告终，把网站卖给了投资商后，受聘成为网站的运营人。深圳教会了小张活得开心最重要，他不想一辈子都为了赚钱忙碌，错失路上的风景。

Disaster Area for Depression

On October 23, 2015, Guosen Securities President Chen Hongqiao hanged himself out of depression. He was the child of a poor family, but changed his fate through hard study, becoming wealthy entrepreneur, training more than ten thousand high-level managers. The field of finance is a disaster area for depression; founder of the Yongjin group of companies Wei Dong jumped to his death in front of his family off a 9-storey balcony, leaving behind 10 billion in assets, and an unsolvable mystery. In the face of a large amount of money, people rethink the value of life.

One Must Be Happy

There is a popular line in many Hong Kong films: "In order to be a good person, you must be happy." Mr. Zhang thinks about this to comfort himself. He came to Shenzhen 20 years previous to work, and after a period of time started his own venture, creating a website. As it was failing, he sold it to an investor and was hired to operate it. Shenzhen taught him that being happy was important—he didn't want to spend his whole life busying himself with earning money, missing the scenery on the way.

Culture and Life

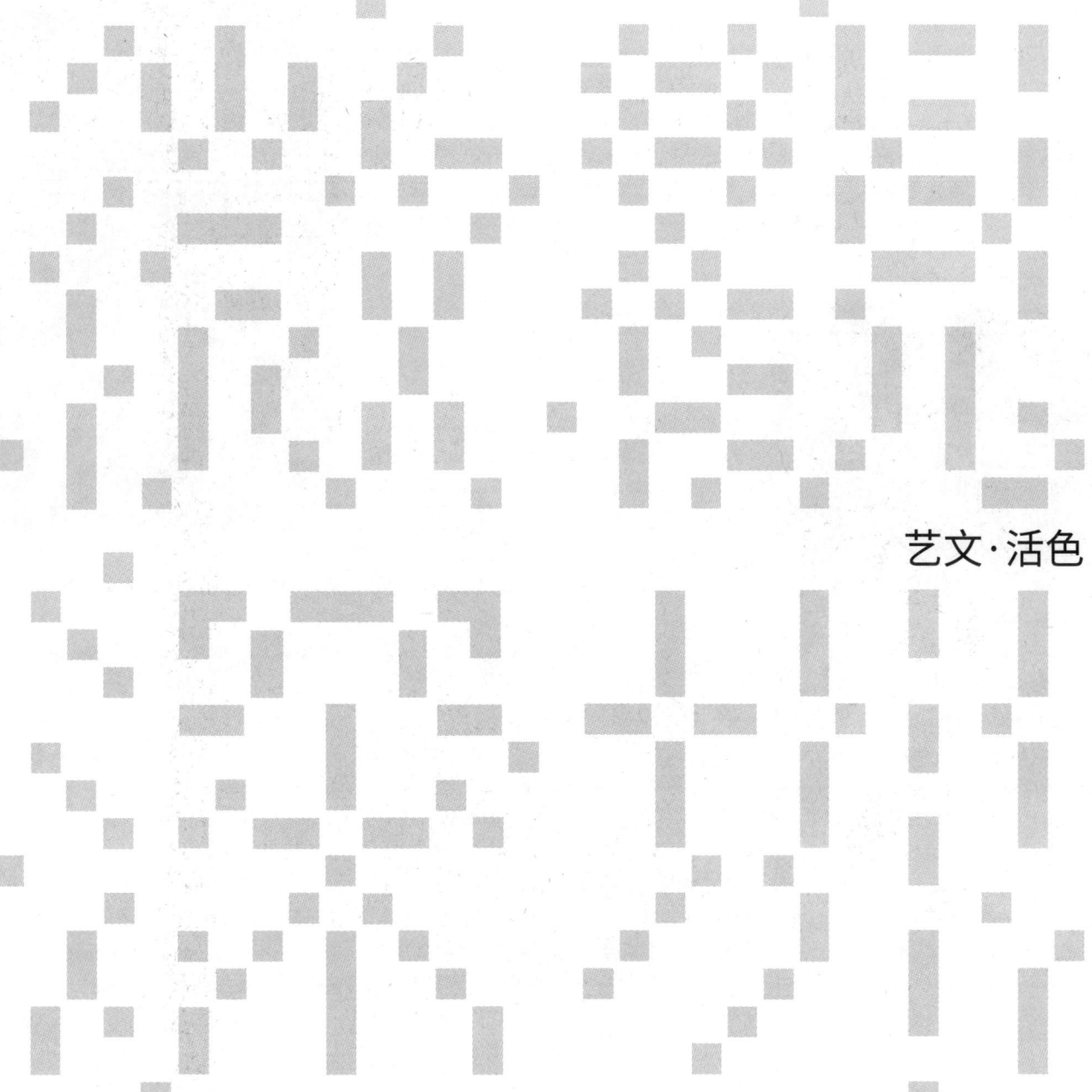

艺文·活色

咸水歌 001

咸水歌又叫疍家渔歌，流传在海上渔民间，带着一点儿甜甜的海腥味儿。一首《海底珍珠》是疍家仔的"撩妹"之作："海底珍又珠容易稳，姑有妹，今日拿鱼无到就无么精神。么花开花红花绿衬，兄又哥，我哥拿鱼无到就上街聊下悠闲。"世间情不分海陆，水上的爱情也能荡漾出火辣辣的激情。

Saltwater Song

The "Saltwater Song" is also known as the song of the Dan, a tribe of Cantonese who speak a distinct dialect. It's a tradition among those who live on the water here, and carries the flavour of the sea. One such song, *Pearls of the Deep Sea*, in the tone of teasing girls by a deep-water pearl diver, describes a life in one of these traditional villages. "Life is good when the catch is good, the flowers bloom red and the trees grow green. Worries are few, and the pace is slow." Land and sea are equally comfortable, and passions burn hot.

万丰粤剧 003

万丰粤剧是宝安沙井街道万丰村潘氏一脉兴起与传承的，自最初对粤曲的喜好，之后发展成为粤剧的一个根据地，迄今近600年历史。潘耀扬为清代重臣，晚年致仕归里，在万家朗村"将军第"之侧，修建了一幢"八音楼"，四时召戏班演戏，为万家朗构筑了浓郁的粤曲氛围，渐而养成了万丰人对粤曲之雅好。

Story of Spring

"There's an old man who drew a circle near the South China Sea, and an old man who wrote a poem there…" Jiang Kairu wrote *Story of Spring* in Shenzhen. "The spring wind blows over China, and the spring rain moistens the old courtyards." This beautiful song swept all of China, and the "old man" described became a statue at Lianhua Hill, which now casts its guarding gaze over Shenzhen.

春天的故事 002

"有一位老人在中国的南海边画了一个圈，有一位老人在中国的南海边写下诗篇……"随着这个圈的画下，初到深圳的蒋开儒写下了《春天的故事》。"春风啊吹绿了东方神州，春雨啊滋润了华夏故园"，美妙的歌曲风靡了大江南北，而那位画圈的老人，则化作一座雕塑站在莲花山上，守护着深圳的春天。

Wanfeng Cantonese Opera

Wanfeng, part of Bao'an District's Shajing Sub-district, continues the tradition of Wanfeng Cantonese Opera. Here, from a place where Cantonese opera was enjoyed, to an origin of a specific form, Wanfeng's tradition has about six hundred years of history. Pan Yaoyang was an important minister in the Qing Dynasty, who in his later years retired from his position and returned home, where he built the Bayinlou, or "building of eight sounds", where operas were performed year-round, making opera a big part of the local culture. These performances would gradually evolve into what is now Wanfeng Opera.

ICIF

There are many cultural affairs going on in Shenzhen; the International Cultural Industry Fair, which started in 2004, is one of them. Traditional Chinese culture is one of introversion, and low-key refinement. Western culture is one of high-profile displays. The ICIF takes place in May of every year, where the two cultures meet and interact. It attracts a huge number of participants and observers. It's an institution that makes the city more confident, and more exciting.

文博会盛宴

深圳文化盛事多，创办于2004年的深圳文博会是其中之一。中国的传统文化讲究低调内敛，酒香不怕巷子深；而西方文化向来高调张扬，生怕别人不知道。如此，在每年5月的文博会上，中西文化的交流与碰撞总能收获一些意想不到的惊喜，吸引无数人参与和参观。这座城市因而更加从容自信、光彩照人。

文化 +

一夜之间，深圳文创产业如春笋般开始蓬勃起来。各类"文化+"就像正在烹饪的大盆菜，"文化+科技""文化+旅游""文化+创意""文化+金融"等新食材，无论你加了什么调料进去，万变不离其宗，都带着自己独特的味道。"文化+"这只新生的大鹏，正充满生机地在鹏城上空翱翔。

Culture +

Overnight, all kinds of cultural industry activities have sprung up like bamboo shoots in spring. All kinds of "Culture +" activities are about, such as "Culture + Science", "Culture + Travel", "Culture + Innovation", and "Culture + Finance". No matter what condiments you add to a dish, it still retains its original identity. These "Culture +" activities are like a newly hatched roc flying over the city, full of life.

中国油画第一村

大芬村位于布吉街道,是个方圆仅0.4平方千米的岭南小村,经过20多年蝶变升华,现已成全球最大的油画生产和出口基地,创造了占领世界油画市场60%份额的奇迹。最初由香港画商来此租用民房从事油画生产、销售,随着日益增多的画家进驻大芬村,"中国油画第一村"成了国内外知名的文化品牌。

Oil Painting Village

Dafen Village is situated in the Buji Sub-district. It has an area of only 0.4 square kilometres. Over the course of more than two decades, it has grown and transformed, and now is the world's largest producer and exporter of oil paintings, accounting for 60% of the total world market. It was originally rented by art dealers from Hong Kong to produce and sell oil paintings. As time went by more and more painters moved to Dafen, making "China's number one oil painting village" famous throughout the country as well as abroad.

观澜街道大水田村是个雅致的客家小村，20世纪20年代，从村里走出一个青年陈烟桥，他手拿画笔和刻刀，成为中国新兴版画的领军人物，当年深受鲁迅先生教诲、器重。因着他的原因，这里成为全国版画创作基地。来自世界各地的版画家，在客家排屋里奏刀有神，一批批版画杰作飞向世界。

奏刀有神的客家排屋

Skill with a Knife

Guanlan Sub-district's Dashuitian Village is a beautiful Hakka town. In the 1920s, a young Chen Yanqiao set out with a brush and carving knife in his hand, and became one of the leaders in the realm of new Chinese woodcuts. He was taught and appreciated by Lu Xun. Because of him, this place became a centre for woodcuts. Carvers and painters from all over came here, living in this Hakka settlement and producing amazing works that travelled throughout the world.

九天十八井，十阁走马廊

鹤湖新居即深圳客家民俗博物馆，始建于清乾隆年间，占地约2.48万平方米，是全国占地面积最大的客家民居建筑之一，有"九天十八井，十阁走马廊"之称。围墙高大坚固，月池整洁明净，古树苍劲雍容，人们置身其中，蓦然间仿佛穿越时空，重回历史，浸润在宁静而神秘的意境中。

The Hakka Settlement

The Hehu Xinju ("Crane Lake New Residence") is a museum of Hakka culture in Shenzhen. It was built during the reign of the Qianlong Emperor in the Qing Dynasty, and has a footprint of 24,800 square metres. It is one of the largest Hakka residences in existence. The outerwall is tall and solid, central court is clean and bright, with old trees standing mightily. Standing inside, one feels as if one has travelled through time to re-experience history, soaking in the quiet and mysterious atmosphere.

Guan Shanyue Art Museum

The Guan Shanyue Art Museum is situated at the foot of the beautiful Lianhua Hill; it's a comprehensive national-level museum. With the mountain at its back, it's shaped like a crescent moon, evoking imagery of Guan's given name, which means "mountain and moon". It is the museum with the largest and most complete collection of Guan's works, which were donated by this artist of the Lingnan painting school before his death. The museum also planned and acquired a series exhibition of numerous famous Chinese artists of the 20th century, and is now a shared art space for the citizens of the city.

半圆如月

关山月美术馆坐落在美丽的莲花山下，是一座综合性国家级美术馆。它的背面靠山，馆身半圆如月，隐喻关山月先生的名字。它收藏关山月先生的作品为海内外最多、最全，均为这位岭南画派大师生前捐赠。美术馆还策划、引进了20世纪中国美术大师和名家系列展览，如今已成为市民共享的艺术空间。

Shiqu Baoji

In November 2012, the "*Shiqu Baoji*, Unrivalled Elegance—Liaoning Provincial Museum Collection of Ancient Chinese Calligraphy and Paintings" exhibition opened at the Shenzhen Museum. *Shiqu Baoji* ("stone canal and box for books") represents a very important collection of Chinese paintings and calligraphy, comprising very important works from the imperial household collection at the height of the Qing Dynasty. The exhibits were national-treasure level items, including calligraphy works from Zhang Xu and Huai Su. Zhang's *Four Ancient Poems* is a beautiful and harmonious work; the brushwork is unforgettable.

《石渠宝笈》

2012年11月，深圳博物馆"石渠宝笈 旷代风华——辽宁省博物馆藏中国古代书画名品展"隆重开展。《石渠宝笈》作为我国书画著录史上的集大成者，汇集了清皇室收藏最鼎盛时期的所有作品。展品是国宝级的藏品，开展之处是张旭、怀素的草书。张旭大草《古诗四帖》，浑然一体，其中五色笺令人难忘。

梦想奏鸣曲

到过深圳音乐厅的人们都知道，它的外墙有"黄红青白黑"五种颜色，暗含中国传统"五行"的理念，内里的金树大厅和对面深圳图书馆的银树大厅遥遥相望，架起一座艺术的桥梁。每逢周末，音乐厅内高雅的交响乐演出和一墙之隔的音乐广场上热闹的通俗演唱会和谐呼应，响彻梦想的奏鸣曲。

Dream Sonata

Everyone who goes to the Shenzhen Concert Hall knows that its outer walls have penta colour: "yellow, red, blue, white, black" which symbolises the "five elements" of classical Chinese culture. The Golden Tree Hall within offsets the Silver Tree Hall of the Shenzhen Library across the street, forming an artistic bridge. Every weekend, the orchestra puts on an amazing performance that's separated only by a single wall from the music square's popular music; it's a resounding dream sonata.

何香凝美术馆

华侨城，深南路边上的浓荫丛中，一座简洁的天桥将参观者引入美术馆的天井中庭。何香凝美术馆是中国第一个以个人名字命名的国家级美术馆，也是继中国美术馆之后的第二个国家现代博物馆。馆内天棚透明，参观者可以在蓝天碧云下，漫步观赏何香凝的书画，间或能够欣赏其他美术展览和精品典藏。

He Xiangning Art Museum

In Overseas Chinese Town, amidst the lush foliage at the side of Shennan Road, a clean and simple overpass carries visitors to the open-air central atrium of the museum. The He Xiangning Art Museum is the first national-level museum named after a person, and is the second museum of modern art in China. The ceiling is transparent so that visitors can appreciate the beautiful blue sky as they walk around appreciating her artworks, as well as the beautiful works of other artists also collected there.

相"儒"以"墨"

"相儒以墨"艺术空间是南山的文化地标,这里有紫砂茶具沏出天地乾坤大,这里也有丹青笔墨染来岁月流金长。媒体人暖暖瞳打造了它,她说:"这是文人雅集之处,也是艺术交流中心,更是你我的会客厅。"她梦想着几时归去,可做个闲人,对一张琴、一壶茶、一溪云……

Mutual "Ink"ssistance

There is an artistic space named "Xiang Ru Yi Mo" in Nanshan District which is full of boccaro tea vessels and beautiful calligraphic works. It was created by the media personality "Nuannuantong". She says: "This is a place where the literati can gather, as well as a centre for artistic interchange. Even more so, it's a meeting place." She dreams of a return to simple life: a Chinese guqin, a teapot, some clouds in the sky…

凤栖梧桐山

深圳河的发祥地在梧桐山,此山跨越三区,与香港隔河相看。或许因为它是"九龙戏珠"的风水宝地,又或许是由于山中有九棵古树组成的情人林的传说,招来各路艺术家入驻,如凤栖梧桐,使得山里往来无白丁,在热闹与清幽之间转换,也让"艺术小镇"渐增浓浓的文化氛围,诱人前往一探。

Source

The source of the Shenzhen River is at Mount Wutong. The mountain crosses through three districts, and looks out across Hong Kong. This is the site of legends, which attracts many artists to live here, just as the phoenix rests in the tree. Nobody here is illiterate. In contrast with the noisy city, this is a place of quiet and beauty steeped in culture. It's worth having a visit.

火神的画

"人似秋鸿来有信,事如春梦了无痕。"深圳艺术家樊鸿宾的青花瓷作品《春梦》以人民币 700 万元拍卖成交。他创作的每一件陶瓷作品都诉说着一段动人的故事,色彩的对比和展示的故事总能带给观众强烈的震撼。美的东西总是逃不掉追随的目光,他的瓷板画被赋予文艺的内涵,被称作"火神的画"。

Paintings of the God of Fire

"People are like swans; they leave traces of their passing wherever they go. Affairs, however, are like spring dreams—they leave no trace at all." This is a phrase from Su Shi, a Northern Song poet. Shenzhen artist Fan Hongbin ("hong" means "swan") produced a porcelain panel painting that sold over 7 million yuan. Every one of his porcelain works tells a moving story; the contrast of the colours and the story displayed always give the viewer a strong feeling. Beautiful things always attract the gaze; these porcelain paintings are imbued with intense artistic intension, and have been called the "paintings of the god of fire".

Girl and Wife

Mr. Chen, who lives at Baishizhou, stands upon his veranda, and looks out at the Window of the World. He's observed the site for many years; the oldest cultural theme park in China to him looks like a graceful and slender young girl in the daytime. It has different beauties when viewed from different angles. At night it looks like a young married woman full of emotion; characteristics of various ethnicities adding to her attractiveness. Brilliant fireworks and the scents of the beer garden intoxicate the observer.

少女和少妇

住在白石洲的陈先生，站在阳台，能看到世界之窗的大半景点。经过多年近距离的观察，在陈先生眼里，这个国内最早的文化主题公园，白天是个婀娜多姿的少女，不同的角度有不同的美好；晚上是位风情万种的少妇，各国民族的风俗让她增加了无限的吸引力。璀璨的烟花，啤酒广场的酒香，都令人陶醉。

素人画家

素人画家这个称谓源自法国，指没受过正统艺术训练，凭感觉和直觉作画的人。何氏姐妹分别为诗人、电影人，她们是孪生姐妹，但画风迥异。"起哄或者望呆——素人画家何鸣何云双人展"，让很多观众留意她们的不同。绘画令她们在丙烯的颜料中殊途同归、完美融合，她们眼里的世界、心中的世界谜团重重。

Sunday Painter

The concept of a "Sunday Painter" originated in France. It's a term that refers to someone without formal artistic training who relies on their feelings and perceptions to create works. There are two He sisters, a filmmaker and a poet; they are twins, but have widely different styles. The exhibition "Kick up a fuss or hope to stay—Sunday Painters He Ming and He Yun" shows observers just how different they are. Painting allows them to reach the same destination via different routes, achieving a perfect melding. The world in their eyes and hearts is full of mystery.

杨梅红了

教育在深圳人眼里有多重要？因女儿找不到一处满意的学画场所，来自西安的杨红梅夫妇两人遂创办杨梅红艺术教育机构，除了教女，亦可育人。美院毕业的杨红梅出版了多本画作，她的文字纯真剔透："能不能骑着木马浪迹天涯？能不能用一个开关控制情感？能不能用一滴眼泪将你融化？"

Ymm Art Education Group

How important is education in the eyes of the people of Shenzhen? Because their daughter couldn't find a painting school that satisfied them, Yang Hongmei and her husband, a couple from Xi'an, came to establish the Ymm Art Education Group; aside from their own daughter, they could also teach others. Yang, a graduate of the Academy of Fine Arts, has published a number of painting books. Her prose is pure and incisive: "How far can you get riding a rocking horse? Can you use a switch to control your feelings? Can a tear melt you?"

以心治印的民间艺人 019

深圳人多才，从事技术工作的帅飞，在枯燥的工作之余，迷上了篆刻。其作品曾入展深圳书法篆刻年度展，现鬻印自给。自2000年年初，帅飞的作品开始崭露头角，许多佳作被国内知名艺术、民俗博物馆等广为收藏，不急不躁、禅风独具的"帅飞禅印"为深圳人所喜爱。

Shuai Fei Zen Seals

The people of Shenzhen are multitalented. Machinist Shuai Fei, in the off time from his boring job, became obsessed with making seals. His works were exhibited at the annual Shenzhen Exhibition of Calligraphy and Seal Cutting. Starting in 2000, Shuai's seals came onto the scene, with numerous excellent works being collected by famous art and culture museums in China. They have a cool, Zen kind of flair, and "Shuai Fei Zen Seals" have become quite popular in Shenzhen.

缺钱、缺人、缺设备 020

《深圳特区报》1982年5月24日创刊，从决定办报到试刊，深圳首份报纸在缺钱、缺人、缺设备等不具备办报条件的环境中诞生。报纸诸多创举：内地首张竖排繁体字报，首张彩色胶印报，深圳办报、香港印刷。报纸印出后，编辑、记者还兼任发行员，将报纸送到读者手中。

Money, People, Equipment 020

The *Shenzhen Special Zone Daily* was first published on May 24, 1982. During its test run, it came into being in an environment where it lacked money, lacked people, and lacked equipment. It was the first newspaper in the mainland of China with a vertical typesetting in traditional characters, and the first full-colour offset-printed paper. It was produced in Shenzhen and printed in Hong Kong. After it was printed, the editors and reporters delivered it themselves.

第一份合资日报 021

中国第一份合资日报《深港经济时报》，因刊号问题半途而废，遂更名《深星时报》卷土重来。《深星时报》由《深圳特区报》和《星岛日报》联合创办，星岛新闻集团胡仙投资，合资办报的激情，就荡漾在当年深圳八卦岭的办公楼里。现与《香港商报》整合，多年荣膺"香港最受欢迎十大中文报章"。

First Joint-Invested Newspaper

China's first newspaper that operated as a joint venture was the *Shenzhen Hong Kong Economic Times*. Due to problems with its publication number, it folded, and gradually reappeared as the *Shenxing Times*. The *Shenxing Times* was jointly published by the *Shenzhen Special Zone Daily* and *Sing Tao Daily*, funded by Sally Aw of the Sing Tao News Corporation Limited. The paper was popular, and rocked offices in Bagualing when it came out. It's now been merged with the *Hong Kong Commercial Daily* and has held a spot in the "top 10 Chinse-language publications in Hong Kong" for years running.

《深圳青年》一纸风行

一本蓬勃的杂志，一代青年的回忆。《深圳青年》1988年在特区诞生，在风中亮出自己的旗。很多年轻人读完杂志，把杂志塞进包裹就来了特区。创刊社长王京生，后来成为深圳文化的掌舵人，再后来成为国务院参事。"这里的握手更有力，这里的微笑更持久"，一度成为陌生青年的接头暗号。

SZYOUTH

A copy of this bright magazine brings back memories of youth. *SZYOUTH* was established in the Shenzhen SEZ in 1988, and its flag flew high and bright in the winds of the city. Young people in many places headed out for Shenzhen after reading a copy of the magazine. Founder of the magazine Wang Jingsheng later came to be the helmsman of cultural industry in Shenzhen, and went on to work for the State Council. "Handshakes are stronger and smiles last longer here" went on to become a contact signal for young strangers on the streets of Shenzhen.

Manuscripts Prices in 1993

In 1993, prices paid for manuscripts in Shenzhen became a big topic. An activity from the *SZYOUTH* kicked off the auction market for manuscripts in China, a new step in China's opening up and reform. The activity had a series of impacts for intellectual property in China, and left a mark on the history of Chinese cultural development and intellectual property.

1993 文稿竞价

1993年深圳文稿竞价成为年度重要新闻，此次由《深圳青年》杂志策划主办的活动，开启了中国文稿拍卖第一槌，"给文人造个海"震动全国，被称为"中国改革开放中的又一创举"。这次活动给中国知识产权领域带来一系列深刻的影响，在中国文化发展史以及知识产权史上，都留下历史印记。

杂志"黄埔军校" Whampoa Military Academy of Magazines

《影视双周刊》是20世纪90年代媒体圈的一道风景，是中国境内最早的全铜版纸、全彩印刷刊物。娱乐刚刚进入中国境内，它即与港台杂志接轨，被评为"中国最有影响力百强期刊"。杂志虽为官办，但内容颇"接地气"。杂志曾网罗深圳办刊精英，停办后，人员被各家挖走，因此被戏称为杂志"黄埔军校"。

Entertainment (Biweekly) was a big thing in the media circles in the 1990s; it was the first magazine to be printed in full copperplate, in full colour, in the mainland of China. The entertainment industry had just entered the mainland of China, and this magazine provided a direct link to Hong Kong and Taiwan magazines. It was praised as one of the 100 most influential magazines in China. It was a government publication, yet had a very "down to earth" feel. The magazine poached a number of very talented individuals from the publishing industry in Shenzhen. After it ceased publication, everyone was subsequently swept up by other powerful parties; for this reason it has been called the "Whampoa Military Academy of magazines".

与众不同的内刊

万科有很多传说，关于王石，关于半山或海滨那些漂亮的房子，《万科周刊》作为最具人文情怀的企业内刊，忠实地用文字和图片记录了那些传说。这本杂志影响力不局限于万科，王石早年为周刊亲自撰稿，对历任主编悉心栽培，使之成为财经企业界最佳读物之一。

A Special Publication

Vanke has many legends about Wang Shi, about the houses on the mid-levels or those abutting the seas. The *Vanke Weekly* is an example of a great internal publication, which faithfully uses images and text to record these legends; it has great influence. Wang Shi himself has written articles for the weekly publications, and has carefully cultivated former chief editors to make it one of the best financial enterprise publications in China.

Middle Bourgeoisie Magazine

In 1995, the only publication that was targeted towards the middle bourgeoisie was *Caiyuan* ("source of wealth"); this was a weekly publication released under *Shenzhen's Investment Advice*, invested in by Switzerland's AG Ringier. The slogan was a bit over the top: "Those who read *Caiyuan* are a cut above the rest." It was laid out horizontally, with a large amount of pictures, and had a hard-hitting reporting style; it was exciting reading for those in the realms that it covered.

You Can't Change Me

Liu Xihong's name is one that can't be ignored when recounting the history of literature in Shenzhen. She is the first writer to win a national literary award from Shenzhen; she published the novel *You Can't Change Me* when she was 25 years old and gained national fame instantly. Then, she suddenly married, moved to France, and dropped out of the scene. She said: "Writing is a personal need; when this need fades, you exit the scene and return to a simpler life. Why would I betray my own wishes?"

中产阶级的《财源》

1995年，放眼全国，公开宣称为中产阶级服务的刊物只有《财源》。这是一份挂在深圳《投资导报》名下的周刊，由瑞士荣格集团投资。其广告语十分张扬："看《财源》人物，自然高人一等。"横排版式、大至半版的图片、穷追猛打的报道手法，令人耳目一新，给业界带来了新的激情。

你不可改变我

在深圳文学的发展史中，刘西鸿是一个不可忽略的名字。她是最早获得全国文学大奖的深圳作家，25岁时发表了小说《你不可改变我》，一夜成名。惊鸿一瞥后，她远嫁法国，作家生涯就此中断。她说："写作是自我需要，当这种需要淡了，退居到更世俗的需要后面，又为什么要违背自己的意愿？"

Oscars of the Capital Market

The "New Fortune Best Analyst Awards" conducted by Shenzhen's *New Fortune* magazine first in 2001 have been called the "Oscars of the Capital Market". This is China's first civilian ranking of financial analysts; the worth of analysts ranked within instantly multiplies. Every year before the rankings people canvass for votes. Once writing poems for voters was quite popular among analysts, just like "I work hard in the stock market, reading surveys, canvassing, currying favour, and writing reports. I stay up past midnight, publish weeklies, and read others' reports".

资本市场奥斯卡

2001年创刊于深圳的《新财富》，其主办的"新财富最佳分析师评选"，堪称资本市场奥斯卡。这是中国第一份专业的民间市场化分析师排名，上榜分析师身价倍增，每年评选都拜票奇招迭出，一度流行写诗拉票："股海辛劳又一年，频调研，勤路演，四月推酒，报告短信繁。纵使三更仍未眠，出周刊，紧翻研。"

《街道》的传说

《街道》主办者是粤海街道办事处，名副其实。一份民政服务月刊，却风格犀利，成为当年中国文化先锋和人文趣味的旗帜，聚集了叶兆言、何立伟、韩少功等一批文化精英。出刊54期后，黯然退场，成为风中的传说。

Legend of the *Street*

The sponsor of *Street* is the Yuehai Sub-district Office, deserving its name. This is a monthly civil government publication, but its style is sharp. It became a forerunner for Chinese literary culture, gathering the likes of Ye Zhaoyan, He Liwei, Han Shaogong, and others. It was published for 54 issues and then suddenly stopped, becoming a legend in the wind.

从《街道》走出来的摄影师

当肖全把他为三毛拍摄的肖像送给三毛时，三毛说："肖全，这不是完整，而是完美。"肖全的镜头捕捉过顾城、张艺谋、崔健、杨丽萍等最独特的样子，拍下了《我们这一代》。他是从深圳《街道》杂志走出来的摄影师，他一直在用镜头和世界对话，被称为"中国最好的人像摄影师"。

The Best Portrait Photographer

When Xiao Quan gave the portrait he took of San Mao to her, San Mao remarked that it was "not only complete, but also perfect". Xiao Quan's lens has captured the likes of Gu Cheng, Zhang Yimou, Cui Jiang, and Yang Liping. He shot *Our Generation*, a series of portraits of contemporary cultural figures. He once served as a photographer in *Street* magazine. He uses his lens to conduct a dialogue with the world, and is renowned as the best portrait photographer in China.

"钢琴王子"李云迪 031

2000年，18岁的李云迪获得第14届肖邦国际钢琴比赛冠军，是中国钢琴家在这一享有崇高国际声誉的顶级赛事中获得的最佳成绩。《纽约时报》评："李将优雅与喧闹、冷静与炽热融合于一体，展现出不寻常的天赋光芒。"李云迪师从深圳艺术学校但昭义教授，但教授门下众多弟子在国际钢琴赛事中获奖，堪称钢琴教育史上的奇迹。

"唯有肖邦" 032

2010年是肖邦200周年诞辰，4月，傅聪的"唯有肖邦"钢琴独奏会在深圳音乐厅奏响。作为《傅雷家书》的主人公，其父子之间的感情跨越时空，感人肺腑，温暖人心。傅聪的独奏，从头到尾一言不发，认认真真，一首一首慢慢地倾诉。演出最后，老人家给观众深深一躬，赢得了长时间掌声。

Prince of Piano

In 2000, 18-year old Li Yundi became the champion of the International Chopin Piano Competition. This was the first time that a Chinese took first prize at this prestigious international competition. *The New York Times* critiqued him thus: "Li combines elegance and noise, calm and heat into one body. He exhibits amazing talent." Li studied under professor Dan Zhaoyi at the Shenzhen Arts School. Many of professor Dan's students have won prizes at international piano competitions, a miracle in the history of piano education.

Only Chopin

2010 marked the 200th anniversary of F. F. Chopin, and in April of that year Fou Ts'ong's "Only Chopin" concert took place at the Shenzhen Concert Hall. With *The Fu Lei's Family Letters* as the protagonist, the feelings between father and son crossed space and time, making one feel warmed from the bottom of the heart. Fou didn't speak a single word during his solo performance, playing diligently as the notes of each piece poured forth. At the end he bowed deeply to the audience, and received a long round of applause.

娱乐发祥地

改革开放催生娱乐业,发祥地在深圳。毗邻港澳自然得风气之先,第一家歌舞厅、夜总会、卡拉OK厅都从兹登陆。内地第一代歌星大都在深圳歌舞厅跑过夜场,崔健、杨钰莹、毛宁、陈明均为台柱。曾经有人担心歌舞厅败坏风气,却意外发现歌舞厅竟风行民歌、民族舞,歌舞厅遂得以保留。

Origin of Entertainment Industry

The period of opening up and reform kick-started the entertainment industry in China, with the point of origin being Shenzhen, which is only natural as it bordered Hong Kong and Macao. The first song and dance hall, night club, and karaoke were all here. The earliest big pop stars all came here to perform: Cui Jian, Yang Yuying, Mao Ning, Chen Ming... Previously people worried that song and dance halls would corrupt the culture, but they were surprised to find that in these venues people were singing folk songs, and dancing folk dances, thus the decision was made to let them remain.

"金鹏"短片节

中国国际新媒体短片节是目前中国唯一国家级、国际性短片节,创办于2010年,与北京电影节和上海电影节并列为中国三大国际性影视文化节庆活动,世界各地的电影人会带着作品来这里竞逐"金鹏奖"。深圳虽然年轻,但她的容貌在世界各地电影人的心中,一帧帧地清晰起来。

A Site for Success

In the early 1990s, when media investment wasn't especially hot, Wang Shi managed to make a real successful move with his establishment of the Vanke Film and Television Company. Wang had an excellent eye for talent and hired Zheng Kainan to lead the company. Zheng graduated from the Central Academy of Drama and had previously acted in the stage play *The Second Handshake*. He served as the producer for the television drama *How the Steel Was Tempered* in 1999, which was extremely popular.

Short Films

The China International New Media Short Film Festival (CSFF) is China's only national-level international short film festival, and along with the Beijing and Shanghai film festivals is one of the top three film events in China. Filmmakers from all over the world bring their works here to compete for the "KingBonn Award" ("Golden Roc Award"). Although Shenzhen is a young city, her figure is clear in the minds of filmmakers around the world.

好吃"螃蟹"的深圳人

深圳人好吃"螃蟹",尤以万科为甚。在20世纪90年代初,影视投资尚属冷门的时候,王石率先吃了一只"影视螃蟹",成立了万科影视公司。王石用人独具慧眼,任用郑凯南担纲万科影视掌门人。郑凯南毕业于中戏,曾出演过话剧《第二次握手》,担任1999年播出的电视剧《钢铁是怎样炼成的》制片人,该剧在央视曾热播一时。

Image of Friday

The Huaxia Star Light International Cineplex has conducted a free art film screening every Friday afternoon since 2011, which has been looked favourably upon by art film enthusiasts. At the same time it also conducts all kinds of master lectures, film fora, film critic salons and other activities. There are three major moments in life: being moved, struggling, and release. Film addicts live for these images that document them all. In Shenzhen, their catchphrase is "see you at the cinema on Friday".

Opera Gathering on Saturday

Who says opera is slow and boring? If you come to the "Opera Gathering on Saturday", you'll find opera is quite interesting. This activity was started in 2009, at which time the "Three Highs" were promulgated: high quality, high standard, high level. Famous performers such as Pei Yanling and Mei Baojiu have been guests of honour here. As the days grow shorter, the night lures people. The opera takes place on Saturday, and the fans shows up decked out as whatever they want to be.

光影星期五

华夏星光国际影城自 2011 年以来，每周五下午都会免费放映一场艺术电影，受到众多艺术电影爱好者的青睐。同时还要举办各类大师讲座、电影论坛、影评人沙龙等。世间的蚀骨热情据说只有三秒。一秒动心，一秒挣扎，一秒释怀。看电影的人为之沉溺，光影记录这一切。影迷的口头禅：周五约起，不见不散。

戏聚星期六

谁说戏曲慢，谁说戏曲闷？来到"戏聚星期六"就知道，戏曲非常有趣。"戏聚星期六"创办于 2009 年，创办之初就立下"三高"原则：高品质、高规格、高水准。著名表演艺术家裴艳玲、梅葆玖等都成了"戏聚星期六"的座上宾。白日渐短，夜色撩人。星期六看一台戏，让戏迷锦衣夜行，变成想成为的样子。

剧汇星期天 038

话剧已是深圳生活的一种充氧型呼吸。所以"剧汇星期天"自2011年9月在深圳植根后,每年从4月到12月,都会以"讲好创意、演好戏剧、展好作品、学好表演"的活动模式,在深圳各区进行全方位戏剧普及。声光现场,在熟悉中不舍,唤醒吗,便更亲昵。深圳人的约会方式之一:今天看话剧吗?

金龙玉凤歌舞厅 039

霓虹灯下,美女如云。金龙玉凤歌舞厅坐落于商业中心的凤凰路,港台商人来深吃饭唱歌的首选,一度火爆到限制进入,现在却颓败出一种缓慢的钝痛。在现代摇滚歌舞的冲击下,这个南粤文艺气息甚重的歌舞厅,辉煌不再,原址也已拆除,只剩骨架。时代狂潮,浪奔浪流,在谁的心中起伏够?

Drama Gathering on Sunday

Stage plays are like the oxygen that the people of Shenzhen breathe. "Drama Gathering on Sunday" began in Shenzhen in September 2011, and runs each year from April to December. Emphasis is on innovation, good plays, good production and study of good performance. The plays take place all over Shenzhen. It's always a great time, with sound, light, and intimate feelings exciting audiences. A common way to set up a date in Shenzhen is to ask another to a play.

Golden Dragon, Jade Phoenix

Just look at all the beautiful ladies under those neon lights! The Golden Dragon Jade Phoenix Song and Dance Hall was situated on Fenghuang Road, in the commercial centre of Shenzhen. It used to be the top spot for businesspeople from Hong Kong and Taiwan to eat and enjoy music. It was so popular that they had to cap admittance; now its barren shell is filled with a kind of dull pain. With rock and roll all the rage now, the southern Cantonese sounds have fled, the glory is gone, the site demolished, leaving only a skeleton. Times and trends come and go—it's quite a ride.

"滚石 30" 040

2011 年 12 月 18 日，"春茧"迎来了"滚石 30"深圳演唱会。在 6 个小时里，40 多位重量级歌手轮番登台，伍佰、任贤齐、齐豫、潘越云、周华健等悉数放声，演唱了一首首脍炙人口的经典歌曲，现场 3 万名观众在沸腾中度过狂欢之夜，一同向青春告别。入夜时分，观众不愿散去，激情仍回荡在体育场上空。

Rock Records 30th Anniversary Concert 040

On December 18, 2011, the Shenzhen Bay Sports Centre welcomed the "Rock Records 30th Anniversary Shenzhen Concert". In the space of six hours, more than 40 superstar musicians took the stage, including Wu Bai, Richie Ren, Chyi Yu, Michelle Pan, and Emil Chau. The performances of these classic songs lit the audience on fire, with 30,000 people enjoying an amazing night. Nobody wanted to leave when the concert came to the end, with passion still permeating the atmosphere.

Clouds of the Old Village 041

In 2010, Christian Rand Phillips' "Ensemble Nostalgic Golden Melody National Concert Tour" came alive at the Poly Theatre. In an immigration city, the song *Clouds of the Old Village* really moved the people. Phillips sang the song as the finale of the concert. One could tell that he really had strong feelings when singing this final song; he wasn't just singing, but also recounting. Most of the people in Shenzhen left behind other hometowns to come here, so this narrative of a traveller missing home really resonated with them.

故乡的云 041

2010 年费翔"群星怀旧金曲全国巡回演唱会"在保利剧院举行。移民城市里，《故乡的云》最易打动人心。费翔唱这首歌时已近演唱会的尾声。看得出，费翔颇有伤感的意味，与其说是在歌唱，不如说更是在诉说。深圳绝大多数人都是背井离乡的游子，听他诉说的游子思乡之情，更有共鸣。

Youth Can't Even Handle Me Right Now 042

Memories of youth in the 1970s have Jonathan Lee's songs as the soundtrack. On May 10th, 2014 the 56-year-old musician held a concert in Shenzhen. Even the most gushing of praise isn't too much to describe Lee's talent. He was born for music, and as an old man has strong feelings and loves commotion. His talent has transformed into wisdom, and his former years have become the stuff of legends—he's an excellent model for all of us.

青春留不住的李宗盛 042

70 后的青春记忆，可以说是伴着李宗盛的歌曲一起成长的。2014 年 5 月 10 日，56 岁的李宗盛在深圳开唱。对于李宗盛的才情，用什么样的溢美之词感觉都不过分。他就是为音乐而生的。老男人就这点好，重感情、爱热闹。才情化为智慧，岁月成就传奇，李宗盛给我们树立了很好的榜样。

纪录民国先生的先生 043

一部 10 集纪录片《先生》,共鸣了隔代不相逢的后生们。在波澜壮阔的文化民国、烽火连天的战乱废墟、大江大海的南渡北归里,他们宛如灯塔,各自照亮一方山河。制作人邓康延,西安人氏。容易忧伤,常常感动,也用自己的寻找和发现感动着许多人。

熊出没 044

美丽神秘的森林,五彩缤纷的雪山,奇妙的地下世界,破坏森林的光头强,森林保护者熊兄弟……似乎和深圳毫无关系。然而,这部叫《熊出没》的原创动漫是深圳华强数字动漫有限公司出品的,片中的光头强以华强老板刘富源为原型创作,引发了创作者和观众的共鸣。

Boonie Bears 044

Bear brothers roam the beautiful and mysterious forest, the snowy mountains, the underground world, always protecting. Logger Vick is always at large. It seems like this show has nothing to do with Shenzhen. However, *Boonie Bears* is an original digital animation produced right here. "Logger Vick" is an original creation of the head of the Huaqiang Digital Animation Company which has resonated with audiences and creators.

The Man Documenting the Masters 043

A ten-part series, titled *Master* resonated with people separated by a generation. As the republic surged high and swept forward, as wars raged, as those great masters crossed great distances from south back to north, they shined like lanterns, travelling past mountains and rivers. The producer Deng Kangyan is a native of Xi'an. He's frequently moved with emotion, and uses his own searches and discoveries to move others.

开不败的"琼花" 045

当年她因一双大眼睛被谢晋看中,出演《红色娘子军》女主角琼花,该片创造了 6 亿观影人次,她也成为第一届百花奖影后。1983 年,45 岁的祝希娟举家南迁,担任深圳电视台副台长,并成为该台第一位主持人。后全力推动电视剧创作与制作,被称为"深圳电视剧的拓荒者"。

Unbreakable Flower 045

Fancied by Xie Jin because of her big eyes, the main character Qiong Hua in *Red Detachment of Women* led a production that sold over 600 million tickets; the actress was the first female to win the Hundred Flowers Award. In 1983, 45-year-old Zhu Xijuan moved south to serve as the vice president of the Shenzhen TV Station, and became its first host. She later worked hard on innovation in and production of television shows, and was named a pioneer in Shenzhen dramas.

夜空不寂寞

深圳集中了中国最寂寞的人群,因此《夜空不寂寞》曾是这个城市最火的电台节目。美国作家彼得·海斯勒在《纽约客》上写道:"在深圳,每天晚上大约有 200 万人收听胡晓梅的电台节目,这个有胆识的女子以她的率直震撼了中国人。"胡晓梅,一个带着 450 元闯荡深圳的女子,她的犀利和直接很难让人喜欢。

The Night Sky Isn't Lonely

Shenzhen has some of the loneliest people in China. For this reason, *The Night Sky Isn't Lonely* used to be one of the most popular radio shows in Shenzhen. American writer Peter Hessler wrote in *The New Yorker*: "In Shenzhen, more than two million people listen to Hu Xiaomei's broadcast every night. This insightful woman rocks Chinese audiences with her direct tone." Hu came to Shenzhen with only 450 yuan in her pocket; her incisive and direct nature can be a bit hard to like.

杨争光的电影忧思

杨争光是小说家,也是著名编剧,曾为电视剧《水浒传》总编剧、《激情燃烧的岁月》总策划,如今在深圳成立了自己的电影工作室。深谙文学与电影现状的他,曾批评当下中国电影脱离了文学性,弊病缠身。他说:"中国电影人要自救,首先就要从对书的尊重开始。"

Thoughts of Film

Yang Zhengguang is a novelist, as well as a scriptwriter. He previously wrote for the TV adaptation of *Water Margin*, and has planned out the popular TV series *A Passionate Life*. Now he has established a film studio in Shenzhen. Involved in literature and film, he's previously criticised Chinese films for their loss of literary character. He says: "Chinese filmmakers have to save themselves, and this starts with respecting books."

公园太极拳 048

与其他城市太极拳多为老人健身不同，在深圳所有的公园里，都能看到打太极拳的年轻人。年轻人练习太极拳，不仅仅是为了锻炼身体，也在学习其深邃的文化内涵，悟出太极就是顺势而为。尊老爱幼，知书识礼；累了，就休息；渴了，就喝水。寒来暑往，秋收冬藏，就是如此简单、直接。这就是太极。

Tai Chi in the Park 048

Unlike other Chinese cities where one sees mainly old people practicing Tai Chi, on can see young people in all of the parks of the city taking part. They do it not just for its health benefits, but for its cultural element; awakening to Tai Chi is going with the flow. One must respect elders and love children, read books and understand etiquette. If you're tired, rest; if you're thirsty, drink water. As the summer ends, collect grain in autumn to store for the winter. Simple and direct: this is Tai Chi.

东湖赏菊 049

去东湖赏菊，是深圳人常年的习惯。东湖公园菊花展从1984年开始，每年岁末举办，从未间断。忙碌的深圳人，偶尔能带着陶渊明赏菊的闲适心情，观赏到上百个品种的菊花，也是赏心悦目事。除了赏菊，展会的造型设计也成了关注焦点，菊花组成了"愤怒的小鸟""美丽的金鱼"，让游客叹为观止。

Shenzhen Mill 050

Time wears people down; there is a far-off dream in the heart of everyone in Shenzhen. When portal Sina's travel forum came on-line, as the people there were more stressed than people in other cities, Shenzhen became called "The Mill", because turning a millstone is hard work. The Shenzhen subforum developed into a community of its own right, founded in June 2000, which provides discussion, activity partner searching, a market for second-hand equipment, and other services.

Chrysanthemums at Donghu Park 049

Shenzhen people enjoy going to the Donghu Park each year to view the chrysanthemums. The Donghu Park Chrysanthemum Exposition began in 1984, and has been held at the end of each year without interruption. It's nice for the busy people of Shenzhen to be able to occasionally enjoy some downtime and appreciate the chrysanthemums here; there are more than 100 cultivars displayed. Aside from the flowers, the design of the exposition is also a point of interest, with exhibits such as "angry birds" and "beautiful goldfish" delighting visitors.

深圳磨房 050

岁月磨人，每一颗深圳人的心，都有远行的梦想。当年新浪旅游论坛被戏称为"驴坛"，户外活动爱好者扎堆，因有感深圳"驴友"比别地更辛苦，所以命名为"磨房"，取辛苦拉磨之意。磨房从简单的讨论版发展成了社区，提供论坛、活动约伴儿、二手装备交易等服务。深圳磨房，2000年6月由驴友创建。

"深圳速度"的足球俱乐部 051

Shenzhen Speed

中国足球协会超级联赛始于 2004 年，首届冠军被深圳夺得，大出所有人意料。距此 10 年前深圳足球俱乐部组建，组建当年和次年连续获得乙级联赛冠军，第三年跃入甲级队，在中国足坛创造了从成立到进入顶级联赛的最快纪录"三连跳"，不愧是"深圳速度"。

The Chinese Football Association Super League (CSL) was started in 2004; the first championship was taken by Shenzhen, exceeding all expectations. 10 years prior the team had just been organised, and that year and the next year it won the championship of the second division (CZL); in the third year it entered the first division (CL). Jumping between the three divisions just like that was truly a feat of Shenzhen speed.

奔跑吧，兄弟！

有一种奔跑叫"深马"，有一种马拉松叫"狂欢节"。每年在这个万民开跑的日子里，没人关注冠军是谁，人们更关注的是，谁的装扮最出彩、最另类：有"唐僧"，也有"康熙"；有身穿草裙的"野人"，也有披着狼皮的"狼人"。参与其中的每个人都是评委，他们用奔跑宣泄热情，也释放压力。

Running Man

There is a kind of run in the city called the "Shenzhen International Marathon"; this marathon is almost like a carnival. Every year countless citizens run around the city, nobody looking out for who is the champion. What people pay attention to is how people decorate themselves; there are "alternative" styles: "Tang Monks", members of the *Journey to the West*, "Kangxi", the emperor in the Qing Dynasty, "savages" in grass skirts, and "werewolves" wearing wolf skin. Every participant is a judge; people take place to show their stuff and release pressure.

大运会的主角

2011年，第26届世界大学生夏季运动会在深圳开幕，大运会口号："从这里开始。"参赛国家及运动员均创会之最，中国夺75金，创造新纪录。赛会的一大亮点是志愿者，2万名赛会志愿者、25万名城市志愿者和100万名社会志愿者的参与，让世界各地的运动员宾至如归。志愿者的口号是："我在这里。"

Stars of the Universiade

The 26th Summer Universiade was held in Shenzhen in 2011, with the slogan: "It starts from here." Records were broken, with China taking 75 gold medals. One of the bright points of the Universiade was the body of volunteers, with 20,000 competition volunteers, 250,000 city volunteers and 1,000,000 society volunteers participating, making the contestants from all over the world feel at home. The slogan of the volunteers was "I am here".

来深圳打高球

深圳观澜湖高尔夫球会曾是中国规模最大、档次最高、配套最齐全的高尔夫球会，吸引了"老虎"泰格·伍兹来这里挥杆；亦是中国第一个拥有72洞的球会，中国唯一获得国际高尔夫球巡回赛事认可的比赛球场。有段时间，全国的高球爱好者，会从四面八方定期会聚观澜湖，既为打球，也为会友。

Golf in Shenzhen

The Mission Hills Golf Club at Guanlan Lake in Shenzhen used to be the country's largest, highest grade golf club in China; it even attracted Tiger Woods to play here. It is also China's first golf club with 72 holes, and the only Chinese golf club to be recognised by major international golf tournaments. There was a time where golf enthusiasts from all over the country would come here to play and mingle.

纵横四海 055

国内民间首次大型洲际航海活动是"中国杯帆船赛"的前身，它有一个极浪漫的名字：纵横四海。从浪漫之都巴黎起航，最终抵达深圳，驾驶者均是被朋友们称为"帆船疯子"的深圳人。多年前，他们满怀梦想和期待从全国各地来到深圳；多年后，驾驶自己的帆船到海上去成了他们新的梦想，并实现之。

Overrun the Four Seas

The China Cup International Regatta previously had a much more romantic name, "Overrun the Four Seas". The journey starts in Paris, the city of love, and ends in beautiful Shenzhen. The operators of these vessels are called "crazy boaters" by the people of Shenzhen. Many years ago they came, hopes in hand, from all over the country to the city of the roc. Today, they take their sailboats out into the open ocean, making these dreams a reality.

Index

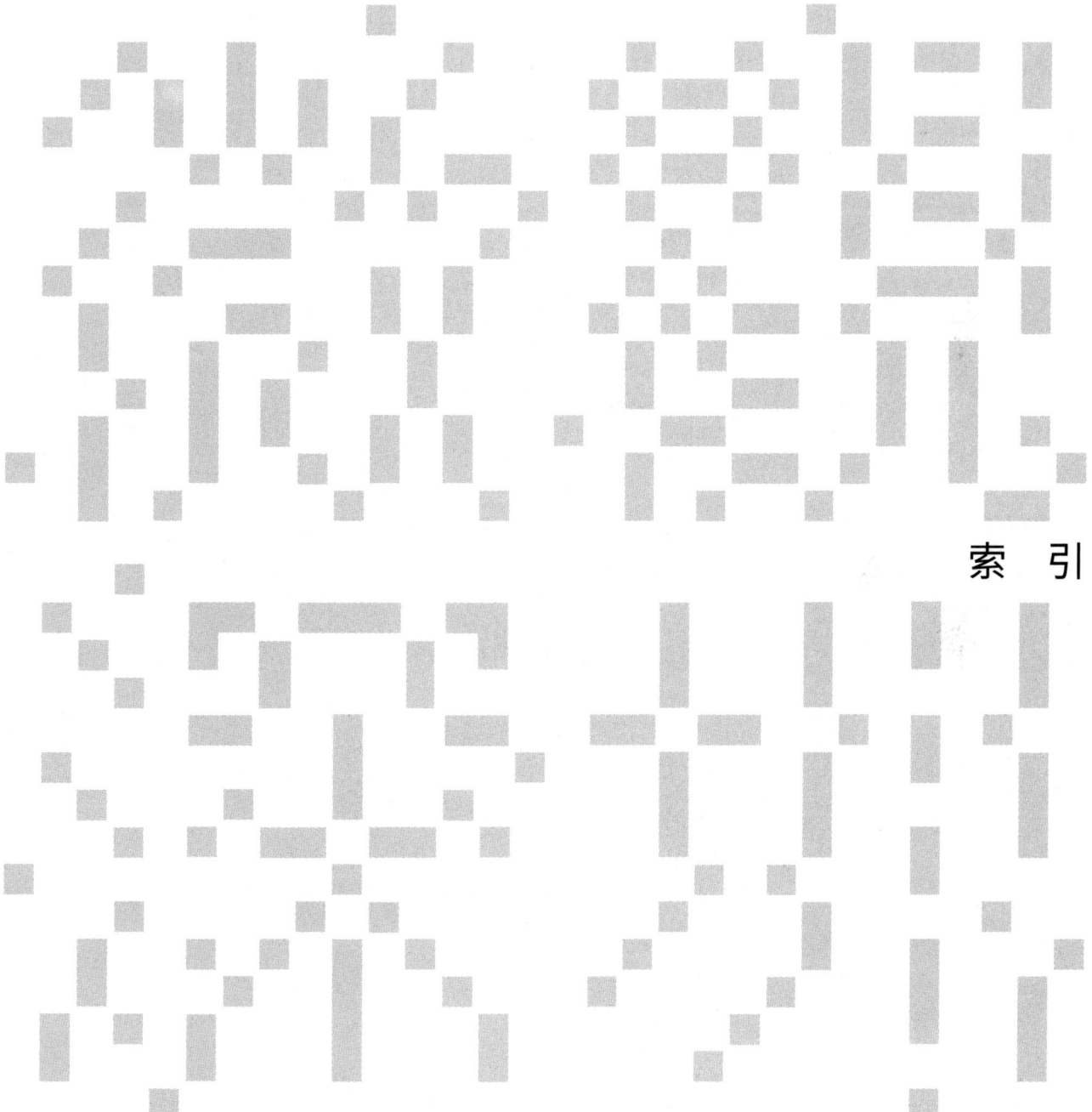

索 引

索 引
INDEX

15 次来深圳的莫言	The Fifteenth Visit	166
1993 文稿竞价	Manuscripts Prices in 1993	221
24 小时书吧	24-Hour Bookstore	175
4 分钱的故事	A Story of 4 Pence	88
600 年的大盆菜	Six Centuries of Poon Choi	100
"8·10" 股疯	The 8 / 10 Disturbance	126
TVB 电视剧	TVB Shows	50

A

爱，会不会是一辈子？	Does Love Last a Lifetime?	98
安置梦想的家园	Home of Dreams	76

B

八卦岭的阅读记忆	Memories at Bagualing	164
坝光遗世独立	Remains of Baguang	24
白龙王喝过的丝袜奶茶	Tea Drank by the White Dragon King	64
半圆如月	Guan Shanyue Art Museum	216
扮猪食老虎	Incognito OG	204
奔跑吧，兄弟！	Running Man	234
比亚迪带电奔驰	An Electric BYD	196
并不物质的小书吧	An Immaterial Bookstore	173
并非一座城的《命运》	A City's *Fate*	164
不讲粤语的广东人	No Cantonese	35
不慕虚荣的深圳人	Don't Call Me Mr. Vain	85
不夜城	Night Activity	64

C

中文	English	Page
财经界第一网红	Financial Internet Celebrity	192
"查理九世"和"朱佩琪"	Charlie IX and Zhu Pei Qi	172
长粽长有	Long Zongzi	99
城头变幻地王旗	New King's Flag	125
城心难寂	In the City	59
吃回忆的酒家	Nostalgic Restaurant	46
赤湾炮台的诉说	Chiwan Bay Left Fort	32
赤湾天后宫的香火袅袅	Smoke from the Temple	5
出门也要靠自己	Rely on Yourself	80
出门迎车公	Che Gong	58
窗外有片相思林	Acacia Forest	19
创客之城	Maker City	140
创投大佬	Venture Capital Boss	187
创意十二月	Creative December	157
创意园的前世今生	Creative Park, Past and Present	155
"创意中国"走出国门	Going Out	156
春风又绿试验田	Forefront of Revolution	79
春江水暖"银"先知	The Banks	70
春天的故事	Story of Spring	208
从《街道》走出来的摄影师	The Best Portrait Photographer	224
从湿地看风水	Feng shui from the Wetlands	6
从"烫手山芋"到"香饽饽"	From "Tricky" to "Beloved"	165
从一张机票开始	Starting with a Plane Ticket	192
翠竹之园	Cuizhu Park	20

D

打工文学	Literature on Labourers	176
大华兴寺隐于观音山	Dahuaxing Temple	6
大鹏所城	Dapeng Fortress	32
大隐于市的戏院	Theatre and the City	43
大运会的主角	Stars of the Universiade	234
大运会魅影	Universiade	159
得宝者安	Bao'an District	33
登顶"地王"为怀乡	On the Peak	77
登上《时代》周刊的女工	Girls in *Time*	98
邓一光的深圳	Deng Yiguang's Shenzhen	176
抵达梦开始的地方	Field of Dreams	43
"地王"	Land King	151
地下工作者	Underground Workers	100
"第五项修炼"和"六顶思考帽"	The Fifth Discipline and Six Thinking Hats	165
第一份合资日报	First Joint-Invested Newspaper	220
"东方神曲"高，深圳和者寡	Oriental Divine Comedy	77
东湖丽苑的第一缕清风	East Lake Feelings	77
东湖赏菊	Chrysanthemums at Donghu Park	232
东门十字街	The Intersection	33
逗利市	Lai See	110
独角兽的阴影	Shadow of the Unicorn	126

F

泛红的毛棉杜鹃节	Rhododendron Moulmainense	18
梵音悠扬弘法寺	Hongfa Temple	12
方形的围屋	Hakka Enclosed Residences	74
风雨伶仃洋	Lingdingyang Estuary	34
凤栖梧桐山	Source	218
福永醒狮	Fuyong Dancing Lion	102
蝠鲼、鸟和蜂巢	Manta Ray, Bird and Beehive	150
父母亲的"情愁"	Parental Melancholy	118

索引 240

G

甘坑小镇的客家凉帽	Hakka Hats	35
尴尬的玩具店	Toy Shop	107
"钢琴王子"李云迪	Prince of Piano	225
港式月饼需要品	Hong Kong-style Moon Cakes: Essential	106
高贵的生活方式	A Noble Lifestyle	177
告别航母明斯克	Goodbye Minsk	133
公园太极拳	Tai Chi in the Park	232
"沟通"	Communication	140
骨子里的文明城市	Cultured City	40
鼓励创新，宽容失败	Encourage Innovation, Forgive Failure	127
故乡的云	Clouds of the Old Village	229
观澜炮楼群	Guanlan Blockhouses	36
光影星期五	Image of Friday	227
归国华侨的光明之地	The Guangming Farm	23
"滚石30"	Rock Records 30th Anniversary Concert	229
滚石不生苔	Rolling Stone Gathers No Moss	185
国际视角下的文艺中心	Global Angle of View	149
国企改革的"深圳模式"	Shenzhen Model	183
国企走出来的培训专家	Enterprise Trainer	193
过番转来的唐人	Hakka People "Turning Back"	106
过街	Crossing the Street	35

H

还在坚持	Holding On	193
海滨栈道任徜徉	A Walk Along the Beach	10
海山公园	Haishan Park	24
海上世界耀明华	World on the Seas	80
好吃"螃蟹"的深圳人	A Site for Success	226
何香凝美术馆	He Xiangning Art Museum	217
和平路上的侨房	Houses on Heping Road	80
红红火火客家年	Hakka New Year	108

蝴蝶谷在梦幻中闪亮	A Dreamy Atmosphere	14
互联网拓荒者	Internet Pioneer	197
花卉小镇的荷兰风情	Dutch Village	13
"花园"深圳	Shenzhen Garden	7
华侨城创意市集	OCT LOFT Creative Market	155
欢声笑语的"大客厅"	Big Hall	71
火神的画	Paintings of the God of Fire	218

J

基围人的基围虾	Farmed Shrimp	107
激情的金蝶	Passionate Kingdee	195
激浊扬清	Cleaning House	132
集装箱世界第一	Number One in Containers	202
纪录民国先生的先生	The Man Documenting the Masters	230
既不凉也非茶	Neither Cold Nor Tea	106
家里的大户室	VIP Room at Home	133
家乡的兰花	Orchids at Home	107
嘉美印刷 典范制造	Jiamei Printing Creates Classics	157
匠心之悟	Masterpiece	147
《街道》的传说	Legend of the *Street*	224
街头的时尚启蒙	Fashion in the Streets	56
解放路的"金三角"	Golden Triangle	41
今天阅读一小时	Read an Hour Today	174
金"基"唱晓	Fund Fun	132
金龙玉凤歌舞厅	Golden Dragon, Jade Phoenix	228
"金鹏"短片节	Short Films	226
九天十八井，十阁走马廊	The Hakka Settlement	216
就是想好好玩一把	Desire to Play	194
巨大中华	The Four Dragons	132
巨资买号为哪般？	Big Number, Big Money	81
剧汇星期天	Drama Gathering on Sunday	228
崛起的大湾区设计群	Dawan District Designers	149

K

开不败的"琼花"	Unbreakable Flower	230
枯燥的畅销书	A Dry Book that Sells Well	155

L

来深圳打高球	Golf in Shenzhen	234
蓝色的抛物线伸向远方	A Long Blue Curve	14
老牌百货的新生	Old Department Store, New Life	204
老帅出山	Here Comes the General	189
离海很远的海滨城市	A Coastal City Far from the Seas	82
李嘉诚的预言	Li Ka-shing's Prediction	58
荔枝公园的秋意	Lizhi Park	13
荔枝花开	Lychees Blooming	14
连锁的魅力	Chain Attraction	204
莲花山的守护者	Guardians of Lianhuashan	46
灵魂入股企业	Soul in Business	191
绿色的红树林	Mangrove Forest	12

M

马行长	Bank Boss Ma	189
马峦山访梅	Plums in Maluanshan	26
马云唯一对手	Jack Ma's Only Opponent	195
麦当劳叔叔来了	Uncle McDonald Is Coming	99
没有悠闲的树叶	Leaves that Don't Rest	133
玫瑰海岸	Rose Coast	25
美哉七娘山	Qiniangshan the Beautiful	41
"门可罗雀"的免费博物馆	Nobody Here Knocking on My Door	166
门口的野蛮人	Barbarians	188
孟父三迁	Mr. Meng's Three Moves	63
梦里依稀当当糖	Boom Boom Sweet	99
梦想在钟声中醒来	Dreams Awaken with the Bell	124
梦想奏鸣曲	Dream Sonata	217

面朝大海，春暖花开	Facing the Sea	27
魔高一尺，道高一丈	As Vice Rises One Foot, Virtue Rises Ten	136

N

南澳鲍鱼在险处	Nan'ao Abalone	111
南方有嘉木	China Southern Fund	187
南粤婚俗重上头	Cantonese Wedding	111
你不可改变我	You Can't Change Me	223
你在深圳还好吗？	Are You Doing Well in Shenzhen?	98
年桔橙黄	New-Year Oranges	112
女人天生爱逛街	Women Love Shopping	60

P

蹒跚的第一次	Staggering Along	136
平面设计在中国	Graphic Design in China	140
平民自助餐	Cheap Buffets	112

Q

企鹅帝国	Penguin Empire	186
企鹅银行	Penguin Bank	125
侨社	CTSOC	47
亲切的"阿"	The Prefix of "A"	113
亲嘴楼	Kissing Buildings	92
青春留不住的李宗盛	Youth Can't Even Handle Me Right Now	229
青青世界	Evergreen Resort	23
区块链布道者	Blockchain Evangelist	187
全民炒股，于斯为盛	Stock Market	83
全民友好型城市	A Friendly Place	83
全球唯一的"建筑双年展"	The Only Biennale	148
全球最大的艺术书墙	Largest Art Wall in the World	151
券业"黄埔军校"	Whampoa Military Academy of the Securities Industry	189
缺钱、缺人、缺设备	Money, People, Equipment	220

R

让魔咒成为传说	Curses to Legends	78
让世界造起来	Let's Make Things	184
让天下不再有孤独的老人	No Lonely Elders	100
人潮人海似蛇阵	Running the Snake Train	76
人生如书 后院读过	Life Is Like a Book	171
人头饭与生果	Weird Food	113
人与城的交集	People and City	91
人与兽的角色互换	Switching Places	19
榕树寿星见证生命	Old Trees	20
"融合"	Merging	141
如火的簕杜鹃	Bougainvillea	15

S

三洲田问茶	Tea in Sanzhoutian	23
"三自"精神源出深大	The "Three-Self" Spirit	88
"杀马特"	So Smart	115
晒布路无布晒	Shaibu Road	42
"山城"深圳	Mountain City	16
山环水抱的大道	The Boulevards	70
山就在那里	That's Where the Mountain Is	87
上帝也无法阻止	God Can't Stop Us	173
上帝之手	God's Hand	195
上海宾馆	Shanghai Hotel	83
少女和少妇	Girl and Wife	219
舌尖上的深圳	Shenzhen on the Tip of the Tongue	88
蛇口老街	Shekou Laojie Street	115
设计让生活更美好	Designing a Better Life	146
设计业的"黄埔军校"	Whampoa Military Academy of Design	147
设计之都的公益精神	Working Hard for the Public Good	148
申奥会徽	Olympic Application Logo	158
伸入深圳的手臂	Extending Reach	56

深二代创业家	Shenzhen Second Generation Entrepreneurs	191
深二代夏春秋	Shenzhen Boy Xia Chunqiu	110
深港"飞地"落马洲	Lok Ma Chau	60
深港通	Shenzhen-Hong Kong Stock Connect	184
深商的"头啖汤"	The First Soup	182
深商教主	Founder of Business in Shenzhen	182
深圳才有家的感觉	Shenzhen Feels Like Home	113
深圳的"潘家园"	Shenzhen's "Panjiayuan"	154
深圳河	Shenzhen River	62
深圳考证的外国人	Taking Tests	89
深圳蓝	Shenzhen Blue	86
深圳磨房	Shenzhen Mill	232
深圳,你被谁抛弃?	Shenzhen, Who Forsook You?	86
《深圳青年》一纸风行	*SZYOUTH*	221
深圳人才日	Shenzhen Talent Day	85
深圳十大观念	Ten Views of Shenzhen	118
深圳时装周	Shenzhen Fashion Week	146
深圳手信	Hand Letters in Shenzhen	85
"深圳速度"的足球俱乐部	Shenzhen Speed	233
深圳湾畔育春茧	Spring Cocoon	150
深圳舞麒麟	Shenzhen Kylin Dance	117
深圳下雪	Snow in Shenzhen	17
深圳墟	Shenzhen Market	42
深圳艺展中心	Shenzhen Art Design Centre	154
深圳中心论	Shenzhen Centrality	166
神秘的"二线关"	Second Border	54
神秘的头狼	The Lead Wolf	190
神奇的气膜建筑	Air-supported Structures	134
神仙树	Mystic Tree	27
生命在于折腾	Life Is a Grind	116
生态广场拥抱幽静	Ecological Park	13
声讯电话	Telephony Services	197
诗意的耳朵——莱耳	Poetic Ears	176

诗意的居住证	Poetic Residence Permit	94
《石渠宝笈》	*Shiqu Baoji*	216
时间就是金钱	Time Is Money	84
实至名归设计之都	A Famous City of Design	144
《市场快报》周刊	*Market Express*	134
首家五星级酒店	First Five-Star Hotel	203
书店里的购书车	Trolleys in the Bookstore	171
书记三问	Three Questions	79
数月亮的大佬	Counting Moons	188
树林里的潜伏者	Lurkers in the Bush	5
双城生活	A Life of Two Cities	62
水晶石顾盼生辉	Crystal Rock	150
"水流柴"上岸	Floating Firewood	45
说吧，乡愁	Feelings for Home	130
"四头四尾"的客家女子	Hakka Women	109
松岗赛龙舟	Dragon Boat Races	116
宋少帝陵	Song Imperial Tomb	44
素人画家	Sunday Painter	219
随处借阅 随处还书	Read Anywhere	170

T

逃港村的陈迹	Things of the Past	64
特朗普的朋友	Trump's Friend	191
特区中的"特区"	A "Special Zone" in the SEZ	47
特区猪油糕的特别之处	Lard Cakes	117
添丁点灯	Light the Lantern	117
通宵畅行的皇岗	Huanggang Doesn't Close	81
图书馆之城	A City of Libraries	177
"土豪式"装修	Tacky Glitz	158

W

| 外地车限行令 | Driving Limitations | 90 |
| 外来工 | Come Here to Work | 118 |

外来和尚会念经	A Monk from Afar Reads the Scriptures	137
外文书店的清凉	Cool Foreign Bookstore	170
万丰粤剧	Wanfeng Cantonese Opera	208
王者荣耀	Glory of Kings	186
围着垃圾桶"打边炉"	Hot Pot	60
"唯有肖邦"	Only Chopin	225
为知识付费	Paying for Knowledge	158
文博会盛宴	ICIF	209
文豪也喜沙井蚝	Oysters of Shajing Town	115
文化 +	Culture +	209
文锦渡口岸	Wenjindu Checkpoint	65
文学博士的"深圳梦"	Literati Shenzhen Dream	171
文字设计在中国	Typographic Design in China	146
问鼎"金顶"的深圳人	I Wanna Be the Very Best	147
我们的员工与众不同	Our Workers Are Different	84
乌石古的外籍员工	Foreign Workers in Wushigu	89
无偿献血	Voluntary Blood Donation	90
无人驾驶首发牌	First Self-driving Car Plate	135
无限延伸的大厦	Limitless Building	153
无约不访，有约守时	Appointments Required	90
梧桐烟云	Clouds on Mount Wutong	18

X

"西涌"＝"西冲"	Xichong	47
西涌情人岛	Lovers' Island	25
溪谷生态园	Creek Valley Park	25
喜新不厌旧	In with the New	50
戏聚星期六	Opera Gathering on Saturday	227
夏雨隔牛背	Patchy Rain	66
先出生，再拿证	Birth Before Certificate	134
咸水歌	Saltwater Song	208
咸头岭文明	Cultured Xiantouling	45
相"儒"以"墨"	Mutual "Ink"ssistance	218

香港 + 深圳 = 香圳	HK+SZ="Hong Zhen"	66
香港电视开禁	TV Shows from Hong Kong	65
香港邮票	Hong Kong Philately	66
小津书房的光影生活	Ozubook's Light and Shadow	177
小区里的午托班	Lunch Care	172
新安古城	Xin'an Ancient City	22
信息两栖人	Amphibious Data	59
熊出没	Boonie Bears	230
休憩的"绿美人"	Resting "Green Beauty"	93
虚拟动漫，活力中国	Virtual Cartoons	156

Y

杨梅红了	Ymm Art Education Group	219
杨争光的电影忧思	Thoughts of Film	231
夜的光源	Night Lights	174
夜空不寂寞	The Night Sky Isn't Lonely	231
一步之遥	One Step Away	126
一旦拥有，别无所求	Fiyta Watch	136
一个人的长征	Long March	92
一呼天下应	CMT, a Call to the World	137
一骑红尘妃子笑	Tribute Item—Lychee	110
一脚回到远古	Back to the Past	22
一念之差	Whoops	135
一桥馨香	Sweet Bridge	58
一条界河波浪宽	Water Works	109
一碗靓汤	One Bowl of Soup	121
以笔为船，横渡商海	Sailing the Seas of Business	193
以深圳人命名的昆虫	Insects Named by a Local	15
以心治印的民间艺人	Shuai Fei Zen Seals	220
抑郁的深渊	Disaster Area for Depression	205
抑郁症更需要关爱	Love for the Depressed	92
因书偶遇	Book Meeting	173
因阅读而受人尊重	Respect for Reading	168

茵特拉根小镇的穿越	Interlaken Is Here	19
饮茶倾解	Drink Tea and Chat	120
有恒乃大	Ever Grand	185
娱乐发祥地	Origin of Entertainment Industry	226
与众不同的内刊	A Special Publication	223
遇见张五常	Meeting Zhang Wuchang	174
粤语难于上青天	Difficulties with Cantonese	67
粤之糖水	Sweet Water	121

Z

杂志"黄埔军校"	Whampoa Military Academy of Magazines	222
在深圳玩雪	Alps Snow World	4
葬我于大海	Bury Me at Sea	112
早产的共享单车	Early Bicycle Sharing	86
早熟的孩子	Precocious Children	121
赠人玫瑰，手有余香	Give Someone a Rose	87
窄屋外的宽阔人生	Narrow Houses, Wide Outdoors	50
展示艺术品的艺术品	Artworks that Display Artworks	149
珍珠养于水贝	Pearls Grow in Oysters	154
知识网红	Intellectual Online Celebrity	62
职业参会者	My Goodies	42
只为遇见你	Just to See You	124
中产阶级的《财源》	Middle Bourgeoisie Magazine	223
中国第一家股份制企业	China's First Share Issuing Enterprise	184
中国电子第一街	The Number One Chinese Electronics Street	200
中国工业设计第一园	The First Industrial Design Park	148
中国境内首个平面设计组织	Shenzhen Graphic Design Association	141
中国科技第一展	China Hi-Tech Fair	137
中国油画第一村	Oil Painting Village	210
中国主题公园之父	Father of Chinese Theme Parks	202
中银大厦和它的孪生兄弟	Bank of China Tower	67
钟声唤醒黎明	Daylight Bell	76
珠宝城与金饰街	Jewelry City and Gold Street	67

资本市场奥斯卡	Oscars of the Capital Market	224
自然的爱与愁	Natural Feelings	17
纵横四海	Overrun the Four Seas	235
奏刀有神的客家排屋	Skill with a Knife	212
最大的风险就是不敢冒险	The Biggest Risk Is Not Daring to Take a Risk	190
最佳试验场	The Best Testing Ground	124
最小的超大城市	The Smallest Supercity	94
最早的军事驻防	The Earliest Military Garrison	41
最赚钱的高速公路	The Most Profitable Expressway	57
做令人尊敬的企业	Form a Respectable Enterprise	196
做人至紧要开心	One Must Be Happy	205

图书在版编目(CIP)数据

微观深圳:汉英对照/胡野秋主编.—北京:商务印书馆,2018
(微观中国)
ISBN 978-7-100-16578-5

Ⅰ.①微… Ⅱ.①胡… Ⅲ.①深圳—概况—汉、英 Ⅳ.①K926.53

中国版本图书馆 CIP 数据核字(2018)第 204071 号

权利保留,侵权必究。

微观深圳
(汉英版)
SHENZHEN: DYNAMIC AND DIVERSE
胡野秋 主编

商 务 印 书 馆 出 版
(北京王府井大街 36 号 邮政编码 100710)
商 务 印 书 馆 发 行
北京中科印刷有限公司印刷
ISBN 978-7-100-16578-5

2018 年 10 月第 1 版　　开本 889×1194　1/16
2018 年 10 月北京第 1 次印刷　印张 17
定价:99.00 元